THE
EARLY CHRISTIAN
ARCHAEOLOGY OF
NORTH BRITAIN

GLASGOW UNIVERSITY PUBLICATIONS

THE
EARLY CHRISTIAN ARCHAEOLOGY OF NORTH BRITAIN

The Hunter Marshall Lectures
delivered at the University of Glasgow
in January and February 1968

BY

CHARLES THOMAS

Published for the
UNIVERSITY OF GLASGOW
by
OXFORD UNIVERSITY PRESS
London Glasgow New York
1971

Oxford University Press, Ely House, London W. 1

GLASGOW NEW YORK TORONTO MELBOURNE WELLINGTON
CAPE TOWN SALISBURY IBADAN NAIROBI DAR ES SALAAM LUSAKA ADDIS ABABA
BOMBAY CALCUTTA MADRAS KARACHI LAHORE DACCA
KUALA LUMPUR SINGAPORE HONG KONG TOKYO

ISBN 0 19 214102 3

PRINTED IN GREAT BRITAIN

GENIO BIBLIOTHECAE
VNIVERSITATIS EDINBVRGENSIS
SCIENTIAE SEMPER
NVTRICIS

Author's Preface

IN THIS BOOK, Chapters 2 to 7 are substantially the same as the lectures given at the University of Glasgow in January and February 1968. I have changed certain passages into a form better suited to the written word, have added some fresh material where appropriate new discoveries have been made during the last eighteen months, and have also excised a few portions dealing with monuments of the ninth, and later, centuries. The original Hunter Marshall Lectures were illustrated with over five hundred slides, most of them from drawings and maps specially prepared for the series. In choosing text figures, I have left out many things which are elsewhere available in print, and have made a careful selection from the remainder, primarily to clarify distributions or the technical aspects of unfamiliar monuments. These illustrations have been redrawn in a uniform hand and style by Dr. Morna MacGregor (Mrs. D. D. A. Simpson), to whom I am most grateful.

The purpose of this short work is the same as the purpose of my lectures. It is to present, as a small return for all the kindnesses I received from a wide circle of friends and colleagues throughout Scotland, during my years at the University of Edinburgh, the results of research in both the field and the library, but in a form specifically addressed to the interested amateur. Though most of my working life has been passed inside the walls of various universities, as both student and teacher, I have been fortunate enough to have an almost continuous connection with extra-mural work and amateur archaeology; I know very well how few books are aimed primarily at the great and informed circle of adult students, and I can see no reason why an introductory survey, like this one, should lose any force through being so directed. For this reason, the references have been confined largely to works in English (even when this involves secondary textual sources) and, as far as possible, to books and periodicals which are accessible at or through a major public library.

My warmest thanks go to Professor A. A. M. Duncan, Professor of Scottish History and Literature, and to the Court of the University of Glasgow, for their invitation to deliver the 1968 Hunter Marshall Lectures, and subsequently to reproduce them in book form. In the field-work and necessary travel lying behind their preparation, I was fortunate enough to receive financial support from the Colt Fund, the Munro Fund, the Russell Trust, and the University of Edinburgh (through the Department of Archaeology, some of whose annual excavations are represented in the text). I was privileged, from 1966 to 1968, to hold a Leverhulme Fellowship, which allowed me to visit a great many relevant, and remote, sites. The names of all the individual friends to whom I owe gratitude for their help, advice, and generosity in this context would (if listed *seriatim*) fill several pages; in thanking them all, I would especially mention my former colleagues Professors Donald Bullough, Kenneth Jackson, John MacQueen, and Stuart Piggott; Drs. Anne Ross (Mrs. R. W. Feachem) and W. F. H. Nicolaisen; Miss Mary-Jane Mountain; and Messrs. B. R. S. Megaw, Malcolm Murray, and Kenneth White. Mr. Robert Stevenson (National Museum of Antiquities of Scotland), Drs. K. A. Steer and J. N. G. Ritchie (Royal Commission on Ancient Monuments, Scotland), Messrs. S. E. Cruden, P. R. Ritchie, and Lloyd R. Laing (Ancient Monuments Inspectorate, Scotland); Miss Campbell of Kilberry, Mr. Tom Henderson (Lerwick), Dr. Dorothy Marshall (Bute), Mr. A. E. Truckell (Dumfries), and many friends in the various Scottish archaeological societies (in particular, Dumfries and Galloway, and Cowal); Miss Rosemary Cramp (Durham), Dr. Douglas Hague (R. C. A. H. M. Wales and Monmouth), Dr. C. A. Ralegh Radford, and Mr. Etienne Rynne (University College, Galway), must also be included. Not least, I owe a special debt of thanks to my secretary, Mrs. P. A. Walker, who had to type the entire lecture-series, and this book, at short notice and among the press of routine work.

The dedication may seem a little unusual, but those who (like myself) have had the run of a really great library will be able to appreciate its point. It reflects my gratitude, not only to the library staff, but to all the past benefactors who have helped to make Edinburgh University Library what it is.

CHARLES THOMAS

University of Leicester
July 1969

Contents

List of Plates

(Plates I, III, V, VIII, Kenneth White; Plate IV, Malcolm Murray; Plate VI, F. M. B. Cooke; Plates II and VII, The Green Studio Ltd., Dublin)

List of Text Illustrations

1. *The Theme and its Background*

LET US IMAGINE that the accident of fate had not preserved for us any of the manuscripts of Bede's *Ecclesiastical History*, or of the writings of Patrick and Gildas, or of the whole body of lives of British and Irish saints composed or redacted before the full Middle Ages. Could we, under such circumstances, hope to reconstruct—from the limited annalistic material, from a few continental sources, from the New Testament and patristic literature, and from the entire field of visible and excavated remains and isolated monuments—an outline of the specifically religious history of our islands from the fifth to the eighth century A.D.?

I hasten to relieve the reader of the apprehension that the chapters which follow may attempt to do this, but I also stress that it would now be possible to build, slowly, a reliable framework for the Christian events of those centuries, using no more than archaeological, artistic, and architectural data. Therein, to my mind, lies the special fascination of this period in the British past. So much that we can today detect through the exercise of archaeological methods—the primacy of the Christian cemetery, the direct Mediterranean contacts, the introduction of full monasticism, and the interplay of art styles in different media—is nowhere explicitly described in what literature has survived. Conversely, much that *is* contained in literary guise alone is not, as yet, reflected in visible or tangible evidence from this period; and much more that would be obscure if not incomprehensible when recovered in the field (I think here, in particular, of the cult of relics) is fairly fully explained for us in written evidence.

In the original six lectures (which are here represented by the next six chapters) a large number of Scottish historians and archaeologists, both students and teachers, gathered to join the lecturer in honouring the memory of David Hunter Marshall, a graduate of the University of Glasgow, later professor of history in the University of Manitoba. A partial contemporary of his, whose name is by no means out of place in a protohistoric context, was the philosopher R. G. Collingwood; a polymath who, using Roman Britain as his platform, sought to demonstrate that in the early centuries A.D. the disciplines of history and archaeology are neither mutually exclusive nor, when used to the full, wholly separable. Collingwood's message is hardly requisite in Scotland, where this dualistic approach to the recent past has for many years been exemplified in the work of men like W. F. Skene, H. M. Chadwick, W. D. Simpson, and F. T. Wainwright, to say nothing of Sir George Macdonald and the extensive circle of Romanists in North Britain. South of Tweed, however, this is still not everywhere the case. In shifting the focus of my own studies, over a decade or so, from prehistoric to protohistoric archaeology, and thus of necessity becoming involved as much with documentary sources as with material clues, it has distressed me to encounter, even today, much mutual incomprehension and untimely suspicion lingering on between archaeologists and historians. The point which has struck me most forcibly is that suspicion tends to arise, not from any failure to appreciate the diverse natures of the evidences *per se*, but from an unfamiliarity with the methods of inference employed in each circumstance.

Archaeology, whether one regards it as an art, a science, or (in modern jargon) a social science, is no more than a set of techniques used to recover information about the otherwise unrecorded, or partially recorded, past. Archaeological writing should be based synthetically and analytically on controlled inferences drawn from all the information so recovered—even if any such inference is at best, as A. L. F. Rivet happily comments, 'a delicate balance of probabilities'. I would not dare to attempt a definition of history —R. G. Collingwood and E. H. Carr each required a book to do so—save to point out that it has an additional dimension; the information about the past which history seeks to provide, or to discuss, has usually (unlike archaeological information) been processed already by a human mind. This does not *ipso facto* equate historical reconstruction with the past as it really was, but it does result in the provision of a fuller, richer, kind of information than anything the archaeologist can hope to offer, and the historian's work therefore carries greater risks and greater rewards. An excavated church is, when all is said and done, no more than an excavated church; there is a limit beyond which inference, however cunningly deployed, cannot legitimately wander. But to read and to reread the writings of men like St. Augustine or the Venerable Bede is to experience the past on two levels—the absorption of whatever factual information is conveyed by the words in themselves and despite the gap of centuries the projection of the writers as persons and the milieux in which, and for which, they wrote. I find so often, as many students do, that it is this second and higher level alone which illuminates certain interpretations and marks others as impossible.

My tribute to the memory of Professor Hunter Marshall, and through him to that long tradition of Scottish learning to which I am personally indebted, will be an attempted exposition of a period in our past (the rise of Christianity, from late Roman times to the Norse invasions) where, of a set purpose, both written and material evidence will be presented as closely linked components. In the title of the book, the expression 'North Britain' is chosen mainly to underline the irrelevance of later political boundaries to early Christian times; it also allows the inclusion, besides present-day Scotland, of Northumbria, Cumbria, and the Isle of Mann, and much of Ireland. The continuous references to events and remains in Wales, Cornwall, parts of present-day England, and the Continent, should not obscure an intentionally greater dependence on evidence derived from north of the Humber.

The Christian reader may find many features of insular Christianity explained below in terms of pagan or prehistoric monuments, and some instances of continuity between pagan and Christian practice argued. These explanations, frequently the least improbable in such little-known byways of the past, follow from the study of religious phenomenology, a study I have found of practical help. This requires, perhaps, a short clarification. The central message of the New Testament, that redemption and the

means of grace were provided for us, the priesthood of all be-
lievers, through God's assumption of manhood and His crucifixion
in the person of Jesus Christ, remains untouched. It is a message
conveyed by the Gospels, by patristic writing, and additionally
through the means of symbols; these apart, it does not and cannot
require any material reflection. On the other hand, the outward
and visible form assumed by humanly constructed burials or
burial-grounds, by the commemoration of dead humans by living
humans, by the retention of skeletal fragments and like trivia as
relics, and by the building of structures specially designed for the
ceremonies of worship, are man's accretions in response to this
message. As such, they are independent of the Word, and for the
most part devoid of direct biblical authority. They are no more
than the handiworks of what Professor Mircea Eliade has called
'religious man'. They are, moreover, the Christian versions of
certain ideas—the doctrine of rebirth, the sacred place, the guar-
dianship and propitiation of the dead, and the efficacy of sympathetic magic—which prove, upon examination, to occur widely
and commonly in the outward manifestations of most known
religions both past and present. My suggestions, that many
external sacral aspects of insular Christianity owe something to,
or are in some fashion rooted in, external sacral aspects of our
pagan Iron Age, arise from some years of study of early Christian
archaeology in the British Isles; they leave untouched the central
core of Christian faith, something not itself explicable in terms of
any particular set of visible religious phenomena. What we shall
attempt to examine, chapter by chapter, is the impact of this
message and this faith upon our countryside and upon our history.
In so doing, we can hardly fail to gain an added appreciation, not
just of a noteworthy segment of the archaeological past, but also
of our first Christians.

Some theatre critic—probably the late James Agate—is credited
with having said that he could stand a *bad* play; the one thing that
really made him shudder was a play with a message. The Hunter
Marshall lectures were not of course conceived as having enter-
tainment value, nor does this book seek to convey any particular
dogma, but there are two major points which I hope will emerge

by the end of the last chapter, and I want to try to sum them up in advance.

The first is that early Christian archaeology (or, as some people fatuously persist in labelling it, 'Dark Age' archaeology), should within its British and Irish setting be a completely unitary study. (By 'British' I imply the adjective corresponding to 'Great Britain', or 'the British mainland'—Scotland, England, Wales, and the adjacent islands; by 'Irish' I mean the adjective proper to unified Ireland, the political Republic and the Six Counties; the entire geographical grouping is 'the British Isles', to which no adjective strictly corresponds, though I shall occasionally use 'insular' for this, as in 'insular Christianity'. This is a tricky usage, which one tries to follow consistently, mainly to avoid offending Irish susceptibilities.) There never was a 'Celtic Church'—the phrase exemplifies what Professor Joshua Whatmough calls 'the extra-linguistic abuse of the term *Celtic*', and rightly so. The word *Celt*, when not describing some variety of prehistoric axe or chisel, means 'a member of a Celtic-speaking, or formerly Celtic-speaking, nation'. The official language of the church in Celtic-speaking parts of the British Isles was Latin, as elsewhere, and the few procedural difficulties (forms of episcopal consecration, the tonsure, and the calculation of the date of Easter) which marked off most of Ireland and North Britain from Christian Europe in the sixth and seventh centuries were the results of peripheral survival, not the outcome of separatist heresy.

The popular archetype of a Celtic saint—ascetic, humbler of the proud and mighty, tireless warrior of Christ, the playmate of birds and animals—reaches its literary peak, not in the jejune and imperfectly constructed Irish Latin lives, but in Bede's prose biography of St. Cuthbert; the biography of a middle-class, and very holy, Northumbrian Angle, composed by the most learned Englishman of the period. Scotsmen in particular should never underrate the strength and tenacity of the Northumbrian heritage; it was a late northern dialect of Northumbrian English which provided the medium for Robert Burns's achievements. What we often tend, in the setting of early Christian archaeology, to regard as 'Celtic art', by which, strictly, we should signify 'an art peculiar to speakers, or former speakers, of a Celtic language' is not in this sense Celtic at all; the nearest approach to a purely Celtic art occurred in the European Iron Age. The general notion of 'Celtic art' in the historic period is derived from the style of the Book of Kells, the High Crosses of Scotland and Ireland, and eighth-century metalwork, still imitated with uneven fidelity in costume jewellery and military trappings. This is a complex blend; of revived Late Iron Age ornament in the north and west of Britain (perhaps continuously maintained in Ireland), of the problematical 'animal style' art of the Picts, of an art style introduced by Germanic-speaking settlers, and of late Classical ornament and motifs brought by trade and contact from the Mediterranean. Of the various centres in which this amalgamation took place, one of the most influential and most fully documented was not 'Celtic' at all; it was early Northumbria.

I am not decrying the Celtic-speaking peoples' contributions to our early history; indeed, as a professed Celtic nationalist and a long-standing advocate of regional devolution, I should find it hard to achieve quite such a degree of objectivity. In any event, the theme of the Celtic contribution is preached, or is supposed to be preached, annually in a number of universities by far abler scholars than myself under the provisions of the O'Donnell Lectures, founded to that very end by a descendant of St. Columba's stock. I merely seek to emphasize, and shall by implication do so in the chapters which follow, the irrelevance of linguistic or national divisions to the consideration of a religion which itself ignored all such barriers. The irrelevance is, if possible, even more marked when we consider the associated artistic achievements.

Unfortunately, the study of British protohistory has long been parcelled out into such narrow compartments as 'the Celtic Church', 'Irish Archaeology', 'The Problem of the Picts', or 'Early English Settlements'. There was admittedly a time when the lack of adequate books at undergraduate level, the frightening vision of untranslated texts in Celtic tongues, and the absence of any sort of corpus for practically all manner of remains, made this approach the only possible one within the normal span of human existence. That day has gone, a happy fact not universally recognized; and those who still prefer to adhere to these partitioned and obsolescent topics, cautiously excised from the body of proto-history, are in no sense fighting in the front line, using what Professor A. J. Allaway has called 'the cutting edge of advancing knowledge'. They might unkindly be described (to continue the analogy) as sheltering in the rest-camps at base. The present struc-ture of protohistoric studies in Britain, and this applies to Ireland as well, may aptly be compared to the position in prehistoric studies before the late Professor Gordon Childe widened all our horizons, and made the idea of a return to the older narrow out-look an unthinkable one. Though Childe's most influential books appeared while he was Director of the Institute of Archaeology, in London, it is significant that the preliminary thinking was done, and the several *ballons d'essai* provocatively released upwards, during his years in the Abercromby Chair at the University of Edinburgh. We need to see the (entire) British Isles as one poten-tial field of study, in protohistory just as in prehistory, and to plan our work undeterred by sources composed in languages other than English, by unfamiliar place-names, by undatable art styles, and by the tiny total of correctly excavated key sites.

My second point is a little more complex. The emergence of Ireland (less the Six Counties) as a politically separate entity has been accompanied, after an initial period of self-adjustment, by the gradual assumption of a surprisingly un-Irish role in *Welt-politik*, a realistic appraisal of internal resources and limitations, and (from our present point of view) a most distinguished tradi-tion of scholarship. I say 'tradition', because of course this long antedates the events of 1921 and 1916; nineteenth-century Ireland, like nineteenth-century Scotland, housed a great many scholars of European stature. In the early Christian interest, one thinks immediately of George Petrie, O'Donovan, Eugene O'Curry, and Whitley Stokes; and the long line of learned Teutons attracted to Irish and Celtic studies. The steady publication (under the aegis of various bodies, in recent times including the Irish Manuscripts Commission, the National Museum of Ireland, the Royal Irish Academy, the Dublin Institute for Advanced Studies, and the Irish universities) of a great portion of the early art, archaeology, history, and linguistics of early Christian Ireland still continues, most of it at a very high level of learning and achievement, and rightly aimed at European rather than just Irish or British markets. Mlle Françoise Henry's recent *Zodiaque* trilogy on early Irish art is a notable example; the Dublin Institute's rather more specialized *Scriptores Latini Hiberniae* series is another, and active interest has long been extended to the far side of the Atlantic.

The not unexpected outcome has been that early Christian studies in the British Isles, whether literary, artistic, or archaeological—and this does not wholly exclude the Anglo-Saxon field—have perforce been dominated by this rich Irish harvest, since on this sort of scale only the material from Ireland is readily available in print. We must also face the fact that neither in western nor northern Britain do we have any centre that begins to enjoy that prestige and support which mark the Dublin Institute; and that the number of students of this period of our past, who are sufficiently trained or experienced to be able to add to the general corpus from other parts of the British Isles, are few and far between.

I hope that, in centring my book on North Britain, I can demonstrate that the British material, less widely known but not all that much less visually spectacular than the Irish finds and sites, both awaits, and deserves, the prolonged researches and full presentation already accorded to so many of the treasures of Ireland. When such a massive task is accomplished we should, I suspect, obtain a view of the development of early Christianity in the British Isles which would have a properly balanced perspective. In a very compressed format, squeezing into six overloaded chapters what could easily be extended into sixteen, I shall try to give a foretaste of that perspective, and to indicate specific areas and subjects in which intensive research could hardly fail to justify the effort, with exciting and formative results. The extensive region, of both islands and mainland, which we know today as the administrative counties of Argyll, Inverness and (Wester) Ross, alone holds enough field-work to occupy a large team over the next fifty years. How many students of the early Christian period who have made the trip to Iona, easily if dearly accomplishable through the MacBrayne fleet, have actually visited Lismore and Applecross as well? Miss Campbell of Kilberry's 'Mid-Argyll Survey', one of the really outstanding field-surveys of our generation, the more so because planned and executed by a highly skilled worker with intimate local knowledge; the astonishingly productive corpus of sites produced for Islay by a devoted team of amateur archaeologists; and the Royal Commission's current Inventory work in the various sectors of Argyll, proffer between them a basis for analytical research, which lops about twenty years of initial exploration off any projected programme otherwise starting from scratch.

2. *The Historical Background: Diocese and Monastery*

CHRISTIANITY BEGAN IN THE HOLY LAND, and its first roots lay in the eastern provinces of the Roman Empire. This is a truism, but it is one that, in discussing any aspect of Christianity in early Britain, we must constantly bear in mind. The transmission of this exotic faith to the British Isles took place, not as any isolated fact of history, but within the framework of continuous contact between the Mediterranean heartland of that Empire and one of its remoter provinces. Before the early fourth century, one can assume that this was largely the work of individual Christians, soldiers or civilians—Greeks, Romans, Syrians, and Africans—who followed the mandate implicit in the words of St. Paul, 'Their sound is gone out into all lands, and their words unto the ends of the world'.[1] Whether or not we choose to take the comments of Tertullian (*circa* 200) or of Origen (*circa* 240) as to the existence of Christianity in Romanized Britain, and beyond, as factual statements or as mere figures of speech,[2] there is now an impressive and slowly growing body of evidence for the existence of organized Christianity in many parts of Britain by the fourth century.[3]

In preparing a distribution map of such clues, we should omit small portable and valuable objects of supposedly Christian character, or those displaying specifically Christian signs and mottoes. Their find-spots may well have arisen from theft, or through loot, or by casual loss in transit. Using such fixed remains as mosaic pavements with Christian symbols,[4] building-blocks with

---

[1] *Epistle to the Romans* 10: 2.
[2] Toynbee 1953, 1–2; Hanson 1968a, 29, n. 3.
[3] Toynbee 1953; Frend 1955; Wall 1966.
[4] e.g. Toynbee 1964 (cf. Painter and Taylor 1967).

Christian graffiti,[1] alleged church-sites,[2] and, from historical sources, the sites of martyrdoms[3] and bishops' seats,[4] it is possible to construct a tentative map (Fig. 1) for late Roman Britain that indicates two major zones of Christian activity. One is the extensively Romanized urban-centred region of southern England, with a south-east bias. The other runs north-west from the legionary fortress and civil settlement at York to the line of Hadrian's Wall, the 'Northern Frontier Zone'.

In the latter area, we have the fourth-century tombstone of the (possibly) Christian Greek, Flavius Antigonus Papias, at Carlisle:[5] another, of one Titius, at Brougham;[6] and from Maryport, a (lost) fragment with a *chi-rho*, probably the corner of a tombstone, that could even belong to the early fifth century.[7] It is just possible that another inscribed stone from Carvoran,[8] of third-century date, relates to a Christian. This western emphasis raises the whole question of the history of Carlisle, with its large and anomalous walled civil settlement[9] at this end of Hadrian's Wall. It is here, in a region less exposed to the irruptions and destructions associated with the Picts and other northern barbarians than the central and eastern stretches of the frontier defence, that we might look for continuity into sub-Roman times of civil life, and with it, some form of organized Christian flock. York (*civitas Eboracense*) apparently possessed a bishop in 314, as did London (*civitas Londinense*), and a third place which is probably meant for *Colonia Lindunensium*, Lincoln.[10] It is quite conceivable that

[1] *JRS* 51 (1961), 193; Wall 1966, 214.

[2] Silchester—*JRS* 52 (1962), 185. Caerwent—*BBCS* 15 (1952–4), 165. Lullingstone—Meates 1955; Toynbee 1955, 5–13 with refs. St. Martin's (Canterbury)—Jenkins 1965; Wilson, P. A. 1968. Lydd—Jackson and Fletcher 1968. St. Alban's—Morris 1968a. One may have to add Poundsbury, Dorset—Green 1968.

[3] Bede, *H.E.* i. 7, i. 18; Morris 1968a.

[4] Toynbee 1953, 4; Hanson 1968a, 31–4.

[5] Salway 1965, 216, no. 20 (= *RIB*, no. 955).

[6] *RIB*, no. 787.

[7] *JRS* 46 (1956), 148.

[8] *RIB*, no. 1828; Watson 1968, 52; Salway 1965, 221.

[9] Salway 1965, 41–5.

[10] Acts of the Council of Arles in 314; text, Toynbee 1953, 4. For Dr. Mann's suggestion that each bishop represented a British *provincia*, see *Antiquity* 35 (1961), 316.

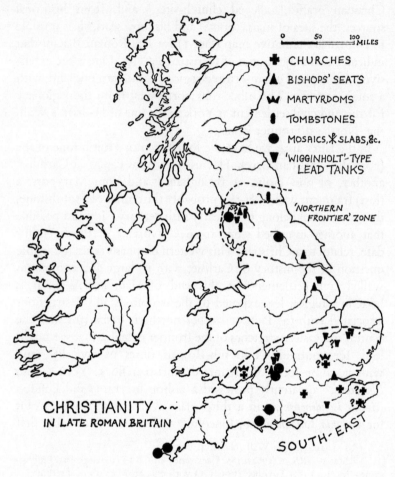

0   50   100 MILES

✚ CHURCHES
▲ BISHOPS' SEATS
♈ MARTYRDOMS
▮ TOMBSTONES
⬤ MOSAICS,✸SLABS,&c.
▼ 'WIGGINHOLT'-TYPE
     LEAD TANKS

'NORTHERN
FRONTIER' ZONE

CHRISTIANITY ~~
IN LATE ROMAN BRITAIN

SOUTH-EAST

Fig. 1.

there were other bishops by the later fourth century, and Carlisle
is a likely claimant for one. For it can now be argued,[1] on the
strength of the recently found Brougham milestone,[2] that there
was a *civitas Carvetiorum* in the Eden valley. Either Carlisle was

[1] I owe both this paragraph and the ideas expressed to the kindness of Dr. J. C.
Mann (Durham).
[2] *JRS* 55 (1965), 224 (no. 11) and pl. xix. 3; the full name of the *civitas* is from
RIB, no. 933.

the capital of this *civitas*, with a territory stretching up to a point beyond Brougham, or else the *civitas* of the Carvetii was confined to the upper Eden valley, with a capital at Brougham or at Kirkby Thore; in which event the argument for Carlisle having achieved city status is very strong. Even if this were not so—and the settlement at Carlisle, after all, covered seventy acres—Professor A. H. M. Jones has pointed out[1] that in other, Eastern, frontier areas of the late Empire, bishoprics were created at important forts or frontier stations. Carlisle would again be a strong candidate on these grounds.

This is directly relevant to the question of what form the Church assumed in Britain, both before and after 400. The consensus of belief today is that, over most of what is now England, Christianity barely survived (and in some regions did not survive at all) the upheavals which appear to have marked the fifth century—upheavals due not only to the Germanic settlements, but also to a period of civil unrest[2] following the Roman withdrawal. On the other hand, Christianity in the north, in Wales, and in the south-west, cannot now safely be attributed (as it used to be) to Christian refugees fleeing to the hills before the advancing Anglo-Saxons. Garrisons, civil settlements, and trading establishments had been established in Roman times in many parts of these less-Romanized regions. The tombstones from the north-west, and other remains from south Wales and Cornwall, indicate that Christianity could have continued (albeit sparsely) from the fourth century into sub-Roman times.

The Church in Roman Britain must, as elsewhere in the Empire, have been diocesan. Bishops ruled from urban seats. Where the Church survived continuously, we have every reason to suppose that such a diocesan structure, initially, survived with it. Bishops, priests, perhaps a deacon, are mentioned on inscribed memorial stones of the fifth and sixth centuries;[3] bishops are also mentioned in the few historical sources, the two best known being Ninian and Patrick.

---

[1] Jones 1964, iii. 295, nn. 10 and 11.
[2] Morris 1966 argues for this.
[3] See p. 102.

Ninian's episcopal status, indeed his very name, is first given to us by Bede, some three centuries after Ninian's traditional lifetime. As both Professor John MacQueen and I have recently set out[1] our not wholly dissimilar views on this difficult topic at some length, I confine myself to the conclusions. Ninian, or Nynia, or Niniavus,[2] was a Christian North Briton, probably a native of the Carlisle area. Having been consecrated, perhaps by another bishop in Carlisle, he was sent to Whithorn, where there was a pre-existing Christian community in need of a bishop.[3] From here, he and his immediate successors administered a diocese which embraced modern Galloway, if no more. I see no evidence that he founded any monastery (in the sense in which we shall shortly define this term), that he had any direct connection with St. Martin of Tours, or that he engaged in personal missionary adventures in his native Cumbria, still less among the Picts in the east and north-east of Scotland.[4] His successors in the diocese probably include those *sacerdotes* or bishops[5] named on a late fifth-century memorial stone at Kirkmadrine in the Rinns of Galloway.[6] I fear, too, that we must reject the notion that the foundations of a small rectangular building, almost certainly a chapel, revealed by the Marquis of Bute and later by Dr. C. A. Ralegh Radford just east of Whithorn Priory church have any direct connection with Ninian. The 'few patches (on) . . . the outer face . . . daubed . . . with a coarse cream mortar'[7] have, over two decades, grown alarmingly (e.g. 'outer face . . . daubed with white plaster',[8] 'rough stone once coated with a white plaster',[9] etc.) but do not suffice to outweigh the objections against this being a principal church, built by Ninian or in Ninian's own time, and known as *Candida Casa*. It is, in my view, a subsidiary chapel of seventh-century (or later) date, constructed when the site at Whithorn had

[1] MacQueen 1961; Thomas 1966a, esp. 112–16.
[2] Anderson, A. O. 1948, postulates this original form.
[3] Thompson 1958.
[4] Thomas 1968a, 117, nn. 8 and 12, for references to main recent writings in the 'Ninianic' controversy.
[5] Dowden 1898. [6] *CIIC* i, 494–5, no. 516.
[7] Radford 1950, 115. [8] Henderson 1967, 210.
[9] So Bulloch 1963, 37.

become a monastery under Irish influence. On the other hand, certain features which may very well be of Ninian's time have now been found at Whithorn, and will be discussed in the next chapter.[1]

A sounder line of evidence is that provided by the various stone slabs and pillars on which, in standard or debased Roman capitals, short funerary inscriptions are hacked out or incised. The use of such memorials is rare indeed[2] for Christians in Roman Britain, but from the later fifth century these occur in some numbers in the western and northern parts of the British mainland. We shall consider later the reasons for this secondary date, and limited geographical range. The inscriptions themselves offer us some unexpected information. They provide the oldest written evidence for insular Celtic languages,[3] apart from a handful of pre-Roman southern British coins, and classical literature. Such linguistic clues, taken in conjunction with epigraphic ones—the extent to which the letters used have devolved from the classical Roman models, for example—allow us to arrange these inscriptions in an approximately dated sequence.[4]

In North Britain, while the oldest instances in both the Carlisle[5] and Whithorn[6] areas belong to the fifth century, others which are known from further north—notably in the central Tweed basin, and around the Firth of Forth[7]—belong to the sixth century. The primary Christian figure of Strathclyde, the person we know as St. Kentigern or St. Mungo, is later in time than St. Ninian; his obit in the *Annales Cambriae* at 612 under the name of Conthigirn(i) need not be discredited. The evidence, which I have rehearsed in greater detail elsewhere,[8] points to a slow spread of Christian ideas northward from the Carlisle and Whithorn areas in the period from 450 to 600, probably through the medium of

---

[1] See p. 55.
[2] *RIB*, nos. 690 (?), 787, 955, 1828, and 1722 (5th cent.); cf., however, Watson 1968.
[3] *LHEB*, chap. 5.
[4] Nash-Williams 1950, 1–16; RCAHMW Anglesey 1937, civ–cxvii.
[5] *RIB*, no. 1722 (= *CIIC* i, no. 498).
[6] *CIIC* i, nos. 516, 517(?), 520.   [7] Thomas 1968a.
[8] Ibid. 102 (map).

conversions at ruling-family level. To the extent that early Christian long-cist cemeteries are found on both sides of the Forth, in the Lothians *and* Fife, the southernmost Picts—Bede's *australes Picti*[1]—may have then come into contact with a church originating in the diocese of Whithorn; and the tradition that Ninian had

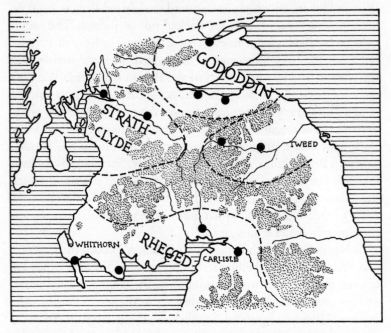

Fig. 2. Sub-Roman dioceses and native principalities in the Lowlands; a tentative reconstruction. The dots represent known, or probable, ecclesiastical sites of the period (cf. Thomas 1968a).

converted the southern Picts may stem in some way from this contact. A church which advances only some eighty miles in two centuries, and leaves such very little evidence of its advance, is not, however, a missionary church.

The clues are slender, the features few; but I would go so far as to suggest that the sub-Roman church in North Britain was a diocesan one. Ninian, of course, Kentigern in Strathclyde, presumably the *sacerdotes* (Viventius and Mavorius) named on the

[1] Bede, *H.E.* iii. 4; cf. Thomas 1968a, 107 (map).

Kirkmadrine stone, the person whose name must be misrecorded as 'Nicolai episcopi' (in the genitive) at Cross Kirk, Peebles,[1] and the bishop Naitan on the newly found stone (also from Peebles),[2] were all diocesan bishops. Their seats were, I suspect, at Carlisle, Whithorn, Glasgow, somewhere in the region of Edinburgh (Abercorn?) and somewhere in the central Tweed basin (Old Melrose?). It is quite impossible to define, with anything approaching a solid line, the boundaries of such dioceses, even if they possessed exact bounds as we understand the term (Fig. 2); but I have hinted at one fairly obvious correlation, with the post-Roman kingdoms of the North.[3] Thus Glasgow would have belonged to Strathclyde; Whithorn and Carlisle between them (divided, perhaps, by the Dumfriesshire river Nith) would have served Rheged; the area around the Forth may be linked with the Gododdin of the heroic poem;[4] and the long valley of the Tweed, 'Greater Tweed-dale', as it has been usefully labelled, with all its subsidiary valleys, should be the lost native state of *Bernaccia*[5] which, like Deira and Elmet further to the south, became submerged (though not without trace) in the later Anglian kingdom of Northumbria.

A point of some relevance is that the names of these episcopal seats may have survived into the seventh century. Bede, whose scholarly interest in linguistics is obvious, and who must have been familiar with four, if not five, languages,[6] gives us the names (with, in some cases, what he considers to be their etymologies) of nearly all the ecclesiastical foundations in the Northumbrian kingdom. These are almost all given in Old English, though it is clear that the list includes some sites which must pre-date the Anglian settlement. A small group possesses non-English names. Thus Abercorn, on the southern shore of the Forth, employed shortly after 680 by Bede's friend Trumwine as a bishop's seat,

---

[1] RCA(H)MS Peebles 1967, ii. 204.
[2] Unpublished; forthcoming, with reading by Prof. Kenneth Jackson.
[3] Thomas 1968a; cf. Hughes 1966, Index, s.vv. 'diocesan episcopacy'.
[4] Jackson 1969.
[5] *LHEB*, 701–5 ('Appendix; The Name *Bernicia*').
[6] Old English; Latin; Greek; probably some Hebrew; possibly some British or Irish in relation to place-names. Cf. Thompson, A. H. 1935, 162–3, 257–9.

and possibly founded some decades earlier as a small Anglian monastery, is given as *Aebburcurnig*, 'the horned confluence', the place where two streams meet at a promontory.[1] Old Melrose is *Mailros*, 'the bare promontory', in an ox-bow of the Tweed.[2] We do not unfortunately know the native British name of Whithorn, though it can hardly have been *Candida Casa*, for which the Old English *Hwitaern* is a direct translation, nor 'Rosnat', which may not even be in Scotland.[3] In the last case, Carlisle, Bede rather pedantically calls this *Lugubalia* in his History,[4] using the British Latin form from some written source. In his Prose Life of Cuthbert, however, he follows the anonymous biographer of the saint in calling it *Luel* which, as Professor Kenneth Jackson shows,[5] represents a *spoken* form [= ləowel], to which in the period around 700 this name would have broken down from the older *Luguvalium*.

Why did these particular names remain more or less unchanged? All four places possessed Anglian monasteries or convents; two were bishops' seats, and Old Melrose was hardly less prominent. I suspect that these were the sites of the principal sub-Roman diocesan churches of the North. Is it just conceivable that others existed, for instance at Abernethy, Glasgow, Paisley,[6] Edinburgh (on the Castle rock), Hoddom, and Peebles?

A picture which diverges a great deal further from the Roman concept of bishops ruling from cities, over dioceses bearing some direct relation to civil administrative divisions, is offered by Ireland at the same period. Here I will do no more than call attention to certain likenesses between the settings of Patrick and Ninian. A careful digest of the Patrician literature[7] does, I think, tend to make one prefer the northern setting and the 'traditional' chronology for Patrick. This would allow him to have been a Romanized Briton from a fourth-century Christian family, like Ninian, from

[1] Watson 1926, 461.

[2] Ibid. 175, 496; air photograph, Chadwick, N. K. 1963, pl. 66.

[3] Wilson, P. A. 1964.

[4] *H.E.* iv. 29.   [5] *LHEB*, 688; Jackson 1948.

[6] Watson 1926, 194 (if from Lat. *basilica*).

[7] Most recent summaries; Binchy 1962, MacNeill (ed. Ryan) 1964, 221–4, Bieler 1968, and Hanson 1968a.

the Carlisle area; and the episcopal diocesan structure of church government would have been the only one with which he could have been familiar. It was, presumably, the one within which he was consecrated. As in the case of Ninian, Patrick's purpose in returning to Ireland was to act as the spiritual head of an existing, if diversified, Christian community. We may assume that he was born in the late fourth century, and died in the middle of the fifth, and that his life thus covered the transition from Roman to sub-Roman times.

There, however, the resemblances between the two men end. They do so because Ireland, much more so than North Britain, was technologically still in the (Late) Iron Age.[1] Ireland was subject to an advanced and intricate social structure, evolved over many centuries.[2] Land, cattle, the dimensions of one's own fortress—these were the outward symbols of wealth and position. Towns were non-existent, and would remain so until peoples of Germanic origin—Scandinavians, Normans, and English—founded them. Far from renouncing all earthly parentage, as the earliest Christians were adjured so to do, an Irishman existed primarily within the framework of his shifting kin-group systems—a state of affairs which will be familiar to any modern Celt, and one which Christianity never wholly overcame.

It cannot too often be stressed that we have no archaeology of the Patrician Church in the fifth century. Inscribed memorial stones of a kind, to be discussed below,[3] do quite probably appear before Patrick's time, but initially in a non-Christian context. The most recent study (and to my mind, outstandingly the best) of the manner in which the Church accommodated itself to the peculiar problems posed by Irish society is that by Dr. Kathleen Hughes.[4] Her conclusions as to the *form* of the Church are that, by the sixth century, within a few generations of Patrick's lifetime, our oldest sources 'quite unambiguously show a church under the rule of bishops. Each bishop held authority within his own *paruchia* . . . the *paruchia* seems to have been co-terminous with the *plebs*'.[5] We can translate *paruchia* here as 'diocese', though

[1] De Paor, L. and M. 1958. [2] Dillon 1954; Thomas 1964, 75, n. 1.
[3] See p. 96. [4] Hughes 1966. [5] Ibid. 50.

later it assumes a rather different meaning (the sphere of influence of a major monastic foundation). Dr. Hughes would translate *plebs* as 'tribe', leaving open the problem of whether the *tuath* (the smallest and most local petty kingdom), or even a sub-division of a *tuath*, is implied.[1] After the sixth century, when the Church in Ireland was monastic in emphasis, we hear far less of these 'tribal bishops' with their (fixed?) dioceses, but Dr. Hughes is emphatic that the system did not disappear at once.[2] The same position seems to have held good in Wales, and, by implication, in Cornwall. In the Life of St. Samson of Dol, composed in the early seventh century, the bishop is pictured as still in authority in south Wales; and Bede's record[3] of the British (Welsh or Cornish?) bishops who, at the same period, met St. Augustine somewhere in the west could also point to a surviving diocesan hierarchy.

It may therefore be supposed that the church in sub-Roman Britain continued to be organized on diocesan episcopal lines; the bishops' seats were linked to civil settlements, or were hard by the seats of secular power; and that the areas over which they held spiritual sway bore some correspondence to native kingdoms. In parts of North Britain, such arrangements appear to have lasted into the seventh century; particularly in Strathclyde, where the medieval diocese of Glasgow must represent in large measure its earlier counterpart. Elsewhere—under the special conditions prevalent in Ireland, in Wales, in the far south-west—the slow process of formal evangelization was impatiently jolted by the advent of a rather different kind of ecclesiastical structure; by the arrival of organized monasticism.

The growth of monasticism in the eastern provinces of the Empire, from groups of fugitive and ascetic hermits in the pre-Constantinian age to the elaborately organized communities of the fourth century, is an increasingly well-documented process.[4]

---

[1] Cf. Binchy's review in *Studia Hibernica* 7 (1967), 219 ('the original episcopal *paruchia* was certainly the *tuath* . . .').

[2] Hughes 1966.

[3] *H.E.* ii. 2 ('episcopos sive doctores proximae Brettonum prouinciae', and 'vii Brettonum episcopi').

[4] A good recent survey is Chitty 1960.

In the furthest West we are concerned with the latter stages. The spread of the monastic idea, northward and westward within the Mediterranean, and beyond, itself presents numerous facets of great interest. The social malaise which affected aspects of religious and intellectual life in the later Empire[1] made this form of Christian involvement particularly attractive to many, offering as it did much that an occasionally very worldly church could not. The prolific literature concerning the Desert Fathers was, we know, of wide and influential popularity.[2] In Gaul, apart from Martin's pioneer monasteries at Ligugé, near Poitiers, and at Marmoutier, near Tours, there were the foundations in the Marseilles area associated with John Cassian and Victor, and the island monastery of *Lerina* (Lérins) established by Honoratus.[3]

If we seek to answer the direct question 'When did monasticism first reach Britain?', we must be clear what, in this connection, we understand by the word *monasticism*. Monks, or nuns, in the sense of individuals who had taken personal vows of continence, chastity, poverty, or like virtues, existed in fifth-century Ireland, Patrick's own writings being the evidence.[4] There must be, at the least, an implication that the same is true of the contemporary Church in Britain, even if the late fifth-century figure *Rioc(h)atus*[5] is not entirely a convincing example of this.

On the other hand, a monastery—in the sense of a permanent, fixed, enclosed community under an abbot, obedient to a Rule, and with such outward manifestations as education, deliberate missionary work, dependent hermitages, and eventually daughter-houses—constitutes a phenomenon for whose presence in Britain or Ireland there is still no evidence before the very end of the fifth century A.D. This statement denies the widely propagated view that the first British monastery (in this sense) was established, about 400 or so, at Whithorn by Ninian, in imitation of Martin at Tours; and it does so for several reasons. The connection

---

[1] Momigliano 1963, *passim*.
[2] Sulpicius Severus, *Dialogues*—'*Postumianus*' (ed.; Hoare 1954, 68–121); Chadwick, N. K. 1955.
[3] Chadwick, N. K. 1955, 142–69; Chadwick, O. 1968.
[4] Hanson 1968a.
[5] *Pro*—Hanson 1968a, 34, 64–6; *contra*—Davies 1968, 136, n. 60.

between Ninian and Martin, or between Whithorn and Tours, is first reported, with reservations,[1] by Bede, and is then only implied. The present tendency is to discount it.[2] There are no indications that any monastery at Whithorn existed until (perhaps) the late sixth century.[3] Our solitary internal source for the Church in Ireland, the group of writings generally agreed to be Patrick's own, is (as Professor Christine Mohrmann has shown)[4] devoid of those technical Latin terms which would betray the presence of full-scale monasticism. No such monastery, among those archaeologically examined, has yet shown signs of an origin older than the last decade or so in the fifth century, and few are as old as this. Gildas, who was writing in the sixth century, probably about 540, can be used (with care) as some kind of authority for the earliest church in Wales, and, as Professor W. H. Davies concludes, 'the monastic element seems small (*scil.*, in western Britain) at the time of the composition of (Gildas') *Epistola*'.[5]

The short answer, as I (an archaeologist) see it, is that full monasticism was introduced first to south-west Britain, apparently directly from the Mediterranean, in the latter part of the fifth century. The fashion was doubtless reinforced from southern Gaul, Aquitaine, and (northern?) Spain, during the sixth century, this later link having some pronounced literary and artistic content.[6] If monasteries first appear in the south-west, and along the south coast of Wales, prior to 500, they occur in Ireland in the first half of the sixth century, spread to the Irish settlements in the north-west by the later sixth century, and were introduced to Northumbria (thence to other English kingdoms and, eventually, the Continent again) after 635. The precise manner in which the ideas and intentions that led men to found such monasteries were transmitted to Britain and Ireland from the Mediterranean, and indeed the narrower chronology of any such transmission, are matters of obscurity. They are also matters on which fresh light can only now be thrown by archaeological inquiry.

---

[1] *H.E.* iii. 4.   [2] Grosjean 1958; MacQueen 1961; Hanson 1968a, 58.
[3] Thomas 1966a.   [4] Mohrmann 1961, esp. 47–8.
[5] Davies 1968a, 142 (where *Epistola* = *De Excidio Britanniae*).
[6] Cf. Hillgarth 1961, 1962; Werckmeister 1963.

It would take a separate book to support this thesis, and I must confine myself here to the most important evidence. Sherds of exotic wheel-made pottery have, over a good many years, been recovered from a number of post-Roman sites in Ireland and west Britain.[1] Their non-Romano-British, and presumably imported, character has long been accepted by most workers, though identification in such precise terms as those of Late Roman B and Late Roman C red wares of the Mediterranean, and as known types of East Mediterranean amphorae and jars, was only first propounded (by myself) in 1957.[2] Subsequently, detailed work by Dr. John Hayes, working in the Mediterranean, and petrographic and mineralogical analyses by Dr. David Peacock, have confirmed these identifications and have permitted much closer estimates of date, and of geographic origin. The fine red wares (our Class 'A' imports) are, in the main, platters or low bowls, some of which bear stamped crosses and other early Christian symbols (Fig. 3). These may have been brought back by pilgrims returning from Egypt, or the Levant, or have been included in some form of casual sea-trade. The wine containers (our Class 'B' imports) are mostly of three distinct kinds (our 'B i', 'B ii', and 'B iv' varieties), and presumably held wines. Years ago, Heinrich Zimmer marshalled most of the available evidence for such an import trade,[3] commencing with the Old Irish word *fín* as a loan from Latin *vinum*, and including many references—some, unfortunately, too vague or general to bear much weight—to the existence of this traffic. The wine was, it is usually assumed, originally intended for the Eucharist, though from the varied find-spots some of it seems to have been diverted to secular ends. The implication is one of direct, if casual or irregular, trade. Wine-jars of our types 'B ii' and 'B iv', which may have come in this case from Syria or Palestine, begin in the fifth century and are current, 'B iv' to the mid sixth, 'B ii' to the mid seventh. Type 'B i', which is almost certainly Aegean—perhaps from wine-exporting islands like Rhodes and Chios—is current from early in the sixth century (Fig. 4).

[1] Thomas 1959, with refs.
[2] Thomas 1957.
[3] Zimmer 1910; cf. Vendryes 1920.

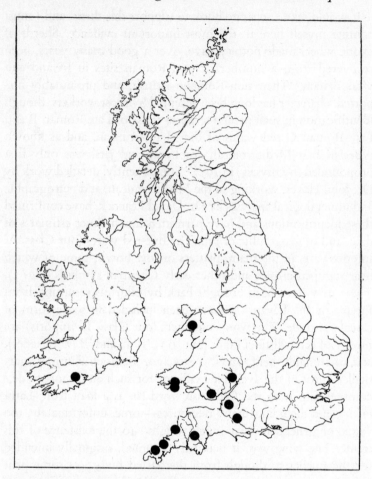

FIG. 3. Distribution (1969) of Class A imported wares in post-Roman Western Britain and Ireland.

It is doubtful if this trade continued until the Arab control of the Straits of Gibraltar (711).

If we make a distinction, as I think we now must,[1] between *primary* find-spots in Britain—coastal sites, where this exotic pottery was directly obtained from traders—and *secondary* ones,

[1] Thomas 1969, 29, n. 14.

inland, where wine-jars or platters were later transferred by exchange, or loot, or gift, the crucial primary context is Tintagel, a monastery occupying a high promontory (now nearly sea-eroded into an island) on the north Cornish coast.[1] Pottery recovered here in pre-war excavations included the early type

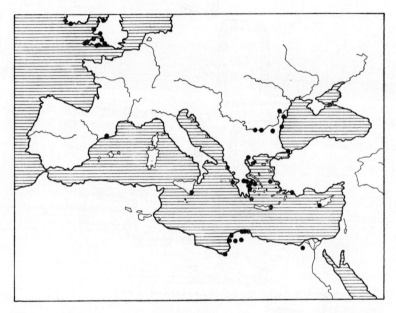

FIG. 4. Distribution of Class 'B i' imported ware (amphorae) in Britain, Eastern Europe, and the Mediterranean; 5th–6th centuries A.D. (after Hayes and Thomas).

'B iv', as well as Late Roman B, cross-stamped sherds of Late Roman C, and numerous 'B i' wine-jars. This is the earliest archaeologically dated full monastery in Britain (with individual sherds of Late Roman C perhaps as early as *circa* 480), as well as being the one closest, in sea-route terms, to Atlantic Europe and to the Mediterranean. Tintagel has a complex history. The clusters of monastic cells are not, as one-roomed structures almost always tend to be in western Britain at this period, circular; they are

[1] Radford 1935a, 1935b.

rectangular in plan (Fig. 5), and this, too, looks like a Mediterranean innovation.[1] The monastery appears to have been deserted after the eighth century, and was partly reoccupied with a secular

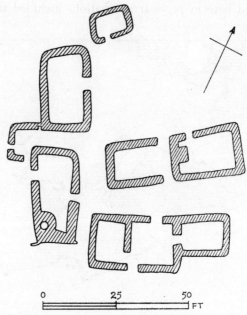

TINTAGEL , SITE D : LIVING CELLS
AFTER RADFORD

FIG. 5.

castle in the twelfth. The name 'Tintagel' is not Cornish; it may be Norman-French.[2] The original name is thus lost. If, as I suspect, it was *Rosnant*—'the promontory by the valley' (there is a long deep gorge inland on the east flank of the original headland), we may have here the mysterious 'Rosnat' or 'Rostat', presided over by Maucennus or Maucannus; a monastery at which, it was later claimed, such early saints as Enda of Aran, Tigernach of Clones, perhaps even St. David, were educated, Maucannus being identi-

[1] See Radford 1962, figs. 2 and 3 (plans).
[2] As first suggested by Henry Jenner.

fiable as the north Cornish patronal saint, Mauchan or Mawgan, of medieval hagiography.[1]

The detailed distribution of imported pottery of classes 'A' and 'B' on the coasts of Cornwall and Devon, and on those of south and west Wales, does suggest some close connection with the pattern of the earliest monastic houses (Fig. 6). In Ireland, this is harder to demonstrate. Monasticism in Ireland is fairly and firmly associated with the sixth century. A connection between central and southern Ireland, and south Wales, is not only posited by the chronology of the spread of full monasticism; it is a recurrent theme in both secular and religious literature.[2] So few of the major monasteries in Leinster or Munster which might have been founded at this time are available for any kind of field investigation, however (with churches, graveyards, and towns now occupying their sites), that it is difficult to pursue this line of inquiry archaeologically. Finian or Vinnianus, either Finian of Clonard (who died about 549) or Finian of Moville (who died about 579), is credited with a Penitential which refers, obliquely, to organized monastic life.[3] Finian of Clonard, in particular, is seen as one of the earliest monastic founders. Ciarán traditionally founded the monastery at Clonmacnois in the 540s.[4] Columcille or Columba established houses at both Durrow and Derry in the later sixth century.[5] Aran Mor, Devenish, Kildare, and Bangor are among other major monastic foundations which, traditionally, also originated in the sixth century.

It is, at this point in time, possible to say something about the physical form assumed by actual monasteries. They were generally enclosed. Adomnán's Life of Columba (written in the 690s),[6] the Rules and Penitential of St. Columbanus (from the beginning

---

[1] Wilson, P. A. 1964, listing refs.; cf. Watson 1926, 159, 496.

[2] O'Rahilly, C. 1924 (see also review by Vendryes, *RC* 41, 486); Kenney 1929, 257, 364, 376.

[3] Bieler 1963, 3–4, 75–95 ('A decision between the two alleged authors seems impossible' (p. 4); but (ibid., n. 3) F. of Clonard is perhaps regarded as the favourite).   [4] Kenney 1929, 378.

[5] Derry in 546 (A.U.), Kenney 1929, 424; Durrow is rather later, Anderson and Anderson 1961, 88–9.

[6] Reeves 1857; Anderson and Anderson 1961, 109–12.

Fig. 6. Imported Mediterranean pottery (Classes A and B) and major early monasteries in Wales and south-west Britain.

of the seventh century),[1] and a host of minor Lives and similar sources,[2] refer to something called *vallum*, or *vallum monasterii*. In Britain this is to be interpreted as meaning (jointly) an earthen bank and an outer quarry-ditch, surrounding or enclosing a

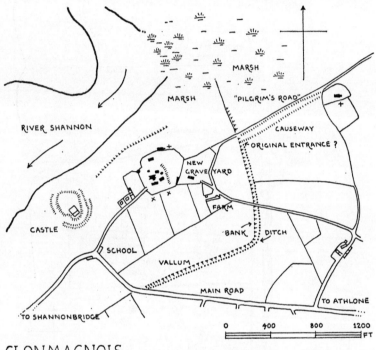

CLONMACNOIS

FIG. 7. Plan based on selective field-survey, 1958 and 1963.

monastery; and constituting a spiritual and legal, though hardly a militarily defensible, boundary between the monastic establishment and the world outside it. Old Irish terms, used in the same context—*lis* and *ráith* implying a bank of earth, *caisel* certainly and *dún* probably a stone-built rampart—are, like the Latin *vallum*, borrowing from the secular vocabulary.

Fieldwork at Clonmacnois, which lies on the bank of the river Shannon in co. Offaly (Fig. 7); on Iona, where the foundation-date

---

[1] Walker 1957, 154–5, sect. viii, 178–9, sect. 26; Bieler 1963, 106–7, sect. 26.
[2] Petrie 1845, 445–52; Plummer 1910, I. xcviii; Champneys 1910, chap. 2.

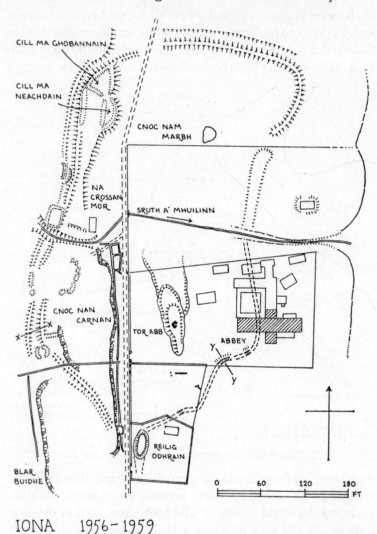

IONA   1956-1959

Fig. 8. Plan based on full-scale survey 1959; copyright, Russell Trust Excavations.

of 563 is an acceptable one (Fig. 8); and on several other larger sites, shows that some at least of the sixth-century foundations possessed *valla* enclosing large areas of approximately rectangular shape. In the case of Clonmacnois and Iona, such areas are of some ten acres or more, and would afford room for agricultural plots as well as for monastic buildings. The Iona *vallum* bank and ditch, which has been sectioned at several points, differs in detail as between these points. The west side is a large crudely constructed affair with a bank, ditch, and little outer bank, but the south side

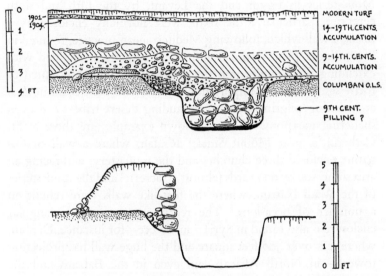

FIG. 9. Iona; section of the Columban vallum and ditch as excavated (above) and reconstructed (below), at point just south-west of Abbey church (see y-y on plan, fig. 8).

is more regularly executed, with a stone facing on the outer side of the single bank (Fig. 9). Another instance would appear to be at Glendalough (second half of the sixth century?), the foundation ascribed to Coemgen ('Kevin'), where Mlle F. Henry has provided a plan showing the extent of the monastic enclosure.[1] It is just conceivable that the early monastic enclosure believed to underlie Glastonbury Abbey, in Somerset, where one side of a massive vallum ditch has been encountered at two points,[2] is also within this class.[3]

[1] Henry 1964, 50, fig. 5.
[2] Radford 1957a; cf. *Med. Arch.* 2 (1958), 189.
[3] This site, unlike the smaller one on Glastonbury Tor (Rahtz 1968b) has, for some reason, failed to yield instances of the 'A' or 'B' imported wares.

The whole concept of this very large, free-standing, near-rectangular enclosure is alien to western Britain at this period—the only counterpart would be a Roman legionary marching-camp, which can hardly be relevant—and it may derive, like the idea of the permanent monastic establishment, from the East. Monasteries in Egypt and the Levant, by the fifth and sixth centuries, particularly the sixth, were normally enclosed by a massive wall which, following Mediterranean practice, resulted in a rectilinear plan. Justinian himself is sometimes credited with extending this practice into the provision of what amounted to fortresses, protecting important churches with their communities and visiting pilgrims against marauding desert tribes, and even sheltering garrisons. The best-known examples are those at St. Catherine's, near Mount Sinai;[1] R'safah, where a wall of this nature enclosed three churches and the monastery, embracing an area some 400 by 600 yards (almost 50 acres);[2] and the monasteries of the Wadi Natrun, where the fort-like walls were rebuilt on a number of occasions.[3] The rectangular or near-rectangular enclosure is also found in Syria;[4] in Greece—for instance, Daphni, where it is over 300 feet square and the huge wall has projecting towers[5]—in North Africa;[6] and even in the Balkans and the Caucasus.[7]

Whether or not this oriental concept of the monastery as a veritable fortress of the soldiers of God underlies the appearance of simpler but related *enceintes* in Atlantic Britain—and on present evidence it is hard to think of another explanation—many monasteries in Ireland and Britain were established in extant strongholds or fortified positions. These tend, naturally, to be pre-Roman Iron Age forts or (on the British mainland) Roman works. It must not

[1] Croly 1843; Krautheimer 1965, pl. 97.

[2] Krautheimer 1965, 187, pl. 96.

[3] Curzon 1849, chap. 7; Sawyer 1930; cf. also Deir el-Medinah near Luxor—Van der Meer and Mohrmann 1958, fig. 582.

[4] Lafontaine-Dosogne 1967, fig. 30 (plan); Lassus 1947, *passim*, and Van der Meer and Mohrmann 1958, fig. 294.

[5] Krautheimer 1965, 187.

[6] e.g. Tebessa—Krautheimer 1965, 187, fig. 59; cf. Van der Meer and Mohrmann 1958, fig. 352.

[7] e.g. Etchmiadzin, Soviet Armenia.

be assumed that such locales were chosen specifically for their defensive capacities—there is no example of a monastery being successfully defended against (say) Norse pirates—and two reasons for such choices come to mind. The first is that the strict physical aspects of a monastic rule could more readily be enforced within given limits, marking an area within which an abbot's word was supreme. In the *Rules* of Columbanus, for example, a penance is specified for those who go *extra vallum id est extra sepem monasterii* without a superior's leave.[1] The second is that deserted forts and earthworks, whether on hill tops or sea-promontories, appear from a great many literary instances[2] to have been in the personal gift of local rulers; perhaps through ancestral inheritance, or because such sites are normally on marginal land. This is particularly so in Ireland, where land tenure was governed by complex circumstances. Lives of saints abound with instances of *reguli* or chieftains making grants of such ready-made enclosures to monastic founders, as acts of piety or in the hope of spiritual intercession. Bede quotes cases of Roman shore-castles being handed over to saints. In north Wales, St. Cybi is given the Roman fort at Holyhead by king Maelgwn. There appear to be comparable examples of such reuse in western Europe at this same period.[3]

There are other such reoccupations which have left no such literary records. St. Molaise's monastery on the island of Inismurray, co. Sligo,[4] occupies what looks like a much older stone cashel. St. Mochaoi's at Nendrum, co. Down,[5] is an even clearer instance, the cashel being originally a triple one. At Dundesert, co. Antrim, which is now ploughed out, a church and burial-ground may have represented the remains of a small monastery (the name-element *disert* suggests this) in a bivallate rath of substantial proportions.[6] The natural fortress of Cashel, the ancient

[1] Walker 1957, 144.
[2] Plummer 1910, i, introduction; ibid. 44, 89, 184; Wade-Evans 1944, 248.
[3] Sulpicius Severus, *Dialogues*—'*Gallus*' (ed.; Hoare 1954), cap. 8 (monks, *circa* 400, in a fort at Amboise); and Columbanus' monastery in a ruined Roman fort at Annegray (Walker 1957, xxiii).   [4] Wakeman 1893.
[5] Lawlor, H. C. 1925; ASNI Down 1966, 292–5, pls. 77 to 81.
[6] Reeves 1857, 181–2; *disert* (Lat. *desertum*) in the sense of 'deserted place, hermitage, monastery'.

centre of Munster, is possibly another example, the lowest courses of the visible religious *enceinte* representing older secular defences.[1] At *Rathceltchair*, the ancient focus of Downpatrick, co. Down, the present cathedral (successor of much earlier religious activity) stands mainly within a prehistoric hill-fort.[2]

Ard-macha, the centre of the modern Armagh, was a rath given to Patrick by king Daire, or so the (late) Tripartite Life of the saint informs us.[3] In Britain recorded cases of royal gifts are those of the Roman fort of *Vindomora* (Ebchester, co. Durham) to Ebba —the parish church stands in the south-west angle of this fort;[4] Bede notes two such, by king Sigbert of the East Angles, to Cedd at *Ythancaestir* (probably the shore-fort at Bradwell-on-Sea, Essex,[5] and to the Irishman Fursa at *Cnobheresburg* (the shore-fort at Burgh Castle, Suffolk, excavated in recent years but not yet published).[6] If the tradition of king Maelgwn's grant of Caergybi, Anglesey, to St. Cybi is historical, it should be rather earlier; Maelgwn was one of the kings addressed by Gildas *circa* 540.[7]

The foregoing sites are all hill-forts or 'free-standing' constructions. There are also promontory-forts (if on high coasts, usually called 'cliff-castles'). These are strongholds where an effective defence can be made by cutting a bank and ditch across the landward neck, and so obvious and economic a mode of fortification was widely current in Atlantic Britain, and Ireland, throughout the Iron Age. Tintagel, as it was in sub-Roman times, is an excellent representative of this class; the great ditch, further enlarged in the Middle Ages for secular purposes, yielded sherds of imported Class 'B' pottery.[8] In North Britain, Deerness in Orkney (the original name, and patron, of which are not known) may stem from seventh- or eighth-century Irish missions in the

---

[1] Particularly on the E. and NE. faces.

[2] Reeves 1847, 354, note K; ASNI Down 1966, 98–9, pl. 15.

[3] Stokes 1887, i. 229; cf. 17th-century plan of Armagh, shown in Henry 1964, 42–3, fig. 2, and see now Norman and St. Joseph 1969, 118, pl. 69.

[4] Plummer 1896, ii. 236.

[5] *H.E.* iii. 22; Plummer 1896, ii. 178.

[6] *H.E.* iii. 19; Plummer 1896, ii. 171 (also Ministry of Public Building and Works excavations, *Med. Arch.* 3 (1959), 299; 5 (1960), 319; 6 (1961/2), 311).

[7] RCAHMW Anglesey 1937, lxviii, xci, 31–4.

[8] Radford 1935a, 401.

northern isles;[1] the *vallum* bank, as at Iona, seems to have an outer facing of stone. Dr. W. D. Simpson argued that the tip of the high promontory at Dundarg, on the north coast of Aberdeen, held the scant remains of a small monastery of pre-Viking date.[2] There are others in Northumbria where, following the mission from Iona to Lindisfarne in the 630s, surviving seventh-century monastic remains should always be seen as potentially of Irish or western British character. St. Abb's Head, Coldingham, Bede's *Coludi urbs*,[3] looks older than this period, and is perhaps (as O. G. S. Crawford suggested)[4] the *gaer golud* (= *caer*, 'fortress', +*Colud*) in the early Welsh poems collectively known as the *Book of Taliesin*.[5] The actual rampart, inside a large ditch, is peculiar in that the stones appear to be cemented together with a hard mortar, conceivably indicating a sub-Roman date (Fig. 10). Old Melrose, Bede's *Mailros*,[6] also a mid seventh-century foundation, occupies an inland promontory (*ros*) in a great U-bend of the Tweed, cut off by a substantial *vallum* bank and ditch which runs right across the neck (Fig. 11).[7]

Island localities were especially appropriate for the smaller 'eremitic monasteries', which will be discussed shortly, but were employed for larger foundations too, as we saw in the case of Inismurray. Islands in lochs and estuaries could be chosen, as well as those in the sea. One of the best-known is Inis Cealtra in Lough Derg, co. Clare, which may date from the sixth or seventh century; it would require major excavations to disentangle the various earthworks now visible.[8] The extension of monasticism from Ireland to western Scotland in the later sixth century, and to the Western and Northern Isles in the seventh, provides other examples. Iona is obvious; less well known is St. Mo-Luóc's foundation on Lismore, which should be seventh century,[9] and there is

---

[1] RCAMS Orkney and Shetland 1946, ii. 240, fig. 328.

[2] Simpson, W. D. 1954; Simpson, W. D. 1960.

[3] *H.E.* iv. 19, iv. 25.   [4] Crawford 1934.

[5] But not in the canon ascribed to Taliesin, and probably later; cf. Williams 1968.   [6] *H.E.* iv. 27.

[7] RCAMS Roxburgh 1956, ii. 323, no. 620 ('linear earthwork').

[8] Macalister 1916, 7 (plan); De Paor, L. and M. 1958, pl. 10.

[9] Reeves 1857, xliii. 298, 371, 460; Groome 1892, iv. 259.

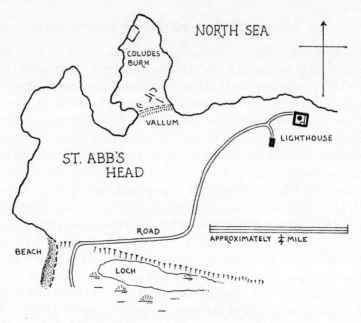

FIG. 10. The seventh-century monastery at Coldingham or 'Coludes burh'.
Plan based mainly on small-scale air photography.

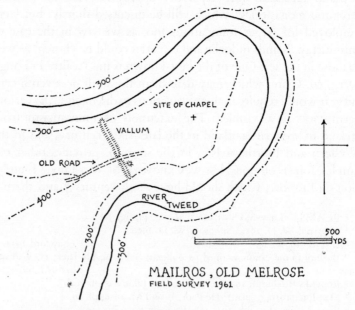

FIG. 11. Plan, greatly simplified, from a new field survey in 1961.

apparently a monastery of Columba's period on Tiree which has yet to be found.[1] In the Northern Isles, Birsay, on a tidal islet, has claims to be a full monastic foundation,[2] and parts of an earlier curvilinear *vallum* wall have been traced below the Norse and

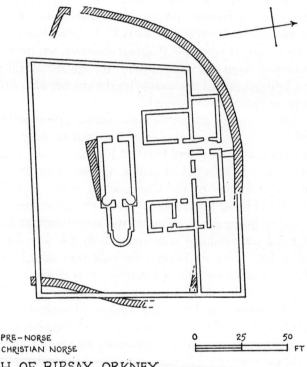

	PRE~NORSE
	CHRISTIAN NORSE

0   25   50   FT

BROUGH OF BIRSAY, ORKNEY
1961 : AFTER CRUDEN AND RADFORD

FIG. 12.

medieval rectilinear precinct (Fig. 12). Birsay may have been the principal monastery in Orkney. In Shetland field-work in 1967 led me to think that Papil, on East Burra, is the principal monastery for (at any rate) the southern half (see Fig. 71, p. 155).

Lindisfarne or Holy Isle, off the Northumbrian coast, was founded by Aidan, from Iona, in 634–5,[3] and though the medieval

[1] Anderson and Anderson 1961, 106, 118.
[2] Cruden 1965, 23, fig. 1, 30, fig. 3.   [3] *H.E.* iii. 3 et seq.

priory and its surroundings have largely obscured any earlier lay-out, there are grounds for suspecting that the first monastery, like its exact choice of locality, was modelled physically on the mother-house. The little-known Coquet Isle, further south, was according to Bede[1] a monastic house of some size. The Isle of Mann offers another instance, the monastery now believed to underlie the medieval cathedral on St. Patrick's Isle, Peel harbour.[2] Off the Welsh coast, Bardsey Isle (Caernarvonshire) was probably a full monastery from the sixth century, though the Royal Commission's investigators were unable (in the absence of excavation) to locate or define any remains.[3]

Our last group of what we must continue, provisionally, to call 'full monasteries' comprises those not sited in older secular forts or earthworks, nor placed to take advantage of such natural isolation as may be afforded by islands, nor indeed the few very large early foundations of the Clonmacnois type. This last group includes all those where there is reason to suppose that a monastic enclosure (normally curvilinear) was constructed at or not long after the establishment was founded. In the accessible series of rather late Lives of Saints—the collection edited by Charles Plummer under the title of *Vitae Sanctorum Hiberniae*,[4] the Welsh group from Brit. Mus. Cottonian MS. Vespasian A. xiv of the twelfth century,[5] and the collection known generally as the *Codex Salmanticensis*[6]—there are continual and repetitive references to saints who surround their monasteries with banks, or ditches, or both, the manual work being done by the founder in person, by the brethren, and by well-disposed helpers.

Though the plans of such enclosures are often distorted by facets of local topography, there is some evidence that the ideal was a circular one; an ideal rarely attained on the ground. The connection may be both with the curvilinear form assumed by most pre-Christian fortifications in Britain and Ireland, and with

[1] Bede, *Prose Life of Cuthbert* (ed. Colgrave 1940), cap. 24.
[2] Kermode and Herdman 1914, 112–13; Ashley 1958; Craine 1958.
[3] RCAHMW Caernarvonshire 1964, iii. 17–20.   [4] Plummer 1910.
[5] Wade-Evans 1944; cf. Hughes 1958, 197.
[6] Heist 1965.

the 'sacral circle' that, as we shall find, seems to characterize so many cemeteries and specialized individual graves in early Christian times.[1] This 'circular' goal was a conscious one, and is rationalized in several ways. The most striking is the plan of Tech Moling, the monastery of the seventh(?)-century saint Moling or

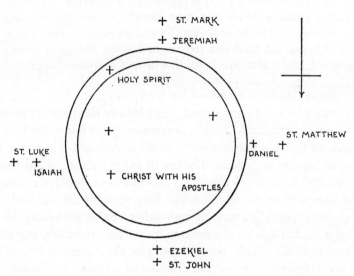

SCHEMATIC PLAN OF TECH MOLING, CO. CARLOW:
MONASTIC ENCLOSURE AND NAMED CROSSES

ADAPTED FROM BOOK OF MULLING, MS. TRIN. COLL. DUBLIN 60

FIG. 13.

'Mullins', co. Carlow, which occurs in the eighth-century 'Book of Mulling';[2] it has an added interest in being our earliest authority for the Irish custom of allotting names to individual free-standing crosses (Fig. 13). There is also a very curious passage in the Tripartite Life of St. Patrick (not before the ninth century), which has generally escaped comment. As the preceding passage refers

[1] See p. 58.
[2] Lawlor, H. J. 1897, 183 ('no corresponding physical traces seen'); Henry 1940, 102, fig. 37. On the connection between the Book and Tech Moling, Kenney 1929, 633. See also Hughes 1966, 149.

to Armagh, one can suppose that the passage in question does so as well. It reads (Whitley Stokes's translation):[1]

> The way in which Patrick measured the *ráth* was this: the angel before him and Patrick behind the angel, with his household and Ireland's elders, and Jesu's staff (*bachall isu*—a reference to a crozier) in Patrick's hand... In this wise, then, Patrick measured the *ferta*, namely, seven score feet in the enclosure (*lis*) and seven and twenty feet in the great house and seventeen feet in the kitchen and seven feet in the oratory; and in that wise it was that he used to found cloisters always.

Great caution must be used in interpreting any part of the Tripartite Life as a factual record, but I believe this to be an attempt to attach Patrician authority, in retrospect, not just to the foundation of the monastic enclosure (*ráth*) at Armagh, but to the circular lay-out in general. The use of *fert*, a form of burial-place,[2] *ráth*, and *lis* (usually a chieftain's enclosed homestead) as synonyms is comprehensible, since circular forts and circular monastic enclosures naturally resemble each other; and a monastery of the type at Armagh would contain cemeteries, churches, and other structures all within one *vallum*. The dimensions given of the 'great house' (*tech mór*; the principal church, probably), the kitchen, and the *aregal* (*airecal*, or oratory), ought to refer to a single, but vital, dimension in a rectangular building of customarily fixed proportions, either a length or a breadth.[3] The seven score feet of the enclosure might be argued to be a diameter of a circle, but I have wondered if it is not a radius. The remarks about the angel, Patrick, and the staff or crozier in Patrick's hands suggest, to any prehistorian, a version of that immemorial mode of laying-out a circle in the field. One man (Patrick) stands at the centre, with an end of a line held against a stick (his staff); another (the angel), keeping the line taut, goes before, or walks around, thus describing the circumference, marking it as he goes with heel-prints or twigs or pebbles.[4]

---

[1] Stokes 1887, i. 237.   [2] See p. 66.
[3] Richmond 1932, with refs.; esp. 101–3.
[4] An Early Bronze Age instance—Snail Down, Wilts., in *WAM* 56 (1955), 133, fig. 2, 137, 144.

Examples of full monasteries, large and small, which appear today to have been original constructions are quite common, and a selection must suffice. In a lot of cases, the addition of medieval precincts, or the enlargement of a burial-ground, has confused the initial outline, and it may take excavation to establish it. A not uncommon dilemma is the existence of a whole cluster of confused earthworks, visible both from the air and on the ground, where one senses the focus of the primary enclosure, but cannot clearly demonstrate it. Instances are the island monastery of Inis Cealtra, mentioned earlier;[1] Seirkieran in co. Offaly, associated with the *other* Ciarán, St. Ciarán of Saigir, and possibly of sixth-century origin;[2] and the interesting complex of banks and enclosures at Cerne Abbas in Dorset,[3] some of which must belong to the early monastery here.

Oval, ovoid, or near-circular enclosures occur widely. In north Cornwall, the large curvilinear churchyard at St. Kew represents the monastery of *Landocho* or *Landoho*, connected with the fifth- or early sixth-century saint Docco.[4] Maughold or Kirk Maughold in the Isle of Mann was clearly one of the island's principal monasteries (Fig. 14), and one stretch of the present precinct wall preserves the original enclosure.[5] Kingarth, on Bute, the monastery of St. Blane or Blaan, has never been planned as a whole, but seems originally to have been a large roughly bean-shaped enclosure.[6] In the far north-west, St. Maelrubha's foundation of *Apurcrossán*, Applecross, in Wester Ross, is now almost entirely ploughed out for forestry; but in field-work in 1964 I was able to trace the oval enclosure (Fig. 15) which marks this early (probably seventh-century) foundation.[7]

The post-635 spread of Irish Christian practices into Northumbria, and thence beyond, affords several examples. Abercorn, Bede's *Aebbercurnig*,[8] still displays traces of a fairly compact curvilinear enclosure, perhaps from the mid seventh century. Sectioning of part of the bank, within the present kirk-yard, in 1967

---

[1] Macalister 1916.   [2] Kenney 1929, 316; Raftery 1944, pl. xiii.
[3] RCHME Dorset 1952, i. 74–85, plans on 78, 80.   [4] Doble 1927.
[5] *MAS* iv. 10, fig. 7; Megaw 1950.   [6] Hewison 1893, 166, 192.
[7] Reeves 1859; Knight 1933, ii. 207–25.   [8] *H.E.* iv. 26.

revealed little beyond the strong probability that it had once been stone-faced; centuries of subsequent burials had caused too much disturbance. Faint remains of what may have been a substantial,

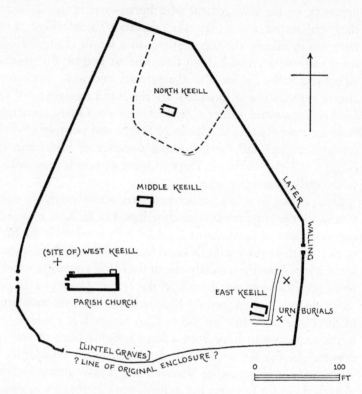

MAUGHOLD CHURCHYARD:
SIMPLIFIED PLAN FROM M.A.S 4TH REPORT (1915)

FIG. 14.

curved, raised causeway-bank were noted in pre-war excavations around the foundation at Whitby, Bede's *Streanaeshalch*, which dates from 657.[1] The little monastic foundation which Bede[2] calls *In Getlingum* is now the church and churchyard of Gilling (Yorks. N.R.); and here, too, it is still possible to make out the greatly

---

[1] *H.E.* iv. 23.   [2] *H.E.* iii. 14, iii. 24.

eroded traces of a small circular enclosure. Finally, in Mercia, there is the early eighth-century monastery of *Briudun*, Breedon-on-the-Hill, Leics., where details from an eighteenth-century estate map may give a clue to an original oval *vallum* largely coterminous with the defences of an Iron Age hill-fort.[1]

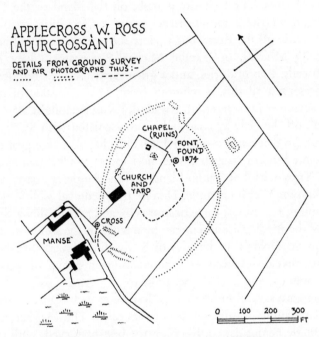

APPLECROSS, W. ROSS
[APURCROSSAN]

DETAILS FROM GROUND SURVEY
AND AIR PHOTOGRAPHS THUS :-
......   ::::::   - - - - -

CHAPEL
(RUINS)

FONT,
FOUND
1874

CHURCH
AND
YARD

CROSS

MANSE

0   100   200   300
FT

FIG. 15. Plan based mainly on visible features in field survey, 1963.

If we regard all the foregoing as representing, with variations, monasteries of pre-Viking date in the accepted sense, we must distinguish one other class which reflects a notably ascetic element in the early British and Irish churches. These are small communities which had, intentionally, very little contact at all with the outer world; they were not, as Iona or Lindisfarne or Clonmacnois were, the foci of their own *paruchiae* and the eventual centres of well-defined personality cults. Most of these small ascetic

[1] Gray estate plan, 1781, Leics. County Record Office; I am grateful to Mr. Richard Potts for showing me this.

houses are on islands or in remote and isolated parts. While each no doubt possessed its abbot, or *praepositus* (a senior brother, 'prior'), the total human complement is not likely to have exceeded a dozen. It is necessary to coin paradoxical terms like 'communal hermitage' or, better, 'eremitic monastery'[1] for these establishments. The type-site is Irish, on the island of the Great Skellig, a sea-girt pyramid of rock some 700 feet high, set out in the Atlantic off the Kerry coast. Here the tiny monastery known as Sceilg Mhichíl, or 'Skellig Michael',[2] contains a bare half-dozen cells, two oratories, and a graveyard; the very remoteness has preserved all this, a religious fossil, in a rare state of near-completeness. Time has dealt less kindly with Ardoileán, or 'High Island', off the Galway coast, which is associated with St. Feichin of Fore (mid seventh century);[3] it had a chapel, a group of cells, and some kind of circular cashel, perhaps a pre-Christian stronghold. Ynys Seiriol or 'Puffin Island', off the Anglesey coast,[4] is the best-known Welsh example. Despite the medieval additions and alterations, remains of three or four cells, and presumably a chapel below the medieval church, can be traced. In the south-west the site on St. Helen's in the Isles of Scilly, linked with St. Ilid or Elidius, revealed within its little enclosure a group of huts, an early oratory, and later chapel (Fig. 16).[5]

There are several in south-west Ireland as well. Oilean-tSenaig or 'Illauntannig', on the cluster of isles called The Magherees off the Dingle peninsula, co. Kerry, is the best-preserved, with three huts and two oratories inserted into what looks very like a pre-Christian cashel.[6] Mlle Françoise Henry's other instances on the Kerry mainland—some of which are not, in my view, really 'eremitic monasteries', even as she herself defines this term—will be considered again under another heading.[7]

---

[1] So Henry 1957, 146–54.

[2] RSAI Guide 1905, 137–46; Mason 1936, 107–15; De Paor, L. 1955; Henry 1957, 113–29 (bibliography, 113).

[3] Macalister 1896; RSAI Guide 1905, 45–53.

[4] RCAHMW Anglesey 1937, 141–4.   [5] O'Neil 1964.

[6] Dunraven 1875, i. 38, 41–2; RSAI Guide 1905, 118; Champneys 1910, 16–22; Norman and St. Joseph 1969, pl. 52.

[7] See p. 82.

In the north again one might include Sgor nam Ban-Naomha ('The Crag of the Holy Women') on Canna, which has[1] never been properly examined but falls within this class (Fig. 17). The site on Skye known as Annait[2] occupies a thin tongue of land

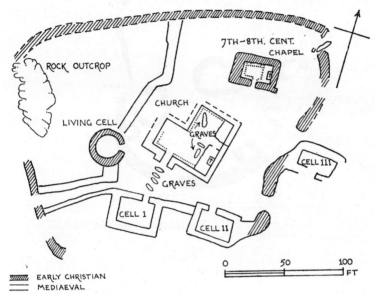

7TH–8TH. CENT. CHAPEL

ROCK OUTCROP

CHURCH

LIVING CELL

GRAVES

CELL III

GRAVES

CELL 1

CELL 11

0   50   100 FT

EARLY CHRISTIAN
MEDIAEVAL

ST. HELENS, ISLES OF SCILLY
AFTER JACKSON AND O'NEIL (1965)

FIG. 16.

between two precipitous river-gorges (Fig. 18), with two or three cells and a tiny chapel inside what is almost certainly an older earthwork;[3] it has the distinction of having been visited by Boswell and Dr. Johnson, who toyed with the idea that it was a temple to the Egyptian deity 'Anaitis'.[4]

The eremitic monasteries, of which the above are a fair selection, should be dated (if this is at all possible) to the seventh

[1] RCA(H)MS Outer Hebrides and Skye 1928, 217, with plan.
[2] Ibid., 149–50, with plan.
[3] I am grateful to Mr. Euan MacKie (Glasgow), for communicating the results of his own re-survey of this site.
[4] James Boswell, *Journal of a Tour to the Hebrides*, etc. (1785), entry under 17 September.

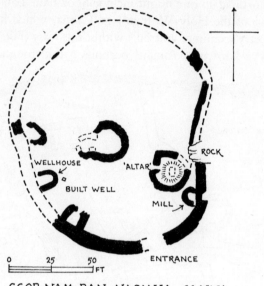

SGOR NAM BAN-NAOMHA, CANNA
R.C.H.M. INV. PLAN

FIG. 17.

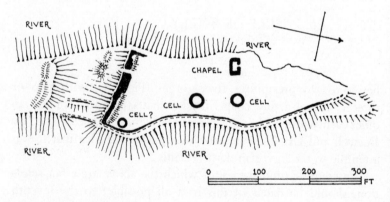

ANNAIT, SKYE
PLAN BY E. MACKIE. ECCLESIASTICAL STRUCTURES
ADDED FROM INV. AND FIELD WORK

FIG. 18.

century, rather than to the sixth. They partly correspond to the hermitages, often the cave or cell of a solitary, which one finds loosely attached to other monasteries in various parts of Europe and indeed Britain. In this particular case we seem to have 'group hermitages', and the connection with any major house is seldom clear.

In summary we see that, though we possess hardly any archaeology of the church in Britain in its purely diocesan stage—the late Roman and sub-Roman period—the addition of full monasticism during the sixth century gives us a very wide range of tangible and visible evidence, so far little explored. The real shift of emphasis in our religious sequence comes, not with the end of Roman Britain, but in some such phase as the latter part of the sixth century. It was then that the scales began to tip and the monastery began to replace the older territorial diocese as the dominant unit in insular Christianity. In the next chapter we see how there grew up a pattern of developed cemeteries; sites which may have borne something of the relationship to larger monasteries that parish churches did to cathedrals in the full Middle Ages.

3. Cemeteries and Chapels

IN THIS CHAPTER our main concern will be with burial practices and the development of the first cemeteries, a topic on which it is difficult to find guidance in print. Chapels (by which I mean the first small churches in the north and west of the British Isles) are already partially covered in existing literature, though some new aspects require discussion; they will be the subject of only a concise analysis here, and we shall regard them as adjuncts of cemeteries and other Christian sites, not as an isolated architectural class.

The treatment of the dead in the early centuries of Christianity is a complex matter. In north-west Europe it is here, above all, that the early Christian debt to pagan ritual and to non-Christian concepts is apparent. We need not, fortunately, rehearse in detail the lengthy tale of what happened to the dead in prehistoric Britain. It will suffice to stress that, by the fourth and early fifth centuries A.D., the dead were almost all being *inhumed* throughout Britain and Ireland. This means that the bodies were placed in graves dug into the ground; graves with or without such elaborations as stone linings and cappings. Individual bodies could be buried *extended*—that is, lying full-length; or *contracted, crouched,* or *flexed*—with the knees raised towards the chin. The longer axis of the grave could lie in any compass direction. Only among the Picts of northern Scotland is there any evidence[1] for the persistence of cremation, with the remains placed in a short cist, or box-like hole in the ground.

Normal Christian treatment, as today, involved the inhumation of an extended corpse, unaccompanied by that selection of objects (*grave goods*) so characteristic of pagan and prehistoric societies. The longer axis of the Christian grave lies east–west—i.e., is

---

[1] Wainwright 1955, chap. 4; some possible cases in *ECMS* III.

oriented—and the head is customarily at the west end. The grave need be no more than a body-length hollow in the ground or bedrock (*dug grave*); or the same, with its sides lined with stone slabs (*cist-grave* or *long cist*) and sometimes with a capping of similar slabs (the term *lintel grave* is used for this form).[1] Wood-lined graves, or graves with wooden coffins, do occur, but are not very common;[2] and there are some instances of interment in full-length, shaped, one-piece stone coffins or *sarcophagi*.[3] Dug graves and long cists are the predominant types. There are exceptions to these generalized remarks; some apparently Christian graves have been found in which the long axis lies north–south, most Germanic-speaking peoples continued to deposit grave-goods with the dead even after their conversion to Christianity, and so forth. The general picture none the less still stands.

If we concentrate entirely on the archaeological evidence we can best approach it under two headings. The first concerns the cemetery, the fixed consecrated area for groups of burials. The second, which is more complicated, deals with the special treatment accorded to certain individual graves.

In Roman Britain we can detect the shift of fashion from cremation to inhumation (a shift common to most of the Roman Empire) during the third century.[4] The cemeteries from which such information is derived were situated, in conformity with Roman law, outside towns and settlements—commonly alongside roads. The classic picture of this is drawn from Trier, in the Rhineland, where the pattern of later churches and cemeteries depends very largely on the siting of the burial-grounds of the Roman era.[5] In Britain, such urban cemeteries, and those in rural settings too, could occasionally be enclosed inside a wall or bank;

[1] Notably in the Isle of Mann. For a plea for standard terminology, see Ohlson 1968.

[2] Gallows Hill, Carlisle—Salway 1965, 216; Rochester, Kent—*Med. Arch.* 5 (1961), 309; Cronk yn How, Isle of Mann—Bruce and Cubbon 1930; York—RCHME Eboracum/Roman York 1962, 84–5.

[3] *H.E.* iv. 19 (reused Roman one, near Cambridge); Ancaster—Wilson, D. R. 1968.

[4] Collingwood and Richmond 1969, 166–72.

[5] Böhner 1958, ii, map iii (at back).

though most of these Roman walled cemeteries occur in south-east England.[1]

The earliest rural cemeteries in post-Roman Britain that we yet know date from the sixth, or conceivably the late fifth, century. Some—notably in the Scottish lowlands and in south-west England areas, peripheral to the truly Romanized zone—are unenclosed, yield burials of the lay populace (men, women, and children) in large numbers, and must have served large and scattered communities over many generations. Cannington, on the north coast of Somerset, with (originally) over a thousand burials in dug graves, is a good example.[2] The Parkburn long-cist cemetery at Lasswade, Midlothian, the full extent of which is uncertain (Fig. 19), is another.[3] But alongside these sprawling open cemeteries there are others which are enclosed, by a rude stone wall, by a low bank with an external quarry-ditch, even (as with monasteries) by some pre-existing earthwork; and these enclosed burial-grounds are invariably oval or circular in plan.

There is growing evidence that these cemeteries, in particular the enclosed ones, antedate any other form of Christian structure in the countryside of post-Roman Britain, and can thus be viewed as the primary field-monuments of insular Christianity. I am slightly less certain about the sequence in Ireland, though there is no reason why such burial-grounds should not have begun in Patrick's day. The enclosed circular aspect is the really important characteristic. Some instances would be the cemetery of dug graves recently found within a hill-fort (Fig. 20) at Trohoughton, Dumfries,[4] perhaps going back to the era of St. Ninian; the pair of odd little burial enclosures at Hartlaw, Berwickshire;[5] a great many small 'cillins' or 'cellurachs', as they often now are called, in the remoter parts of Ireland;[6] and others to be described below.

Such primary field-monuments, enclosed cemeteries which were not, however, subsequently elaborated with anything more than the odd cross-incised slab or pillar, or occasionally a 'special

---

[1] Collingwood and Richmond 1969, 172–3; Jessup 1959 (survey).
[2] Rahtz 1968a; cf. *Med. Arch.* 8 (1964), 237.
[3] Henshall 1958.   [4] Simpson and Scott-Elliot 1964.
[5] Stuart 1866.   [6] Examples in Henry 1957.

grave', we can describe as being *undeveloped*. We can distinguish from these a larger class of cemeteries, to which oratories and chapels, internal divisions, and living-huts, were eventually added, leading in many cases to medieval church sites and, in parts of

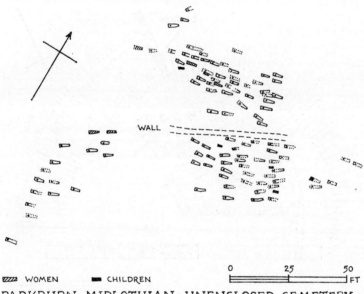

WOMEN   CHILDREN

0   25   50 FT

PARKBURN, MIDLOTHIAN : UNENCLOSED CEMETERY
AFTER HENSHALL (1958)

FIG. 19.

Cornwall, Wales, and southern Scotland, to parish churches surrounded by their graveyards. These, in contrast, we must call *developed cemeteries*. But before we try to analyse the nature, and the sequence, of any such development, we must explore another problem; why so many early burial-grounds *are* enclosed, and why the enclosed area tends to be circular or oval in plan.

I cannot do more than outline all the instances from British prehistory where the sacred place, be it funerary or merely religious, assumes circular form. These monuments extend over at least three millenia, beginning with the neolithic henges (and perhaps some causewayed camps),[1] continuing through the entire

[1] Piggott 1954, chaps. 2 and 11.

corpus of round barrows of all kinds,[1] and including localized groups of stone circles,[2] enclosed cremation cemeteries,[3] and the numerous sorts of megalithic tombs from New Grange downwards that possess a basically circular ground-plan.[4] The circular

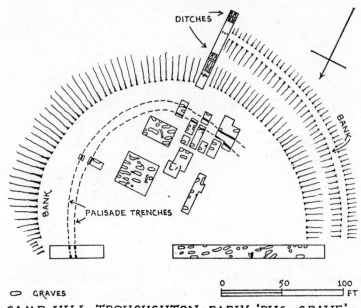

CAMP HILL, TROHOUGHTON : EARLY 'DUG-GRAVE' CEMETERY

AFTER SCOTT ELLIOT AND SIMPSON

FIG. 20. An early cemetery from Dumfries-shire located inside a deserted palisaded Iron Age hill-fort.

sacred place, if we choose to make this an isolated concept, occurs over most of the Old World, and beyond. Mircea Eliade's clear and cogent exploration of this very intricate phenomenon has brought out its main points.[5] This sacred circle, whose boundary (whether wall, bank, fence, ditch, or any visible barrier) separates the holy from the profane, if necessary the dead from those still

[1] Ashbee 1960.   [2] Thom 1967.   [3] Piggott 1962, 94–6.
[4] Daniel 1950, Daniel 1960; Piggott 1954, chaps. 5 to 9.
[5] Eliade 1961.

alive, is in itself a hierophany, an instant revelation of holiness. It is an archetypal model of the world (compare the various meanings of the Latin word *mundus*);[1] only within the circle can contact be effective between our own sphere of reality and that of others, for instance of the dead. The internal or central posts and pillars so common in prehistoric versions of the circle symbolize, through what Eliade calls 'ascension myths',[2] the modality of such contact.

The contention that the idea of the sacred circle not only existed in prehistory, but was maintained continuously into historic times, has in the past been advanced through some extraordinary by-ways of literary endeavour; on long straight tracks, indeed, which sped swiftly onwards through Gates of Horn to the furthest limits of inference. In advancing the idea yet again I am all too conscious of exposing myself to well-merited ridicule. I do so after full consideration of Eliade's extensive writings (none of which refers directly to this particular problem) because the enclosed circular cemetery, though not necessarily peculiar to early Christian Britain and Ireland, is so constant and striking a feature there that some underlying reason for its long existence must be sought. I believe this to be, at any rate, the least improbable.

One factor not hitherto cited in this line of argument is an important one—the extent to which such cemeteries are imposed upon, and are often spatially coterminous with, pre-Christian burial-grounds. This is far from generally known and some of the numerous occurrences must be listed.

A small burial-ground, to which a chapel had been attached, at Cille Aroo on the north end of Colonsay, yielded three short cists, two of which contained contracted inhumations with Bronze Age pots.[3] The famous 'Catstane' cemetery near Kirkliston, W. Lothian, contained a short cist with a cremation as well as the rows of oriented long-cist inhumations (Fig. 21).[4] Two Berwickshire sites, the Hartlaw complex, and another at Addinston,[5] which seems to have been unenclosed, produced a mixture of

[1] Eliade 1954, 15–16; cf. *Thesaurus Linguae Latinae*, xiii ('M'), s.v.
[2] Eliade 1958, 108–9, 122; Eliade 1961, 47–51.
[3] Anderson, J. 1907, 449–50; Grieve 1923.
[4] Hutchison 1866.   [5] Stuart 1866; Rosehill 1871.

remains; at Addinston, oriented long-cist inhumations, presumably Christian, were found scattered among contracted burials and small cremation cairns (Fig. 22).

In Selkirk, of the two or three early unenclosed and undeveloped cemeteries in the neighbourhood of Yarrow church, that at Warrior's Rest[1] had an uninscribed standing-stone close to some

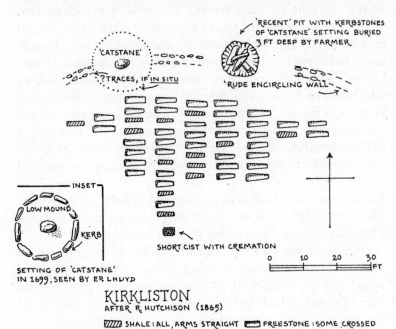

SETTING OF 'CATSTANE' IN 1699, SEEN BY EDᴿ LHUYD

KIRKLISTON
AFTER R. HUTCHISON (1865)

▨ SHALE : ALL, ARMS STRAIGHT   ▨ FREESTONE : SOME CROSSED

FIG. 21. The 'Catstane' cemetery at Kirkliston, probably enclosed, with a 'special grave', but plan is based on inadequate excavation records.

eight oriented cists, graves which appear to have cut through some Middle Bronze Age burials. In the little enclosed developed cemetery (circular wall, tiny chapel) at St. Ninian's Point, Bute,[2] inhumation graves which lie north–south are reported as being overlain by oriented extended inhumations of obviously Christian character; and the presumably non-Christian graves also seem to antedate the circular enclosing wall (Fig. 23). At Whithorn, the

[1] RCAMS Selkirk 1957, 113–14.   [2] Aitken 1955.

recent excavations conducted by Mr. P. R. Ritchie[1] below the east end of the Priory church have revealed various oriented dug graves, with greatly crushed skeletons, which one can regard as probably being, not only of the period of Ninian, but also indeed

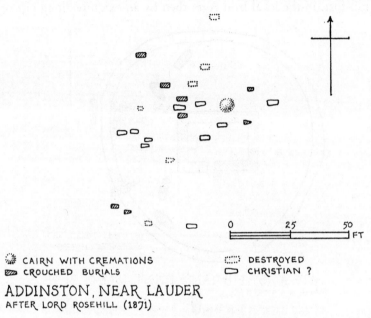

CAIRN WITH CREMATIONS   DESTROYED

CROUCHED BURIALS   CHRISTIAN ?

ADDINSTON, NEAR LAUDER
AFTER LORD ROSEHILL (1871)

FIG. 22. An apparent instance, from an old excavation, of a Christian unenclosed cemetery sited upon a pagan burial-area.

as the *raison d'être* for the ecclesiastical foundation at this precise point in the burgh. These graves have disturbed what may be cremations of the Roman period.[2]

The list could be multiplied from a wide area, and we might add just a few from outside North Britain. At Killygony, co. Down, an enclosed but undeveloped cemetery still exhibits two substantial, almost megalithic, stone cists of prehistoric type inside the burial-area.[3] In the Isle of Mann there are two interesting

[1] To whom, as to Mr. S. E. Cruden (A.M.I., Scotland), I am grateful for permission to refer to this.

[2] *The Scotsman* (Edinburgh), 'Week-end Magazine', 4 May 1965.

[3] ASNI Down 1966, 93.

occurrences. One (Fig. 24) is from the late Gerhard Bersu's excavations at Balladoole.[1] Chapel Hill, Balladoole, was successively occupied, firstly by a group of prehistoric burials, both cremations and inhumations, some in cists; then by a small univallate hill-fort, in the local Iron Age; then by an extensive long cist or

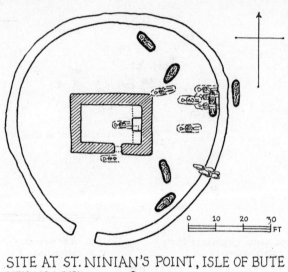

SITE AT ST. NINIAN'S POINT, ISLE OF BUTE
AFTER W.G. AITKEN
PHASE 1 — NON-CHRISTIAN?   PHASE 2 — CHRISTIAN

FIG. 23.

'lintel grave' cemetery of Christian type; and finally by a pagan Norse boat-burial immediately above the long cists. The other is the developed cemetery at Keeill Lingan, Marown, where the chapel sits immediately above some cists with fragments of charcoal and cinerary urns, and of which it was written that 'it was evident that this had been a cemetery of the Bronze Age before it was converted to Christian uses'.[2] From the region of Padstow, on the north Cornish coast, come our last two instances, both of which seem to imply successive Roman and early Christian use. The first, at Trevone Bay, consisted of a Christian long-cist cemetery, attached to a chapel, these cists lying above an earlier series

---

[1] Bersu and Wilson 1966, 1–4.   [2] *MAS* i. 15–16.

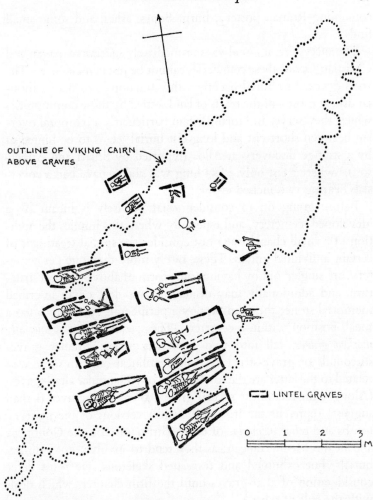

OUTLINE OF VIKING CAIRN
ABOVE GRAVES

⊏⊐ LINTEL GRAVES

0   1   2   3
├──┼──┼──┼──┼──┼──┤ M

CHAPEL HILL, BALLADOOLE
AFTER BERSU (1946)

FIG. 24.

with north–south alignment, inhumations, and objects of Roman
date (fibula, sherd of samian, etc.). The second, at Penmaine,
St. Enodoc, explored before 1850, was also attached to a small
chapel, the Christian graves being confused with a lower level

containing Roman pottery, burnt bones, ashes, and some small finds.[1]

The successive, if not always immediately successive, pagan and Christian uses of these cemeteries cannot be just coincidence.[2] The areas devoted to burial occupy a tiny fraction—less than a thousandth, at most—of the tracts of land settled by those communities which they serve. In North Britain particularly a temporal overlap between short-cist and long-cist burial seems to be hinted at by a strange discovery at Alloa (reported by Stuart and Anderson),[3] where a cist only 3 feet long was said to have had a cover-slab bearing two incised crosses.

Before going on to consider what precisely is meant by a 'developed' cemetery, and especially where this implies the addition of a small chapel, we must consider the special treatment of certain individual graves. These, rarely more than one per cemetery, are singled out by having some form of above-ground structure, and additionally may display a cross-slab, or an inscribed memorial stone; they can occupy a peripheral, but more often a focal, position within a cemetery. The *special graves*, or *specially marked graves*, fall into two main categories: circular grave-surrounds or grave-structures, and rectilinear ones. In some way related to the latter are the small square or rectangular altar-graves. (Along with rectilinear special graves, these altar-graves (I shall suggest) represent the Irish and British versions of the martyrs' tombs and *cellae memoriae* of early Christianity on the Continent and in the Mediterranean; as they tend to involve, not primary burials, but exhumed and translated skeletons, we must defer consideration of altar-graves until the fifth chapter, which deals with the cult of relics.)

The circular grave-structure—the primary burial contained within, or beneath, some form of small circular ditch, wall, or mound—may possess the same symbolic and ritual value as the curvilinear cemetery. It has a specialized history, since the com-

---

[1] Trollope 1860.

[2] For an instructive recent discussion on pagan/Christian continuity, see *Norwegian Archaeol. Review*, 2 (Oslo 1969), 3–32.

[3] Anderson, J. 1876.

parative material indicates a north-west European Iron Age background. The isolated grave of a notable person is a frequent Iron
Age feature. 'Chariot burials', regular pits with square or rectangular ditches around them, extend right across from central

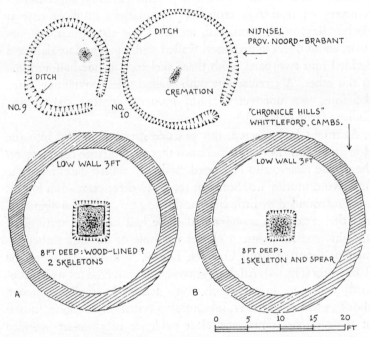

PRE-ROMAN IRON AGE CIRCULAR GRAVE-SURROUNDS
NETHERLANDS AND EAST ANGLIA

FIG. 25.

Europe into Yorkshire, between the sixth and third centuries
B.C.[1] Small or medium-sized *circular* surrounds, though less pub-
licized, also occur (Fig. 25). At a pre-Roman, Iron Age cemetery
in the Netherlands, Nijnsel (Noord-Brabant), grave no. 10, which
holds a cremation, lies within a circle about 16 feet across, defined
by a shallow ditch.[2] Grave no. 9 is similar, but smaller. Below
two very shallow mounds at the 'Chronicle Hills', Whittleford,

[1] Stead 1961; Piggott 1968, 62-3.   [2] Hulst 1964.

Cambs., were found related features; circular areas 22 feet in diameter, enclosed by crude 3 feet high walls of chalk lumps. In the centres were small (5 feet square, and 4 feet square) pits, 8 feet deep; one pit held two skeletons, the other a single skeleton with a spear.[1] On a smaller scale the large and virtually unpublished[2] cemetery of Iron Age crouched inhumations in short cists at Harlyn Bay, north Cornwall, included one cist which was circular, about 6 feet in diameter, walled with upright slate slabs and divided into two parts, with three skeletons in one half and one in the other. A circular cist with walled sides, containing three skeletons, was uncovered about 1900 on another coastal site, Gullane (East Lothian).[3]

As might be expected, this practice survived locally into the Roman period. In the Netherlands there is the large cemetery on the Gaalse Heide, also in Noord-Brabant,[4] which dates from the first two centuries A.D. Some of the sixty-three cremation burials were surrounded by little circular ditches, 7 to 10 feet in diameter, and the excavators wondered if these had not held settings of upright wooden posts. A clearer example of this last embellishment is reported from Overton Down, Wiltshire,[5] also of the Roman era (Fig. 26). All three grave-circles, covered (as at Whittleford) with very low mounds, were defined by shallow ditches, about 15 feet in diameter, surrounding central cremations; in two of these ditches there was clear evidence of close-set wooden uprights. Another possibly relevant site is at Brettenham (near Thetford), Norfolk; here, ploughing revealed a complex pattern of soil marks, and a cremation-burial in a Roman vessel, within an oval area 16 feet by 21 feet, defined by black soil.[6]

It is interesting to notice still later versions, centred on the areas of Germanic-speaking peoples, up to (and apparently into) the broad period of their conversion to Christianity in the seventh and eighth centuries. Circular grave-surrounds are known from Putten, Gelderland (Netherlands), a Saxon cemetery; and from

[1] Fox 1923, 77–9.
[2] Bullen 1912, 108–12, fig. 15.
[3] Richardson and Richardson 1902.
[4] Modderman and Isings 1961.
[5] Smith and Simpson 1964.
[6] Cf. C. B. A. Group 7, *Bulletin of Archaeological Discoveries*, no. 12 (for 1965), 3.

Alemannic cemeteries at Audincourt, at Holzerlingen near Wurtemburg, and at Bernerring, near Basle. Tomb no. 230 from Holzerlingen, for instance, had staggered wooden posts close-set all round the circular ditch.[1] In Britain there are the two recently

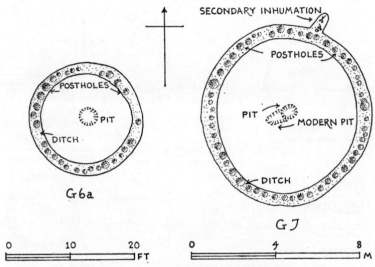

WEST OVERTON, WILTS. : MOUNDS G6a AND G7
AFTER SMITH AND SIMPSON (1964)

FIG. 26. Circular grave-surrounds of the Roman period.

reassessed Anglo-Saxon cemeteries at Chamberlains Barn, Leighton Buzzard (Beds.), known as Leighton Buzzard I and II.[2] Cemetery I is pagan, but cemetery II, for which some such starting-date as *circa* 650 is proposed, should be, despite occasional grave-goods, its Christian successor, only a short distance away. Now in cemetery I, grave no. 17 had around it a small circular ditch, the burial (a male) lying north–south. A similar feature, with a ditch 14 feet in diameter, marks another grave on the outskirts of cemetery II. Both are clearly non-Christian. But within the centre of cemetery II an oriented grave, containing

[1] Salin 1950–9, ii. 58–65 ('sépultures encerclées').
[2] Hyslop 1963.

a presumably converted male with his buckle, knife, and snaffle-bit, is *also* surrounded by a small (16-feet diameter) ditch. This offers a fairly clear case of pagan–Christian continuity.

Given such brackets—from the Iron Age to the seventh century —we might expect to have circular grave features of sub-Roman

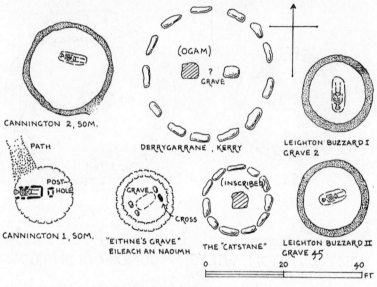

CIRCULAR GRAVE ENCLOSURES

FIG. 27.

and post-Roman date in Britain and Ireland, particularly in those parts where there is a strong element of continuity from the Iron Age, parallel with the Roman occupation of England and parts of Wales and Scotland. Careful search does reveal some examples (Fig. 27).

In the north one might begin with the 'Catstane' cemetery at Kirkliston. Here, the nineteenth-century diggings uncovered part of the low curved enclosure wall, rows of oriented long cists, and the still-visible inscribed memorial stone of the sixth century.[1] But in 1699, when the antiquary Edward Lhuyd saw all this,[2] the

[1] Hutchison 1866.   [2] Ibid. 189.

inscribed stone (the 'Catstane' itself) stood in the middle of a low circular mound about 15 feet across, with a kerb of boulders; and in 1860 the excavators seem to have encountered these boulders, obstacles to agriculture, which had been removed and buried in a large pit close by.

On the island in the Garvellochs group called Eileach an Naoimh,[1] which possesses some problematical remains—perhaps those of an eremitic monastery—there is a structure known as 'Eithne's Grave', Eithne being the mother of Columcille (Columba). Unlike the Catstane circle, where no related burial is definitely known, Eithne's grave is certainly real enough; there are two slabs at the (western) head end, and two marking the feet, one of which bears an incised cross of seventh-century type. This grave is surrounded by a low cairn-like wall, forming a circle with an external diameter of about 16 feet.

A now-destroyed monument on a moor at Derrygarrane South, barony of Dunkerron, co. Kerry, was similar but larger.[2] Here the medium-sized slabs formed a circle about 33 feet across. The reported central grave was flanked, east and west, by two large stone pillars, the western of which bore an ogam inscription of some interest.[3]

In the great unenclosed cemetery at Cannington, Somerset, which was mentioned earlier, there are two features of this kind. No. 1 is a small low cairn, within which was an oriented inhumation, a young person in a cist grave. A large post-socket by his or her feet may have been (who knows?) for a wooden cross, and a well-trodden path seems to indicate constant pilgrimage to the spot.[4] No. 20 is about 20 feet across, a shallow continuous ditch forming a circle, and enclosing a central oriented dug grave with another burial. There can be no doubt that both these formed an integral part, perhaps in some degree the focal points, of the cemetery.

Related to these circular grave-surrounds, if only by sharing a long ancestry into prehistoric times, are the few rectangular

---

[1] Bryce and Knight 1930; Simpson, W. D. 1958.
[2] *CIIC* i. 213–14.   [3] See p. 106.
[4] Rahtz 1968a (and personal communication from Mr. Philip Rahtz).

counterparts. In the Dutch pre-Roman Iron Age cremation cemetery at Nijnsel, at least eight such little rectangular enclosures are
associated with the two circular ones.[1] Stuart Piggott has recently
discussed[2] other cases, including the late pre-Roman Iron Age
ones at Wallertheim (Rheinhessen), and some southern British
instances from Roman times, notably the miniature ditched rectangular surrounds, one with inhumation graves, one with mixed
inhumations and cremations, at Roden Down, Berks. These, he
argues, must be referred to a wider tradition of the rectilinear
sacred site, the 'square ditched enclosure' which also forms a
component of many Romano-Celtic temple lay-outs. Again,
something of this seems to be carried over into Christian usage.
At Poundbury, Dorset, continuing work on an inhumation
cemetery[3] has produced various graves of Christian type. One is
the grave of an adult female, oriented, her head to the west, and
the presence of nails may hint at a wooden coffin. Her grave lies
in the southern half of a small square surround, marked by a ditch
filled with dark soil (in chalk), 3 feet wide and about 1 foot deep;
the square measures 15 feet between ditch centres.

A very similar example has lately come from North Wales, in
the complex of henge monuments and prehistoric remains at
Llandegai, Caerns.[4] A medium-sized inhumation cemetery of
oriented dug graves, in three rows, is flanked on the south by a
rectangular feature. This is a rough slot ditch, marking out an
area internally 12 feet north–south and 14 feet east–west, again
with an off-centre dug grave inside this surround.

No catalogue of these unusual facets of Christian practice, however fragmentary, should omit what is quite the most remarkable
site of all (Fig. 28); site no. I on the Hill of Knockea, co. Limerick,
explored by Professor M. J. O'Kelly.[5] A regular ditch, 6 feet
across and 2 feet deep, enclosed an area roughly 45 feet square.
Inside the ditch was a broad low bank faced internally with a
dry-stone revetment. Inside the bank the central area measures
some 25 feet each way. On the crest of the low bank were found

[1] Hulst 1964, 75, fig. 2 (graves 2 to 8, 11).   [2] Piggott 1968, 74–9.
[3] Green 1967, esp. fig. 10.
[4] Houlder 1968, 217, fig. 1, pl. xxxii. a.   [5] O'Kelly 1967.

the sockets for twenty-six stout upright posts, two of them flanking the entrance-gap on the west side. Within the central area
were at least sixty-six inhumations, of both adults and children;
the great majority were oriented, and this fact, with the general

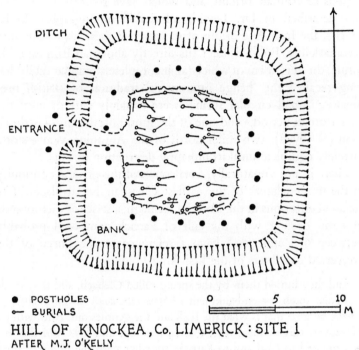

DITCH

ENTRANCE

BANK

● POSTHOLES
○— BURIALS

0   5   10
M

HILL OF KNOCKEA, Co. LIMERICK: SITE 1
AFTER M.J. O'KELLY

FIG. 28.

date of the few associated finds, leaves little doubt that this must
be an early Christian monument. In the terminology that we have
so far employed, Knockea Site I is an undeveloped inhumation
cemetery, enclosed within a ditch and inner bank of approximately square lay-out. These characteristics, to which one must
add the surrounding posts that crown the bank—and there is no
suggestion that they refer to any kind of roof—give us a monument which combines nearly all the features previously examined.
Lastly, under this heading, let us briefly consider yet another
class of monuments which may have reinforced the idea of the

F

'sacred circle', in so far as both the circular enclosed cemetery and the circular grave surround are involved with this specific hierophany. I allude to the small circular shrines—not quite temples, not quite individual mausolea—which are known from various regions of Roman Britain, and which have recently been listed and described in Dr. Lewis's admirable monograph.[1] As he stresses, the Iron Age origin of so many of these little structures is remarkable. Frilford no. 1 sits directly above an Iron Age 'A' shrine, the very form of which (an incompletely annular ditch) has long recalled the 'henge monument' tradition of British prehistory.[2] Small circular shrines were certainly current until the later Roman period,[3] and one of the most noteworthy—Arthur's Oon (= Oven), two miles north of the Antonine Wall—stood virtually complete until its unhappy destruction in 1743.[4]

There is, not unnaturally, a reflection of this general continuity in the nomenclature of the earliest Christian burial-places. Tírechán's collections in the Book of Armagh, a series of memoranda in Latin dealing with the cult of Patrick composed probably between 670 and 700,[5] have a reference to the burial of the converted daughters of the Irish king Loiguire.

> And they buried them by the spring called Clebach, and they made a circular ditch (or embankment—*fossam rotundam*) in the likeness of a *ferta*, because that is what the Irish and the gentiles did. And with us, moreover, this is called *relic*, that is, *reliquiae*, and *fert*. And the *ferta* was granted to God and to Patrick, together with the bones of these holy females, etc.

The word *fert*, here Latinized as *ferta*, originally meant a circular burial-mound.[6] The Glossary of Cormac mac Cuilennáin (died 908), or *Sanas Cormaic*, defines one class of landowner as he who has the right to raise up his *fert* or tomb (*cóir a fhirt dochur*).[7] The much later glossary of Donall O'Davoren (the manuscript is

---

[1] Lewis 1966 (add now Philp 1969).
[2] Cf. Piggott 1968, 64–9; Lewis 1966, 188.
[3] Collingwood and Richmond 1969, 154–74.   [4] Steer 1958.
[5] Kenney 1929, 329–30; Stokes 1887, ii. 300–31.
[6] Binchy, note in *Ériu* xvii (Dublin), 83, para. 11.
[7] Stokes 1862, 10 s.v. *coairt*.

marked 1569) describes *fert* as *.i. ulaid cumdachta* ('that is, the building of a grave'),[1] and again equates it with *cladh*[2]—a word from a root meaning 'dig', with the primary sense of 'bank, mound, earthen rampart', but also with a wide secondary meaning, particularly in Scotland, of 'a burial-ground with a dyke or bank around it'.[3] The equation of *fert*, as early as the seventh century, with the specific and common Christian term *relic(c)*, 'cemetery' (Latin *reliquiae*, 'sacred relics', hence 'place containing sacred relics of martyrs and saints; consecrated cemetery') is of some importance. It suggests that the degree of formal continuity between the circular burial-site of pagan times, and its later Christian counterpart, was actually comprehended.

We can now return to the question of what is implied by the adjective 'developed', in relation to early enclosed burial-grounds. Perhaps a brief summary of the situation might be adduced here. Both enclosed and unenclosed rural cemeteries exist from sub-Roman times onwards, the enclosed form predominating (though, admittedly, enclosed examples are easier to recognize in the field). By the seventh century, if not during the late sixth, the first small churches or chapels, simple rectangular structures, are combined with enclosed cemeteries. These earliest chapels were mainly of timber construction, perhaps also of whatever materials such phrases as *ecclesia terrena* (literally 'earthen church'—this is used by Tírechán of a chapel of Patrick's day) may imply; possibly turf, or wattle-and-daub. In some cases the cemetery evolves within the enclosure around such a primitive chapel; in others, perhaps in most, the chapel is added to the earlier enclosed cemetery. We shall see instances of both.

'Development', then, means the sequence exhibited by all those cemeteries which progress from mere collections of inhumation-graves, first to cemeteries with special graves (either those with such circular, less commonly rectangular, surrounds of the type we have already discussed, or another kind based on the *cella memoriae*—see p. 143 below), and secondly to cemeteries with other features like timber chapels, *leachta*,[4] and even internal

---

[1] Ibid. 90.
[2] Ibid. 91 ('fert .i. cladh').
[3] Watson 1926, 253, 278, etc.
[4] See p. 169.

divisions. Subsequent development involves, usually during the late seventh and eighth centuries, the replacement of wooden chapels by stone ones; often, too, the addition of small dwellings or living-cells for the isolated brethren who appear to have staffed such, by now permanent, places of worship. At this stage of development, particularly in remoter regions, it is not of course always possible to distinguish at once between an enclosed developed cemetery (with a stone chapel and a handful of little round huts) and a small eremitic monastery. Only careful excavation could produce the evidence to satisfy a purist as to this fine distinction; the presence or absence of lay persons (women and children) buried in the cemetery.

We are not in this book much concerned with the church in North Britain, or in western Britain and Ireland, after the eighth century, but I would here point out that this 'developed cemetery' sequence lies behind those hundreds of parish churches, often dedicated in honour of obscure local saints, which stand within their raised circular or oval graveyards even to this day. This statement is especially true of my native Cornwall, where I have devoted much time and print[1] to the elucidation of this sequence. Often, despite the successive rebuildings of the parish church, and despite the rewalling or modern enlargement of the graveyard,[2] the lay-out revealed in older maps, the discovery of some sixth- or seventh-century memorial stone or cross-incised grave markers, and the attachment of some appropriately early place-name element (*cill, lan, merthyr,* etc.) enables one to posit this continuity over some twelve or thirteen centuries.

I pass now to brief consideration of the actual chapels, both as to their place in this sequence and as to their intrinsic character. The contention that the chapel series commences with structures in rough wood, hewn timber, or perhaps wattling, is not in dispute. The evidence, which is largely literary, has been set out by George Petrie, Bishop Reeves, and Dr. H. G. Leask.[3] Early Irish

---

[1] Thomas 1962; Thomas 1967a.
[2] Cf. Beveridge 1911, 292 (on Kilmuir; 'its boundary wall was re-built (in 1901) and extended so as to form a rectangle in place of a circle, as before . . .').
[3] Petrie 1845, 125–7; Reeves 1857, 106, 114, 360; Leask 1955, 5–10.

sources constantly mention wooden chapels, the word *dairthech* (explained as meaning 'house of oak') being commonly employed. A modular proportion—length to breadth as three to two, for example 15 feet by 10 feet internally—seems to have been the rule, at any rate in Ireland, and Leask has shown that this was also true of later stone-built chapels.[1] Bede and other Northumbrian writers, while themselves supplying direct evidence for the timber-stone sequence in the Northumbrian church, in other parts of England, and indeed in the Anglo-Saxon mission to the Continent, also refer indirectly to this succession in Ireland and in the Irish settlements in Britain. Finally, recent field-work has given us actual instances.

Professor M. J. O'Kelly's excavations (1965–6) on the small Church Island, near Valencia, co. Kerry, disclosed three main phases (Fig. 29). In the first I think we can deduce that this isle, employed for an unenclosed cemetery, was enriched by a tiny timber oratory, only some 2 metres by 3, defined by six post-sockets; and there was a circular (6 metres in diameter) wood-framed living-hut close to it. Burials occurred on the north-west and west sides of the oratory, aligned exactly on the structure's longer axis, and a cross-slab (to which an inscription in ogam was later added) may have been set up to mark the grave of the founder of the oratory and the first occupant of the hut, assuming these to have been one and the same person. There seems every reason to date this first phase to the seventh century, and the first use of the isle as a lay cemetery may be still earlier. In the second phase the timber oratory was replaced by a small stone church, internally 18 feet 6 inches by 12 feet 4 inches (proportions of three to two again), which partly overlies the post-sockets of its timber predecessor and also overlies some of the graves of the first phase. Further burials, in phase two, are aligned exactly on the longer axis of the stone building, which is some fifteen degrees off the axis of the timber one. In this second phase the circular wooden hut was replaced by a circular stone one, which largely obliterated the first hut. The little stone chapel is of the oldest known type, and could belong to the first half of the eighth century.[2]

[1] Leask 1955, 6, 49–50.   [2] O'Kelly 1958.

This skilfully executed demonstration of a sequence hitherto only inferred from the literature took place, of course, in a peripheral area—the extreme south-west tip of Ireland—and thus required to be checked elsewhere. We shall discuss this in a

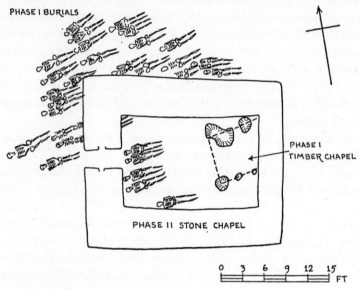

PHASE I BURIALS

PHASE I TIMBER CHAPEL

PHASE II STONE CHAPEL

0   3   6   9   12   15 FT

CHURCH ISLAND, CO. KERRY
CONSTRUCTIONAL SEQUENCE
AFTER M.J.O'KELLY

FIG. 29.

moment. The successive occupation of the same spot by chapels of increasing size, in different materials, must provide the explanation for a phenomenon that we can call 'overlain burials'. This is found where small stone chapels of the eighth, ninth, or later centuries are investigated, and where it is then noticed that extended Christian burials in dug graves or long cists occur, either well below the floor-level or, more significantly, wholly or partly below the chapel walls. Selected instances of this might be St. Justinian's chapel, near St. David's, Pembroke, very badly dug in the 1920s,[1] where an early chapel and some associated burials were

[1] Boake, E. J., *Archaeologia Cambrensis* 81 (1926), 381.

found below a medieval chapel, the head of one early grave being just under the medieval west wall; St. Ninian's Point, Bute, a developed cemetery that we have already noticed,[1] where the little eighth-century chapel overlies at least two graves; and perhaps Keeill Woirrey, Patrick, Isle of Mann,[2] where the numerous early burials below the chapel avoid a central space in which there

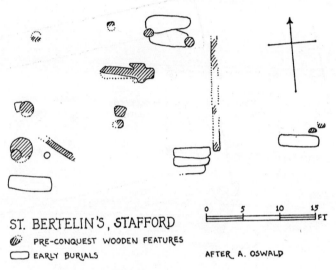

ST. BERTELIN'S, STAFFORD

🕸 PRE-CONQUEST WOODEN FEATURES

⬭ EARLY BURIALS

0   5   10   15 FT

AFTER A. OSWALD

FIG. 30. Skeletal plan of a Mercian (?) timber church, from careful excavation of a largely-destroyed site.

is room for a timber structure of the size of that found on Church Island.

The use of wood for church-building did not altogether vanish; apart from such reminders as the Saxon timber church of St. Andrew, Greensted (Essex), we have two from recent excavations. At St. Bertelin's, Stafford, Mr. Adrian Oswald, working under conditions of appalling difficulty,[3] managed to recover most of the outline of a pre-Conquest Mercian church in wood (Fig. 30); and at Potterne, Wilts., Dr. Norman Davey has produced[4] the plan of a late pre-Conquest church and baptistery, defined by post-sockets and sill-beam trenches.

[1] Aitken 1955.   [2] *MAS* ii. 5, fig. 1.   [3] Oswald 1956.   [4] Davey 1964.

The Church Island sequence can be condensed as: unenclosed lay cemetery—timber oratory and hut, with aligned burials—stone chapel and hut, with further aligned burials. In attempting to demonstrate that this sequence would also hold good in North Britain, I selected, after much search, the small tidal island of

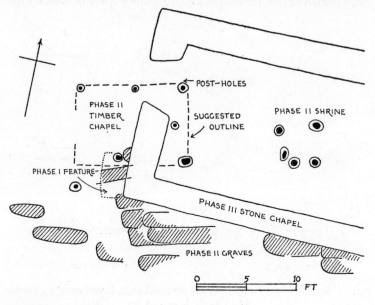

ARDWALL ISLE
CONSTRUCTIONAL SEQUENCE

FIG. 31.

Ardwall Isle, off the Kirkcudbright coast; and in two seasons (1964–5) was enabled (with the help of many kind friends) to confirm this result[1] (Fig. 31 and Pl. I).

The site on Ardwall Isle also began as a rural lay cemetery, of dug graves, and its position in the Whithorn area suggests that it was first in use in sub-Roman times, during the sixth, or just conceivably the late fifth century. I suspect that it was also at first unenclosed. Here, phase 1 was marked by a number of subsequently much-disturbed inhumation graves, around something

[1] Thomas 1967b.

I have interpreted as the below-ground element of a *slab shrine*;[1] a focus that possibly held the translated skeletal remains of some local saint. In phase 2 a small timber chapel or oratory, outlined by post-holes which gave a plan of 11 feet by 7 feet 6 inches (that is, proportions of three to two), partly overlies the rock-cut hollow of the slab shrine—one post-hole goes right *through* it—and displaced some of the primary inhumations. A second-phase series of further dug graves are aligned on the longer axis of this timber structure, and some shallow post-sockets outside its east end may refer to a *corner-post shrine*, a later type than the slab shrine.[2] Both the small timber chapel and a number of the finds rather imply Irish influence, and there is some independent evidence for the idea of Irish secular and religious activity in Galloway from the later sixth century.[3] In phase 3 a stone-walled church, internally 23 feet by 13 feet—this is a little longer than the three-to-two ratio—overlies both the timber structure of phase 2 and the rock-cut hollow of phase 1, and is on a new axis, which (as at Church Island) is still broadly east–west, but about fifteen degrees off the axis of the timber chapel. Still more burials, outside the west wall, are now aligned on this new (phase 3) axis. In a subsequent stage, around A.D. 1000, a few more graves were inserted within this stone chapel, then in ruins, and about the thirteenth century the largely destroyed walls of the chapel were incorporated into the foundations of a medieval hall-house.

Nor are these the only two instances. In the last few years Mr. D. B. Hague has recovered traces of a third example, on the tidal islet of Burry Holms, off the Gower peninsula, S. Wales.[4] Here, below a small and early stone church, which was itself enlarged in the eleventh and twelfth centuries, four large post-holes appear to indicate an earlier wooden chapel, again on a different axis. The site possesses an oval enclosure, and there seem to be inhumations of several phases.

Two further Irish occurrences may be included. In 1967, excavating in the Church of Ireland graveyard at Ardagh, co.

---

[1] See p. 142.   [2] See p. 150.   [3] Thomas 1966a.
[4] *Med. Arch.* 10 (1966), 184; 11 (1967), 281; and personal information kindly afforded by Mr. D. B. Hague.

Longford, Mr. Liam de Paor examined the remains of a small stone chapel of eighth-century type.[1] Apart from a number of modern interments, graves were found *under* the foundations of the stone walls and the early Christian graveyard proved to extend for some distance. Traces, disturbed by burials, of two systems of posts could be recovered; one of these, marked by sockets for posts of about 14 inches diameter, was interpreted as belonging to an earlier wooden structure, but was too fragmentary to give a coherent plan. A very similar situation prevailed at the pair of ruinous early churches at Derry, co. Down.[2] Mr. D. M. Waterman found, below the south church (which may be of ninth or late eighth century date), traces of a timber-framed structure standing on stone foundations. Though this is not certainly ecclesiastical, the context, which includes the presence of a substantial lay cemetery of two phases, suggests that we must at least note it here.

Alongside this increasing corpus of archaeological evidence we can set Bede's comments on seventh-century Northumbria. About 626, the newly converted king Edwin built a little church of timber in York, dedicated in honour of St. Peter. Late in 627 he built 'on the same site, a larger and more noble stone basilica, which was to enclose his earlier little oratory. The foundations were laid, and the walls of a four-sided church began to rise around this little oratory . . .'.[3] But Edwin was killed, and his successor Oswald had to complete the church about 635, adding a *porticus* to it in honour of Gregory the Great. In 669, Wilfrid restored this church, which by then was in a poor condition;[4] we may assume its foundation lies somewhere beneath York Minster. Bede, and the other Northumbrian writers, describe numerous small wooden churches—at Lindisfarne,[5] at *Campodonum*,[6] at Oundle[7]—and among the Northumbrian Angles the transition to a stone technique, which actually began in the latter

---

[1] Preliminary circular, 1967; I am grateful to Mr. Liam de Paor for allowing me to summarize a part of this.

[2] Waterman 1967. [3] H.E. ii. 14.

[4] Eddius, *Vita Wilfridi* (ed. Colgrave 1927), cap. 16.

[5] H.E. iii. 23, iii. 25.

[6] H.E. ii. 14. [7] Eddius, *Vita Wilfridi*, cap. 67.

part of the seventh century, was really due to continental and Mediterranean influence, not to what might be taking place in Ireland or in the far north-west.

In the Celtic-speaking provinces very small single-chambered stone chapels may have originated well back in the seventh century, especially on outlying islands where suitable stone lay all around, and wood was absent. Adomnán's *Life of Columba* reminds us, however, that the community on Iona—an island which is virtually treeless—were prepared (in the late sixth century) to go to Mull, or beyond, and to cut down trees for building purposes, towing them back to Iona behind their boats.[1] In view of the uncertainties, it is safer to ascribe the earliest and most primitive-looking Irish stone churches to the period after 700. The famous oratory of Gallerus, co. Kerry, and the two tiny ones at Skellig Michael, are the current prototypes. The Skellig buildings (Fig. 32) are, externally, high corbelled stone cells of oval form into which roughly rectangular internal ground-plans have been fitted.[2] The Gallerus oratory, which is also complete, is rather more sophisticated. Its end elevation—best appreciated from inside—supports Dr. Leask's thesis[3] that the graceful ogee shape is based on that which results, in a timber-framed structure, from the use of curved crucks as the principal members for united wall and roof (Pl. II).

Many features of the earliest stone churches do seem to be *skeuomorphs*, non-functional imitations in another medium, of elements proper to timber construction.[4] Another kind of cruck, the 'elbow cruck', which gives a near-vertical wall and a straight slooping roof in one stretch, might, if used in opposed pairs, stand out at the gable-ends of wooden buildings; because the planking or framing of the gable wall would either be nailed to the inside of the crucks, or, more pleasingly, slotted or mortised into the thickness of the crucks. These projecting gable elbow-crucks are skeuomorphically reproduced in stone in the (non-functional) *antae* of chapels

---

[1] Adomnán, *Vita Columbae* (ed. Anderson and Anderson 1961), ii. 45.
[2] De Paor, L. 1955 (plans and elevations).
[3] Leask 1955, chaps. 5 and 6.
[4] Ibid., chap. 5.

like Temple MacDara, co. Galway, and many others.[1] Again, the crossed terminals of any pair of crucks, checked into each other and standing out above the plane of the roof-ridge, are reproduced in the well-known stone gable-finials.[2] This particular trick has

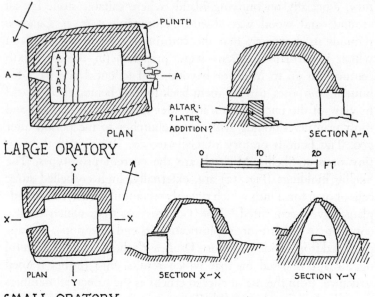

FIG. 32.

a very long history, almost as long as the history of cruck building. An instructive parallel to Irish usage is a depiction (Fig. 33) of a little chapel on a fifth-century mosaic from Thessalonica,[3] in which the crossed crucks are clearly visible. Instances of both curved crucks (West Cross) and elbow crucks (Muiredach's Cross) can be seen on the small stone church-like capitals of the late High Crosses at Monasterboice, co. Louth[4]—double skeuomorphs, since

[1] Leask 1955, 29–30, 55–6, figs. 9 and 10.   [2] Ibid. 46–7.
[3] I owe this to the kindness of Miss Mary Cobley (Truro).
[4] Macalister 1946, pls. xi and xix; Henry 1964, pls. 76, 83, and 90.

these capitals are solid stone copies of wood-and-metal portable reliquaries, which are miniature imitations of churches (see Pl. II). The so-called 'Temple Scene' in the Book of Kells[1] shows, in ornate and stylized form, a church with elaborate gable finials, and one can see such finials also on the very late solid stone shrine,

FIG. 33. A chapel, apparently cruck-built (note crossed gable finials); detail from a fifth-century Christian mosaic, Thessalonica.

itself a full-sized skeuomorphic copy of a house, or church-shaped reliquary coffin, at Clones, co. Monaghan.[2]

The ornamental, often zoomorphic, shapes adopted for these projecting gable-finials in the skeuomorphic copies just listed are also found on the stone finials from early chapels. In addition to those mentioned by Dr. Leask,[3] we have a broken example from the second-phase chapel at Church Island,[4] and—so far, alone

---

[1] Folio 202, v; Henry 1964, pl. 88 (colour).
[2] De Paor, L. and M. 1958, 60.
[3] Leask 1955, 46–7.   [4] O'Kelly 1958.

outside Ireland—the plainer terminal of another (Fig. 34) from the phase 3 stone chapel on Ardwall Isle.[1]

What lies behind this transition from the small timber chapels to the somewhat larger stone-walled ones, and why are most of the latter connected with those cemeteries whose 'developed'

FIG. 34. Ardwall Isle, tip of gritstone finial (scale half size); drawing by Mr. T. D. McArdle.

aspect they initially represent? Apart from the interesting fact that a parallel transition from stone to wood probably took place with regard to another Christian monument, the large free-standing cross, and possibly (as at Church Island) holds good, too, for living-cells associated with Christian establishments, I think the answer may lie partly in a shift of function. The very tiny timber oratories, as at Church Island and Ardwall Isle, quite apart from their relative transiency, are surely intended for the accommodation of one or two brethren alone. These are the people who, in slightly larger bands, inhabited the eremitic monasteries. As we read in Adomnán's *Life of Columba*,[2] and in the two *Lives of*

---

[1] Thomas 1967b, 156–7 (no. 12); I have now (1969) noticed a stone in the collection housed in the crypt at Lastingham, Yorks., which is conceivably half of a large stone gable finial.

[2] Adomnán, *Vita Columbae*, iii. 23.

Cuthbert,[1] such men went out from established monasteries like Iona or Lindisfarne, in the sixth and seventh centuries, to engage in a lonely personal struggle with unseen powers, for the sake of their souls and for the hope of eternal salvation. Our materialist world today might well categorize them all as escapists, mad visionaries, or drop-outs from life and reality. In their own time, such men were the *milites Christi* and, like the Desert Fathers to whom ultimately they owed their inspiration, they were the heroes of the early Church.

The attachment of such a hermit, whose structural requirements would involve no more than a hut or cave and the smallest of oratories (we shall examine a few such hermitages in a moment), to a cemetery is a process we can only tentatively reconstruct. It is unlikely that such a man, if his retreat was in any way accessible, would for long escape the attention of earnest pilgrims; some of these might be at death's door, seeking a miraculous cure, and like the hermit himself,[2] would doubtless request to be buried at a place already sanctified by spiritual power or angelic revelation. A cemetery could thus grow around a hermitage, particularly after the death of some notable saintly solitary, whose grave would in all probability be specially distinguished. Conversely, some solitary brethren, fired with missionary zeal, might attach themselves to an existing cemetery. The cemetery, as we have already argued at length, was the primary field-monument, consecrated in the remote past by an appropriate bishop, perhaps even by Patrick, or Ninian, or Kentigern. Its exact location could be due to local sentiment, to a wish to preserve continuity with some older, albeit pre-Christian, tribal burial-ground, and we have examined the evidence for this, too. Notably with the numerous off-shore islets, there is another factor, preserved in much later Scottish tradition; early graves were of no great depth, and such water-girt sanctuaries were naturally protected from the sordid depredations of wolves and other grave-robbers.[3]

---

1 Colgrave 1940.

2 Cuthbert wished to be buried on the Great Farne; Guthlac of Crowland left or ders for his burial in his own little oratory (*Vita Guthlaci*, ed. Colgrave 1956, cap. 50). See now Burn 1969. 3 Ritchie 1920, 119.

The replacement of the restricted timber oratory by the larger stone chapel goes hand-in-hand with the little skeletal evidence we yet possess. The presence of men, women, and children, as at Church Island, Ardwall Isle, and Burry Holms, shows that the lay population is being served. The new churches are proper little churches in every respect, with their own fixed stone altars; indeed, some of these altars are very complicated, as at Ardwall

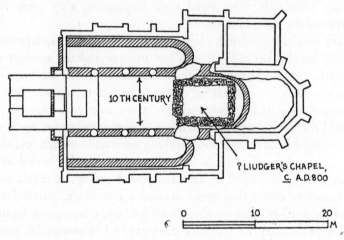

10TH CENTURY

? LIUDGER'S CHAPEL,
C. A.D. 800

0   10   20
M

DUTCH REFORMED CHURCH, ZELHEM, GELDERLAND
AFTER J. YPEY, 1959

FIG. 35. An instance from the Netherlands of continuity on a recently-excavated church site.

Isle, and we must consider this point in another chapter.[1] Is this the point at which the rustic congregation enters the church, instead of standing outside it in the primary cemetery?

The continuity of the sacred place expressed by the superimposition of the stone chapel on its wooden fore-runner is an aspect of religious phenomenology,[2] not only exhibited in a Christian guise by many of our major British cathedrals, but also illustrated by several excellent instances from the Continent. The Dutch Reformed Church at Zelhem, in the Netherlands,[3] has been excavated (Fig. 35), and beneath it, at the start of a long sequence of

[1] See p. 179.   [2] James 1952.   [3] Renaud 1959, esp. 195, afb. 7.

I. Ardwall Isle, Galloway: excavated remains of stone-walled chapel (seen from W.) overlying smaller timber oratory (outlined in black)

rebuildings, was the small (and very Irish-looking!) stone-walled chapel attributed to the eighth-century Frisian, Liudger, disciple of the Anglo-Saxon missionaries, and once a pupil of Alcuin at York. There is also the great Dionysius Church at Esslingen, on the river Neckar, in Germany. Here, in Gustav Fehring's recently published,[1] and technically brilliant, excavation, the initial phase of the long and complicated architectural sequence was another small stone church, built between 725 and 750, whose focal point appears to be the reliquary-coffin of St. Vitalis. The subsequent growth of this sacred place into a large modern town-church is fully demonstrated, stage by stage, through Fehring's work. To return to North Britain, we can see that the siting of the priory church at Whithorn is ultimately due to the fact that, below its east end, lies part of the sub-Roman cemetery of Ninian's day; I have opined elsewhere, with Radford, that any fifth-century church actually used by Ninian must have lain approximately below the crossing, at the east end of the priory church's nave.[2]

One striking fact about developed cemeteries in Ireland and Atlantic Britain is that, from Shetland to Scilly, the same basic plan with only minor variations can be seen. These sites are so widespread in occurrence that we can consider only a sample.

In Cornwall, both St. Helen's (Scilly) and the raised oval churchyard at St. Buryan in the Land's End, are probably eremitic monasteries in origin;[3] almost any Cornish parish church in a curvilinear (original) graveyard which has also produced inscribed stones or cross-slabs of early date could, however, be regarded as a developed cemetery. St. Mawnan, near Falmouth,[4] is a case where the original enclosure-bank, just possibly an older secular work, is still prominent within the graveyard. Merther-Uny, in a remote part of west Cornwall,[5] is an interesting and recently excavated example, initially an oval homestead-enclosure of the Romano–British period, where the development sequence *in toto* does not begin until the ninth or tenth century. The Beacon Hill ('Old Lighthouse') cemetery on the island of Lundy, in the Bristol

[1] Fehring 1967.
[2] Thomas 1966a, 114–16.
[3] O'Neil 1964, 44, fig. 1 (plan).
[4] Henderson, C. 1928, 156–7.
[5] See note in *CA* 7 (1968), 81–2.

channel, is unique in Britain in still possessing four inscribed memorial stones of late fifth- to seventh-century dates; it has a small rebuilt chapel of medieval type and an earlier special grave.[1] In Wales, Cilrhedyn in Carmarthenshire[2] appears, in plan, to be a typical instance. From Ireland one can choose Kildreenagh,

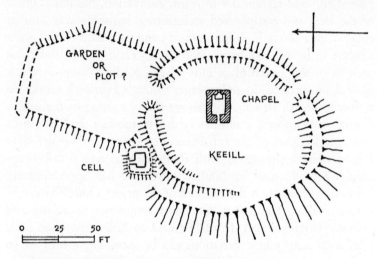

LAG-NY-KEEILLEY, ISLE OF MANN
AFTER KERMODE, 1909

Fig. 36.

Loher townland, co. Kerry, with its small oratory, hut, and what looks like a clerics' burial-area divided off from the larger lay cemetery;[3] and in the north, Maghera, co. Down,[4] where there is a second church outside the enclosure.

There are numerous cases in the Isle of Mann, like Lag-ny-keeilley, Patrick (Fig. 36), with the oratory inside the enclosed cemetery, a single living-cell just outside it, and even a small attached garden-plot.[5] In seventh-century Northumbria we may recall Bede's description[6] of what is today the little parish church

---

[1] Gardner 1960; Gardner 1962; Thomas 1969b.
[2] Bowen 1954, 157-8 (with sketch maps).
[3] Henry 1957, 142-5, fig. 25.   [4] ASNI Down 1966, 306-7, pl. 85.
[5] *MAS* i. 19-24 (with plans).   [6] *H.E.* v. 2.

and graveyard of St. John's Lee, Acomb, perched on a high spur
above the Tyne, just north of Hexham. This was 'a rather isolated
foundation, surrounded by scattered woodland, and by a bank
and ditch (*vallum*), containing a cemetery dedicated in honour of
St. Michael the Archangel'. Presumably it had a chapel or oratory

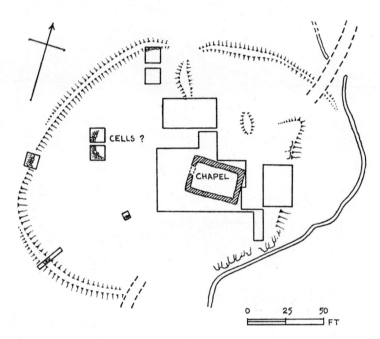

ARDWALL ISLE

Fig. 37. General plan of the developed and enclosed cemetery, Ardwall Isle,
showing position and extent of 1964-5 excavations.

so dedicated, where St. John of Beverley and his friends prayed
during their retreats; and at least one living-cell. Another cell or
hut (*parvum tugurium*) was built within this enclosure (*in conseptis*)
for a poor dumb boy, whom St. John of Beverley wished to cure.
This is a classic description of a developed cemetery, and there are
others in rural Northumbria.

To the west, in Galloway, we have Ardwall Isle (Fig. 37), where
the low stone-revetted enclosure bank (of the second or third

phase) embraces the chapel, the burial-ground, and perhaps some living-cells, since what seemed to be the ruined foundations of one were noticed. Despite extensive medieval alteration, Kirkmaiden in Glasserton parish, and the other Kirkmaiden (Fig. 38), in the Rinns of Galloway, can both still be clearly seen to have begun as sites of this kind.[1] The smaller enclosure within the confines of

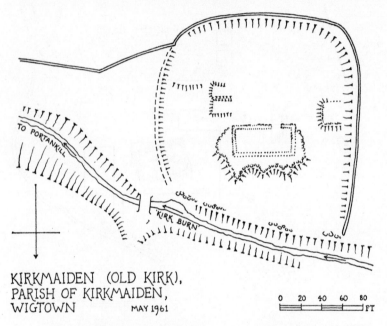

KIRKMAIDEN (OLD KIRK),
PARISH OF KIRKMAIDEN,
WIGTOWN   MAY 1961

0   20   40   60   80
⊨===⊨====⊨===⊨===⊨ FT

FIG. 38. Plan based on visible features in field survey, 1961.

St. Blane's monastery, Kingarth, Bute[2] is an instance, like St. Michael's in the Iniscealtra complex,[3] of a developed cemetery encapsulated in a large monastic enclosure. Relig Oran (Reilig Odhrain) on Iona, enclosed in the ninth century in such a way that its surrounding wall overlaps, from the outside, the great *vallum* ditch of Columba's earlier monastery, is another example. The western Isles, Orkney, and probably Shetland, could between them give us many additional instances.

[1] RCA(H)MS Galloway i, Wigtown, 1912, nos. 2 and 165.
[2] Hewison 1893, with plans.   [3] Macalister 1916, 117–19.

We must be careful, in our examination of the developed cemetery, and particularly in considering the postulated origin of some developed cemeteries as additions to isolated hermitages, not to overlook the very few hermitages—of individual monks—which can still be distinguished here and there. The surviving traces of these ascetic solitaries are, as one might expect, on the remoter fringes of the west. In two probable cases the tiny oratory is more or less combined with the living-cell. This is how I would interpret the remains on North Rona, with its two-stage chapel;[1] the eastern half is the original oratory, and the western half an addition for living purposes. Less well known is the site (Fig. 39) at Luchubran, Pigmies' Isle, off the Butt of Lewis,[2] where oratory and circular cell were linked into one. Other hermits lived from time to time in caves, as Martin of Tours is said to have done,[3] and as later tradition held of Ninian, whose cave at Physgyll was certainly venerated from an early date.[4] Two very similar hermitage sites (Fig. 39) are: Illaunloughan, co. Kerry,[5] with an oratory and separate circular cell, to which what may be the hermit's own tomb (a slab shrine with a rectilinear *cella memoriae* surround) appears to have been added; and St. Cuthbert's Isle, off the southern tip of Lindisfarne (Fig. 40), where the cell is represented by a low circular jumble of stones and where the oratory was rebuilt in the medieval period.[6]

Lastly, let us briefly examine the names used, in Latin and in the Celtic languages, to describe these various forms of cemetery and church.

Cemiterium, literally 'the place of those who sleep', from Greek via Latin, is not often found before the Middle Ages, and Bede's word *clymiterium*, used of St. John's Lee, Acomb, is presumed to be a form of this. I believe the oldest British term to be the noun **lano-* (which occurs in continental Celtic place-names),

[1] Darling 1939, 38–46 and pls.; Nisbet and Gailey 1962, 103–7 (with plan, fig. 2).
[2] RCA(H)MS Outer Hebrides and Skye, 1928, 9–10; Munro 1961, 82–3.
[3] Sulpicius Severus, *Vita Martini* (ed. Hoare 1954), cap. 10.
[4] Maxwell 1885; Radford 1951; Radford 1957b, 152–61.
[5] Henry 1957, 96–8 and fig. 16 (plan).
[6] *Trans. Berwick Nat.* 13 (1890–1), 240, and plan, pl. xii.

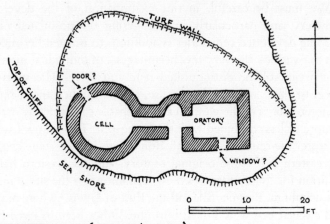

LUCHUBRAN, OR 'PIGMIE'S ISLE'
AFTER MACKENZIE, 1905

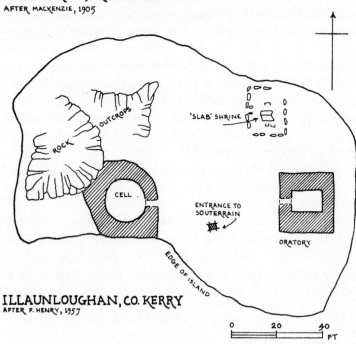

ILLAUNLOUGHAN, CO. KERRY
AFTER F. HENRY, 1957

FIG. 39.

in the meaning of 'flat space, cleared space'.[1] It gives both Welsh *llan* and Cornish *lan*, and by itself, and in compounds, early acquired the secondary meaning of 'enclosure'. *Llan* (*lan*) is so widely employed, invariably in a religious context, that one can infer a semantic development from 'cleared space' to 'consecrated

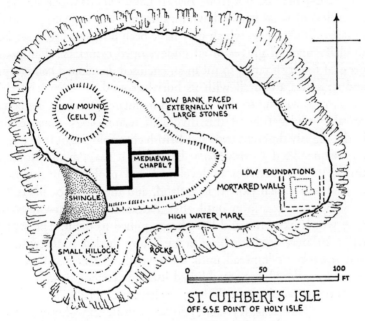

FIG. 40. Plan based on visible features in field-survey, 1964.

cleared space' (= unenclosed cemetery), thence to 'sacred enclosure' (enclosed cemetery) and finally 'church and cemetery' or even 'church site' (developed enclosed cemetery).[2]

The equivalent Irish term, apparently arising in Ireland, and disseminated throughout areas of Irish settlement in Britain, was Old Irish *cell*, later *cill*, a loan (with loss of final unstressed *-a-*) from the Latin *cella*.[3] Though both Aldhelm (*circa* 690) and, in

[1] Cf. *Ogam* 12 (1960), 403–4, 531–2.

[2] Cf. Williams, H. 1912, 266–8, with a perhaps less convincing explanation of the semantics.

[3] Williams, H. 1912, 270.

the next century, Alcuin, use the diminutive *cellula* to mean 'chapel', we are, I think, concerned with an origin earlier than this time. Whether, by the sixth century, *cell* referred to the first timber oratories, or to the living-huts attached to cemeteries, must be a matter of some doubt; and I am inclined to think that the borrowing may be not from British Latin *cella* (if it existed, and regardless of what it may have meant), but from the continental phrase *cella memoriae*, which may have been borrowed to describe specially marked graves in an undeveloped cemetery. The progress of the Irish term, to mean an enclosed developed cemetery, and still later a church with its burial ground, or even 'church' alone, runs parallel to that of *llan* in mainland Britain. One conceivable explanation of this divergent terminology may reside in the slightly different Irish and British chronologies of the cemetery sequence. If British **lano-* begins, as it may, in sub-Roman times, it first describes undeveloped and probably unenclosed cemeteries. If such existed in Ireland, and they are not likely to have become common until after Patrick's day, non-Christian Irish words like *fert* could have been applied to them. The word *cell* > *cill* may not have been in use before the late sixth century, and scarcely widespread until the seventh. By such a time the word *lan-* would have established itself in western Britain as the appropriate equivalent. Where ecclesiastical place-names with the prefix Cil- (Kil-, Kyl-, etc.) do occur in Britain—for example, in parts of Wales, and possibly in east Cornwall—they betray the presence of Irish speakers and Irish Christian settlers rather than the deliberate adoption of the Irish word, and the reverse explanation no doubt applies to a few examples of *lan(n)*, in this sense, in early Irish sources.[1]

Subsidiary terms, some of which we shall encounter in the fifth chapter, allude not so much to the enclosure or any of its buildings, but to the role of the actual cemetery as the repository of corporeal relics (bones) of saints and martyrs. Old Irish *relic(c)*, later (as in Scotland) *reilig*, and the Manx word *rhullick*, are from the Latin *reliquiae*, 'relics' (in this special sense), 'places possessing such relics'. *Relic(c)* is a common word for a cemetery, nearly as

[1] Stokes 1905, 388–9 ('Index of Places & Tribes') s.nn. 'Land-'.

common as *cill*, to which it might be said to act as a synonym. In the *Félire Óengus* (*circa* 800), under 21 July, we read[1] how the high cross of 'Heli martir', the martyr Helius, made great something described as *relicc lechtach*, 'a grave-abounding cemetery', and in the later Notes to the *Félire*,[2] a place in West Meath called *cell Toma* is said to be a *relic*, a clear equation of terms.

The extraordinary and early Irish term *rúam*, derived from *Roma* (Rome), reminds us of the Eternal City's function as the main source of Apostolic relics, like those of St. Peter and St. Paul, traditionally preserved at Armagh since Patrick's time. The Irish *martrae* is, by the eighth century, used to mean 'physical relics, bones'; *martir*, from the Latin *martyrium*, a technical term meaning 'a place possessing a martyr's physical remains', seems later to have acquired the sense of 'a church, or cemetery, holding the physical remains of a named saint or martyr'. The British counterpart is seen in Welsh *merthyr*, Cornish *merther*, both of which occur as the first elements in the names of churches and developed cemeteries (like Merthyr Tydfil, and Merther Uny).

The large number of words—some of them Old Irish, some loans from Latin at early and late stages—used for chapels, churches, and oratories need not detain us; but we must include reference to a curious word, *andóit*, later *annait*. This is found by itself, particularly in Scotland, as a place-name, as well as occurring in compounds; it meant, so W. J. Watson informs us,[3] a patron saint's own church, a mother-church containing the relics of a founder. One suspects that in Scotland *annait* was generally the equivalent of the word *merthyr* (*merther*) in Wales and Cornwall. As the basic idea of primacy and great age seems to be implied, Whitley Stokes was no doubt led, many years ago, to postulate that *andóit* was a loan-word from Latin *antitas*, a shortened form of *antiquitas*.[4] No other etymology has ever been seriously advanced.

---

[1] Stokes 1905, 164.

[2] Stokes 1905, 47. Binchy (*Ériu* xviii. 83) draws attention to an extraordinary gloss in *Coibnes Uisci Thairidne* in which *nemed cille* (Gaulish *nemeton*, 'sanctuary, sacred grove'; see Piggott 1968, 71–2) is interpreted as meaning a Christian cemetery.

[3] Watson 1926, 170, 250–4.   [4] Stokes 1887, ii. 640.

We began, in Chapter 2, with the diocese and the monastery; we have now examined the sequence leading up to the developed cemetery enclosure with its internal structures, the early Christian equivalent of the later parish church, and the subordinate unit in the monastic *paruchia*. In the next chapter, descending to still smaller units, we can examine the various modes by which the individual Christian dead were commemorated.

4. The Commemoration of the Dead

THE IDEA THAT DEATH SHOULD MEAN the complete and final extinction of the individual is one that many people, however outwardly rational, find it distasteful to contemplate. The corollary, that a man's identity is continued in the memory of his name and deeds, or vicariously in the persons of his own descendants, is a concept that can and does find expression in the archaeological record. This is perhaps of special relevance in the Celtic-speaking (or formerly Celtic-speaking) regions of the British Isles, where in former times—as, to some extent, today—people found it hard to consider either themselves or others as isolated beings, divorced from their total environment. It mattered, often very much, where a man was born and raised, from which family or group of families he sprang, and whom he chose to marry. In the days of the full Highland clan-system, in medieval Wales, and in the society affected by the early Irish law codes, these were vital considerations; a man with no kin, and no stake in the land, was not only pitiable but vulnerable.

The Christian admonition to ignore the earthly family and parents of this world when considering the Divine Father of the next may be faintly reflected in Britain in the handful of late Roman Christian memorial stones,[1] with the indifference shown as to the deceased's true age or immediate background. In post-Roman times it was clearly not strong enough to overcome an almost universal desire to identify a dead person by reference to his or her father, and with a constricted range of given names such references may represent an everyday practice, an early form of that which eventually produced surnames of the patronymic class (e.g. Ap Rhys, O'Donnell, MacLachlan, Quilliam, or Richardson).

[1] See p. 11.

These are but a few of the many points which will arise, and which we shall do well to keep in mind, during our brief examination of the ways in which the Christian (and some non-Christian) dead were commemorated in early Christian Britain and Ireland. The subject is fascinating, but full of difficulties. I would at the outset list three major obstacles to fuller study, not all of which have been considered in recent discussions. In the first place, we can discuss only those graves which were marked out, at ground-level or above and presumably at or soon after the time of burial, by some form of memorial, bearing either writing or symbols or both. It is abundantly clear that the proportion of individual Christian burials so distinguished was never very high. Even allowing for the erosion of this total by wilful or accidental destruction over many centuries, it may never have been higher than, say, one-tenth. I would not argue, as I have done[1] in the case of the extraordinary symbol-stones of the historical Picts (which I believe to be gravestones), that Christian memorials are confined to the ruling classes or the higher grades of society; the natures of many of the epitaphs preclude this idea. A strong element of chance must be seen at work here.

Secondly, our discussion centres perforce around surviving memorials in *stone*. Just as, in recent centuries, grave-monuments of wood and of cast-iron have been employed, so too there were almost certainly memorials in wood (in particular, I think, small shaped crosses) in pre-Conquest times. These have failed to survive physically, but they may have partially come down to us in skeuomorphs and flat depictions, and we should not overlook them.

The third and last caveat is that the rules of typology, that is, the principles which archaeologists employ to arrange long series of artefacts of given classes in chronological order (using empirical assumptions about improvement, function, fashion, and imitation) may not really be of much help here. The erection of any memorial to a dead person is a social action by surviving relatives or friends or admirers, with all the implications of ostentation, status, prestige, or superstition. Socially impressive or desirable

[1] Thomas 1964, 41–2.

models will be copied again and again, hyperbole will creep into the wording of epitaphs, and the fickle and swiftly changing workings of fashion are just as detectable in this field as they are in the greater one of female dress. As an object-lesson in the unreliability of pure *form* as a guide to absolute date, it may be pointed out that the older cemeteries of central Edinburgh—both in the Old City and the (Georgian) New Town—exhibit, as far as I can detect, every known form of classical (and pagan) memorial, sarcophagus, stele, funerary tablet, and grave-enclosure, and this includes several miniature temple porticoes and a small red granite imitation of the Pyramid of Celsus.

Why, in this small proportion of cases where early Christian graves were visibly commemorated, were monuments erected at all? We get some direct clues from the wording of the inscriptions. Visitors are urged to pray for the soul of the deceased; they are reminded of his Christian status and, if it was important to his family, his social status as well. Behind this must lurk a number of other motives, some of them clarified more by the study of religious phenomenology than by that of the New Testament. We should think of that perpetual human desire to visit the resting-places of loved ones or old friends; of the great advantage of burial close to a saint, in a clearly defined grave, so as to partake of the benefits of the prayers of pilgrims, and to ensure participation in the Resurrection; of a desire to avoid disturbance of one's grave by subsequent graves, an almost universal risk in permanent burial-grounds; of apotropaic and not wholly Christian symbols on tombstones, intended to keep the dead well under and to ward off predators or evil; and of the long pre-Christian tradition of the upright slab or pillar or post, stretching back to the sacred circle with its internal uprights as a modality of the widespread 'ascension myth'.[1]

During the late Roman period in Britain, those who lived in or visited or invaded the Romanized province would have had ample chance to observe many manifestations of Roman funerary practice—the upright pillar or stele, the elements of portraiture or other pictures, the formulaic inscription set out in horizontal

[1] Eliade 1958, 108-9, 122; Eliade 1961, 47-51.

lines of well-cut capitals, and the set references to Divine powers, to status, parentage or ancestry, and to military prowess. The prestige attached (in barbarian eyes) to these displays of the superior soldiery and *bourgeoisie*, redolent of Rome's seeming permanence and the *potestas* of her gods, is not always appreciated. Two quite discrete schools of stone memorial, neither of them demonstrably Christian at all in the earliest stages, can be argued to have arisen in ultimate imitation of the Roman tombstone. Both later became Christianized, but this fact does not affect their origins.

In Ireland, some degree of contact with the Roman provinces in Britain is certain.[1] Roman objects are more common in early Ireland than is generally suspected—this whole topic is now being reconsidered, particularly with regard to coins[2]—and even if most of these represent the proceeds of piracy or slave-raiding rather than organized trade or civilized visits, interchange at a human level also occurred. It can be suggested that small groups of Irish settlers had established themselves on the Atlantic coasts of Britain within the later fourth century.[3] We also remember that, when Patrick was called by his vision to return to Ireland in 432 or thereabouts, it is thought that he went back to minister to established Christian flocks, some members of which may have been of British origin.[4]

Someone, possibly an Irish scholar and probably during the fourth century, invented a stroke alphabet (Fig. 41) based on groups of long and short lines, set straight or obliquely across a base-line; this is known as *ogam*.[5] It is generally agreed that the ogam structure must have been based on the Latin alphabet as the latter was classified by late Roman grammarians.[6] Initially, ogam may have been intended to convey short messages notched on the angles of portable tally-rods or the like, but by the late fourth century this system of writing, despite its inability to distinguish long and short vowels or any aspirated consonants, began to

---

[1] Ó Ríordáin 1947a.
[2] By Dr. R. H. M. Dolley (Queen's, Belfast).   [3] See p. 221.
[4] Kenney 1929, 309–15; Chadwick, N. K. 1961, 17, 53, 76.
[5] Correctly *ogham*, in Irish.
[6] Jackson 1950, 202–3; LEHB, 151–7; cf. MacNeill 1937, 170–4.

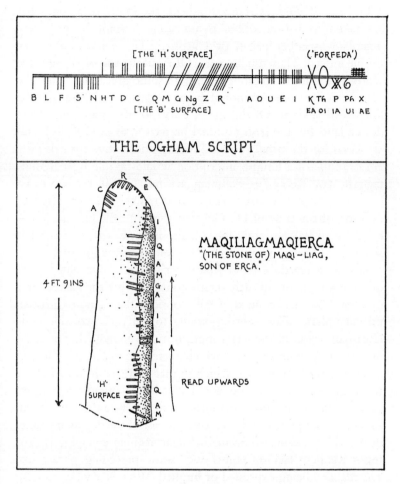

FIG. 41.

appear in Ireland on what can only be called tombstones.[1] If large stones or pillars possessing a naturally sharp and straight edge (e.g. chunks of limestone or slate) were not available, then a long straight line could be incised or chiselled on a flat face, and treated as a base-line for the inscription.

[1] Interestingly, the knowledge of ogam seems never to have been lost: cf. Raftery, B. 1969.

In view of their extreme simplicity the inscriptions on what are taken to be the oldest ogam stones cannot be definitely described as either pagan or Christian. The epitaphs are very simple indeed. They usually read 'Of A, of the son of B', all three words being in the genitive case, with some preceding noun like 'The Grave' or 'The Memorial' being understood. Variants of the link-word MAQQI 'Of the son' are AVI 'of the grandson, of the descendant' (cf. the Irish nominal prefix O', as in O'Kelly), and MUCCOI 'of the tribe'. The use of any nominative form is rare. An example of a longish inscription would be one from Ballin-taggart, co. Kerry (= Ballintaggart no. 9).[1] It reads NETTA LAMINACCA KOI MAQQI MUCOI DOVINIAS, 'N.L. here; (tomb) of a son of the tribe of D'. Contrast this with the brevity of an-other, from Ballingrannig (no. 6), also in co. Kerry: CCICAMINI MAQQI CATTINI, '(Tomb) of C— (tomb) of the son of C'.[1]

Despite a reaction, from Macalister's grossly overstated view of the pagan nature of early ogam stones, to a guarded acceptance of their Christian context, I still consider that a non-Christian primary phase of use, corresponding to the very probable non-Christian origin of the script itself, must be envisaged. The stress on a man's parents or ancestors, characteristic of Celtic society at all stages, is of course one which insular Christianity plainly had to accept and to accommodate; but it is also broadly analogous to the *nomina*, filiation formulae, and tribal-names of Roman funerary inscriptions, and moreover the use of the deceased's name in the oblique case also occurs in pagan Roman epitaphs, as Pro-fessor Kenneth Jackson points out,[2] some preceding phrase like *Dis Manibus* being expressed or implied. Whatever view modern scholars may take, it does seem that (as Macalister frequently emphasized) in early Christian times some people considered ogam stones to be pagan objects. The invention of the very script was aetiologically attributed to a god or divine hero called *Ogma*, perhaps the same as the Gaulish god *Ogmios*; some stones are found with the ogam notches (selectively?) defaced, and with the simple linear crosses added to the stones 'to Christianize them'

[1] *CIIC* i. 156–7, no. 163.
[2] *LHEB* 166–8.

III. (*Above*) Incised cross, 32 mm. long, on beach pebble used as primary grave-marker, from Physgyll Cave, near Whithorn (Whithorn Museum). (*Below*) Incised cross, 173 mm. long, on small slab used as primary grave-marker, Ardwall Isle, phase II burials

IV. (*Right*) Primary cross-slab with pecked-out cross, Iona (original context unknown)

(*Below*) Primary cross-slab with incised outline cross of 'wooden' form, from pre-Viking (?) burial-ground, Holm of Noss, Shetland (Shetland Museum, Lerwick)

(Macalister!); and they are found, surprisingly often, reused in such secular contexts as the slab roofs of pre-medieval souterrains. One is bound, therefore, to suppose that, mostly in the south of Ireland, there was a period in which ogam inscriptions were made and used in pagan contexts—probably during the very late fourth, and fifth, centuries—and that this slowly gave way to a longer period of mainly Christian usage.

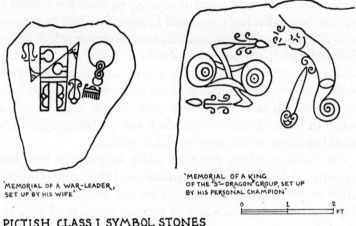

'MEMORIAL OF A WAR-LEADER,
SET UP BY HIS WIFE'

'MEMORIAL OF A KING
OF THE '5'- DRAGON' GROUP, SET UP
BY HIS PERSONAL CHAMPION'

PICTISH CLASS I SYMBOL STONES
(AFTER J. ROMILLY ALLEN)
WITH TENTATIVE EXPLANATIONS OF THEIR MEANINGS

FIG. 42.

If the originators of ogam inscriptions borrowed the idea of *script* from Roman practice, then the *pictorial* nature (Fig. 42) of the oldest group of Pictish stones in north-east Scotland—which exhibit on the flat faces of boulders or pillars a variety of non-Christian symbols (stylized objects, geometric shapes, items from the animal kingdom)—may have been inspired by the pictorial element of Roman tombstones, Roman altars, and the embellishments of Roman monumental entablature. I have argued this in considerable detail elsewhere,[1] though without convincing all fellow students of this period,[2] and will only summarize the argument now. My contention is that a ruling class in Pictish society

[1] Thomas 1964.   [2] Henderson 1967, chap. 5.

H

began, perhaps in the late fifth century, a custom of erecting stone monuments to the dead, analogous to the ogam-inscribed stones of Ireland, but in this case confined to the upper crust of Pictland; whom I believe were the Celtic-speaking descendants of Iron Age settlers, merged with a very much larger population of Bronze Age aborigines who spoke (non-Indo-European) Pictish. The Picts, as a nation, were non-literate, possessed no form of script of their own, and used pictorial symbols on these tombstones to indicate, not individual names and filiation, but such looser concepts as status, occupation, and (like the Irish names which follow the word MUC(C)OI) some sort of tribal descent. No one seriously doubts that ogam stones, hardly any of which are reliably recorded as having been found in direct association with graves, *are* tombstones; no other explanation really fits the 'Class I symbolstones' of Pictland, as these are called, and a whole range of Old World analogies would support this hypothesis.

The Pictish symbols, many of which originate in local Iron Age art, are both stylized and archaic, and their continued currency in post-Roman times must be due to their continuous employment as the vocabulary of personal tattoo markings. The use of these stones appears to originate around the Moray Firth,[1] a region which was not converted to Christianity until the late seventh or eighth centuries. The conversion to Christianity is marked, iconographically, by the adoption of a more elaborate form of symbol-bearing stones which exhibit universal Christian symbols as well as Pictish ones.

We return now to the Christian mainstream. It is strange that so few fifth-century tombstones (Fig. 43) could be described as following directly on from the late Roman Christian group, small as the latter is.[2] We have the fifth-century stone from Chesterholm (Northumberland); BRIGOMAGLOS HIC IACIT, followed by a second name ending in -ECUS.[3] Another of this date, from Whithorn, doubtless from the sub-Roman cemetery, has a long inscription[4] which reads 'We praise the Lord. Latinus, aged 35 years, and his daughter aged 4 years. The grandson of Barrovadus set

---

[1] Henderson 1958.   [2] See p. 11.   [3] *CIIC* i. 475–6, no. 498.
[4] *CIIC* i. 499–501, no. 520; best reading, Radford 1957b, 170–5.

up this memorial.' In west Cornwall there is another fifth-century stone (from Carnsew, Hayle) which somewhat recalls the Whithorn one;[1] it is now grievously defaced but may have been restorable as reading 'Here lately went to rest Cunaide. Here in

'CUNAIDE' STONE, HAYLE: 'LATINUS' STONE, WHITHORN:
AFTER IAGO AND BECKERLEGGE   AFTER RADFORD

FIG. 43. Horizontally-inscribed memorial stones in the late Roman Christian tradition; both of the latter part of the fifth century.

the tomb he (or she) lies. He (or she) lived 33 years'. It is possible that a few of the very early stones from north-west Wales, also employing, as those we have considered do, Roman capitals set out in horizontal lines, could be attributed to this sub-Roman tradition.

Following the conversion of the Emperor Constantine in 312 (as reported by Lactantius and Eusebius) and the so-called 'Edict

[1] *CIIC* i. 457-8, no. 479; cf. Thomas 1953, Beckerlegge 1953.

of Milan' in 313, Christians throughout the Empire officially and widely adopted a symbol, the monogram of the two Greek capitals *chi* and *rho*, like our capitals 'X' and 'P', which are the first two letters (in Greek) of *Christos*, Christ; this six-armed motif was encircled by a version of the classical triumphal wreath. A widely ranging series of inscriptions and graffiti—for instance, in the Roman catacombs and on tombstones—shows the evolution and stylization of the *chi-rho*, as it is often known. British fourth-century examples are represented on the reconstructed wall-paintings (on plaster) from the house-church at the Lullingstone villa in Kent;[1] by the central roundel of the Hinton St. Mary (Dorset) mosaic floor;[2] and, more humbly, by such things as the incised building-block from the Catterick bath-house[3] (Fig. 44).

In the early fifth century, notably in Gaul, Iberia, and the Rhineland, the chi-rho is simplified into an upright cross, like a 'plus sign' (+) in mathematics, the upper arm being looped around to the right to form a 'P' and, still later, partially looped instead to form a little hook like the top of a shepherd's crook. Christian abhorrence of the Cross with its connotations of our Saviour's death and of criminal punishment, despite the fourth-century abolition of crucifixion, may have delayed this particular evolution into a simpler form. In Britain, the early, six-armed, or 'Constantinian' form of the chi-rho has a markedly Romanized distribution during the fourth and early fifth centuries. It is a distribution which differs notably from that of the later, 'looped cross', form of chi-rho current in the fifth and later centuries, a distribution pattern which must include insular derivatives of the sixth and seventh centuries. This latter spread is clearly connected with the Atlantic coasts of Britain and Ireland. With it we must also consider a much larger group of inscribed tombstones—in south-west England, in south and north-west Wales, and in southern Scotland—still, for the most part, employing Roman capital letters set out in horizontal lines, and such universal Christian formulae as HIC IACIT ('Here lies . . .'), but with other, novel, features.

---

[1] Meates 1955, 137–45.   [2] Toynbee 1964.
[3] See p. 11, n. 1.

These stones, the dates of which range from the later fifth to the earlier seventh centuries, do not occur in Ireland. Here, ogam stones, now assuming general and in some cases rather idiosyncratic Christian character, take their place. There is broad agreement that with these later memorials we have to deal, not with

HINTON ST. MARY, DORSET
CENTRAL ROUNDEL, MOSAIC

LULLINGSTONE, KENT
PAINTED WALL-PLASTER FROM 'HOUSE CHURCH'

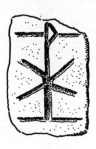

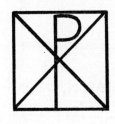

MOTIF (SIX TIMES) ON RIM OF LOST SILVER CUP:
R. TYNE AT CORBRIDGE

CATTERICK, YORKS.
ON A BUILDING SITE

FIG. 44. Instances of the *chi-rho* motif in late Roman Britain.

any question of continuity from Romano-British Christianity, but with the influence of the church on the Continent—in Gaul, especially. Impressive evidence for this belief has been marshalled, notably by Nash-Williams;[1] there are specific forms of wording used, special terms, a stone (in north-west Wales) which may commemorate a Gaulish immigrant,[2] and another reciting a Gaulish consular date (of 540).[3]

---

[1] Nash-Williams 1950, introduction; cf. *LHEB* 159, 163–5.
[2] Ibid. 63, no. 33 (= *CIIC* i. 311–13, no. 325).
[3] Ibid. 93, no. 104 (= *CIIC* i. 372, no. 396).

The inclusion, on a number of these later stones, of references to Christian status and occupation—such terms as SACERDOS, PRESBYTER, and probably EPISCOPUS and DIACONUS—shows us an organized episcopal church (of the kind envisaged, in regard to sub-Roman North Britain, in the second chapter). This is

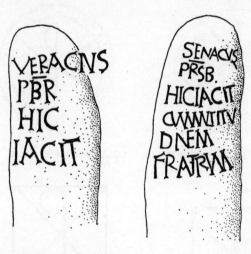

ABERDARON, CAERNS:
1 "VERACIUS PBR (= PRESBITER) HIC IACIT"
2 "SENACUS PRSB (= PRESBITER) HIC IACIT CUM MULTITUDINEM
FRATRUM"
AFTER NASH-WILLIAMS

FIG. 45. Memorial stones (late fifth or early sixth century) showing the specific title of *Presbyter, Presbiter*, 'Priest'.

notably so in southern Scotland; and also in north-west Wales (Fig. 45), where one or two other terms (MAGISTRATUS, MEDICUS) hint at real continuity in the form of settled civil existence.[1]

Something of the evidence for this postulated contact with Gaul was shown in Chapter 2; the British cleric Faustus at Lérins, Patrick taking ship with traders from Ireland to Gaul, and the bare fact of the spread of monastic ideas. Archaeology can now suggest that sea-borne trading contacts, providing a background

[1] Discussion, Foster 1965, 216-17.

for Christian contacts at a personal level, cover this period. A widely diffused type of imported pottery found in Britain and Ireland, quite separate from the Mediterranean red wares and wine-jars discussed earlier,[1] is that known as 'Class E'. This is a high-quality kitchen or domestic ware, of a grey or whitish colour, wheel-made, mass-produced, and fired almost to 'stoneware' hardness. 'Class E' pottery was, for some years, thought to have come from the Middle Rhine area,[2] a source which would certainly pose some historical problems. I have recently suggested (and this is to some extent confirmed by Dr. David Peacock's petrological work)[3] that a much more likely source-area is the Saintonges region of Aquitaine, the French Atlantic coast, and that this ware was produced by surviving Gallo-Roman ateliers under nominal Visigothic and later Frankish suzerainty (Fig. 46).

Likely points of export would then be Bordeaux, La Rochelle, and the minor Gironde ports. In the case of Bordeaux, the Gallo-Roman *Burdigala*, there is an independent link with Ireland. The famous schools of Burdigala in the late Empire[4] were almost certainly known to the Irish in Patrick's day; and whether or not we credit, with Zimmer, the idea of an exodus of men of learning from Gaul in the face of fifth-century disturbances fleeing to such relative havens as Ireland, the occurrence of an Irish form of this place-name *Bordgal*, both as a place-name in Westmeath and Kilkenny and as an actual noun (meaning 'meeting-place, place of assembly') takes on, as J. F. Kenney remarked,[5] 'a peculiar significance'. Others[6] have marshalled the evidence for equivalent literary contacts at this time, contacts which may of course have been influential in the initial westward spread of monasticism.

There is also a hint of North African influence in some sixth-century British epitaphs.[7] Rather rarely, we find in Wales and Cornwall the noun MEMORIA, used with a personal name. We have (Fig. 50) MEMORIA VOTEPORIGIS PROTICTORIS (South

---

[1] See p. 23.   [2] Thomas 1959, *passim.*
[3] Peacock and Thomas 1967.
[4] Chadwick, N. K. 1955, index, s.n.; Haarhoff 1958, 46–9.
[5] Kenney 1929, 140–3; cf. Stokes 1905, 304, index, s.n.
[6] Chadwick, N. K. 1955.
[7] Nash-Williams 1950, 10, 107, 191, 205.

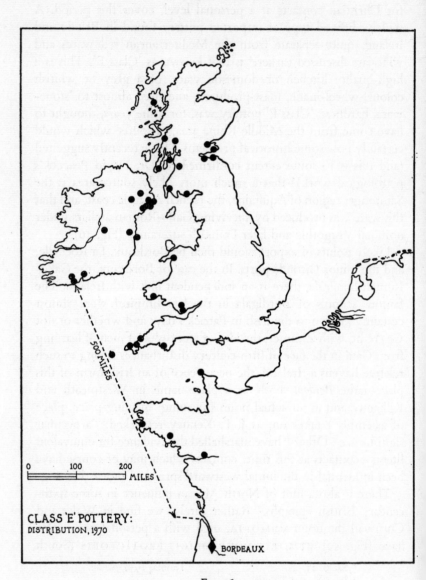

CLASS 'E' POTTERY:
DISTRIBUTION, 1970

0   100   200   MILES

500 MILES

BORDEAUX

FIG. 46.

Wales, mid sixth century);[1] INGENUI MEMORIA (Fig. 47) in east
Cornwall (early sixth);[2] and, from Yarrowkirk in the Scottish
Borders, the early sixth-century epitaph commencing HIC MEM-
ORIA PERPETUA.[3] With these go two Welsh stones, both early

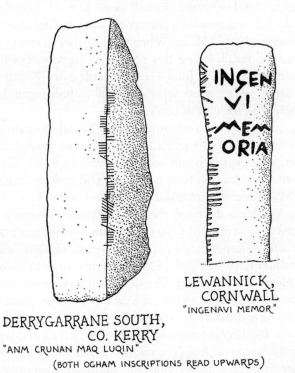

LEWANNICK,
CORNWALL
"INGENAVI MEMOR"

DERRYGARRANE SOUTH,
CO. KERRY
"ANM CRUNAN MAQ LUQIN"
(BOTH OGHAM INSCRIPTIONS READ UPWARDS)

FIG. 47. Monolingual (left) and bilingual (right) ogham-inscribed stones, both
late fifth or sixth century.

in the sixth century,[4] containing the words NOMINE and NOM-
ENA, both following a name in the genitive. MEMORIA is here a
technical term, related to the Latin *reliquiae* and *martyrium* that lie
behind the words *relicc* and *martir* mentioned early in connection

[1] Nash-Williams 1950, 107, no. 138 (= *CIIC* i. 342-3, no. 358).
[2] *CIIC* i. 443-4, no. 466.
[3] *CIIC* i. 491-3, no. 515; best reading, RCAMS Selkirk 1957, 110-13.
[4] Nash-Williams 1950, 169, no. 279; 205, no. 370.

with names of cemeteries. It means not just 'memory' ('In Memory Of'), but something more like 'martyrial shrine, special grave, tomb'; and it is particularly common by the sixth century in both Italian and North African epitaphs. NOMENA (correctly NOMINA, plural of *nomen*, 'name') came to mean something like *reliquiae*, 'the remains (of a martyr or saint or Christian)', and is also found in North Africa. When we note these terms in Atlantic Britain, and recall during this period the import of 'Class A ii' red wares, which Dr. John Hayes regards as of North African provenance, we see a link which we shall consider again below in the context of the cult of relics.

Related to these two terms is another, found in ogam epitaphs over a limited area of southern and south-west Ireland; it occurs in inscriptions which begin with the word ANM, literally 'name' but perhaps better translated (as in later Old Irish) as 'inscription'. Eoin MacWhite has mapped these,[1] and some little time ago Joseph Vendryes discussed their significance.[2] Whether (as one suspects) ANM translated NOMEN, NOMINA, in the sense of 'name of', or with a deeper meaning ('person by the name of, inscription of, remains of, *reliquiae*'), this looks again like an echo of continental or North African usage. The stones whose inscriptions contain ANM could be Christian ones; at least three possess simple incised crosses which could be contemporary with the ogams (this is not often so), another[3] commemorates someone called COLMAN who is described as AILITHIR ('the pilgrim'), and another stood in the odd circular setting at Derrygarrane South, co. Kerry, mentioned earlier[4] (Fig. 47).

The addition of crosses of any kind, or of other non-literate symbols, to Christian memorial stones, and the rise of yet another class of stones exhibiting crosses but no form of script (Roman or ogam), are matters involving formidable problems of chronology. Fifth-century tombstones, like the Whithorn LATINUS stone and the Hayle CUNAIDE stone, bear epitaphs composed entirely of lines of lettering; they have no crosses. The earliest 'pictorial' addition is, in any event, not the cross, but the second (hooked or

---

[1] MacWhite 1961.   [2] Vendryes 1956.
[3] *CIIC* i. 186–8, no. 193.   [4] See p. 63.

looped plus-sign) form of the chi-rho symbol. The best two instances of the latter, both probably before 500, come from what must have been a subsidiary church or cemetery in the Whithorn diocese, a (now lost) site at Kirkmadrine in the Rinns of Galloway.[1] Both display (Fig. 48), within an outline circle, equal-armed

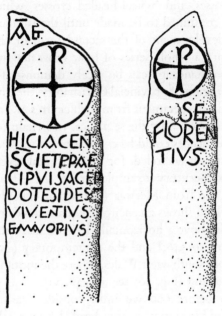

KIRKMADRINE, WIGTN?
AFTER MACALISTER

FIG. 48.

crosses with expanded terminals (the arm-ends), the uppermost arms having the crooked additions representing the *rho* of the chi-rho.

The significance of this embellishment, added to the mere lines of lettering, cannot be overstressed. Not only does the chi-rho, encircled or not, seem to have been the most important of several factors leading to the eventual common use of small initial crosses on memorial stones; it may also have been the avenue through

[1] *CIIC* i. 493–6, nos. 516–17.

which the plain cross, as a universal Christian symbol, was introduced and popularized in post-Roman western Britain and Ireland. The circular surround (which was maintained, notably in the long-lived Whithorn school of crosses, as an integral part of this design) underlies most if not all of the later schools of so-called 'ring crosses' and 'wheel-headed crosses' which, over much of Britain, continued to be made until the Romanesque era.

The development of the second form of chi-rho, in its plain circle, into a whole series of basic cross designs (some encircled, some free-standing) can be nicely demonstrated (Fig. 49) from another region of provincial Christianity, the Rhineland. Approximately dated specimens from such centres as Trier and Mainz can be arranged to show the sequence. In Britain (outside Galloway) partial sequences could be constructed from Cornwall, where the chi-rho is not encircled, for the sixth and seventh centuries. Isolated sixth-century examples from the Atlantic coasts would include one from Mertola (Portugal), epitaph of the presbyter *Britto*, which shows an encircled equal-armed cross with expanded terminals above a horizontally lettered inscription bearing a date equivalent to 546;[1] and the contemporary (?540–550) *Voteporix* stone from south-west Wales, where the motif is just a plain linear cross in a ring (Fig. 50; see also pl. vi).

Again before 600 we must consider various tombstones in which the inscription is now headed by a small cross (not a chi-rho, but an outline or linear cross) in such a way that the cross forms the first 'letter', as it were, of the epitaph. The CONINIE stone from Manorwater, Peebles,[2] of the later sixth century, is an example. During this century we can also reckon that ogam inscriptions were accompanied by small simple crosses (usually near the top of the stone) and that, as a number of people have suggested, older ogams—this includes those presumptively pagan ones from the fifth and late fourth centuries—were now given such additional crosses, often with the lines which form the crosses cutting through ogam notches. It is perfectly possible, though

[1] Bruce 1889.
[2] *CIIC* i. 486–8, no. 511 (the initial cross is *not* a chi-rho; cf. *PSAS* 70 (1935–6), 35 ff.).

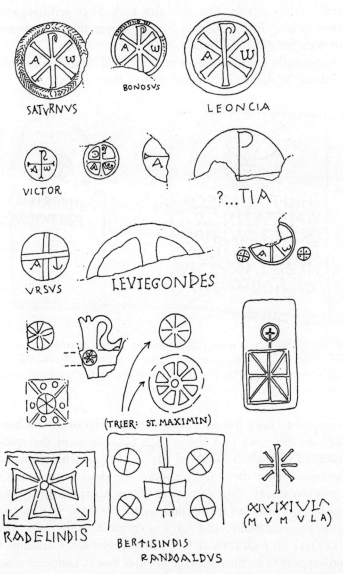

FIG. 49. Sequence showing development of cross from encircled 'chi-rho' motif; Rhineland, late fourth to seventh centuries. Tombstones from Mainz (Alte Peterskirche, Friedhof, Kantel, and Albanskirche cemeteries) after Behrens, 1950.

hardly demonstrable, that this also took place with regard to
stones bearing inscriptions, in Roman letters, that had originally
not been accompanied by any such cross-symbols.

Some sixth- and seventh-century inscribed stones from southern
Scotland, Wales, and Cornwall possess their inscriptions set, not

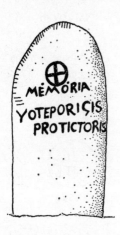

FIG. 50. Sixth-century memorials headed by crosses derived from the 'chi-
rho' motif, (left) Mertola, Portugal, (right) Carmarthen, Wales—the ogham
reads *Votecorigas*, the Primitive Irish equivalent of the (genitive) name in
Latin letters.

in horizontal lines, but *vertically* down the pillar or slab. When we
examine these, we find that a high proportion of the epitaphs
disregard the older formula of HIC IACIT (x), with the name in
the nominative; they commemorate the dead in such terms as
CONETOCI FILI TEGERNOMALI (from Cornwall), (CON)TI-
GERNI FILI TIGERNI from Lundy, CAMULORIGI FILI FANNUCI
from Pembrokeshire, and (as a mixture of styles) HIC IACIT
CARANTI FILI CURITANI from Roxburghshire. Common features appear to be the use of the genitive case (a Latinized second-
declension ending in -*i*) throughout, the final letter I often set
horizontally in relation to the inscription; the inscription, in one
or more lines, set vertically (i.e. one turns one's head over,
normally to the right, to read what is lettered); the occasional

persistence of the HIC IACIT opening even when ungrammatically followed by a string of genitives; and the occasional presence of an initial cross (now at the *top* of the first line).

This distortion of the older, Romanized, style not only reflects the influence of Irish Christian memorial practice, but largely defines, through the distribution of such instances, the areas of

FIG. 51. Sixth-century inscriptions from Guival, Cornwall, with Irish personal name (*Quenatauci*).

secular Irish settlement in post-Roman Britain. The formula, in Latin letters, 'Of-A FILI Of-B' exactly transliterates the ogam formula 'Of-A MAQQI Of-B', and the vertical setting must copy the normal vertical setting, up and down the edges of a stone or an incised base-line, of ogam tombstones. Indeed, in certain cases, like the rather transitional inscription (Fig. 51) on a sixth-century pillar near Penzance, Cornwall, QUENATAUCI IC DINUI FILIUS, 'Of-Q here, of-D the son',[1] the dead man's name (*Quenataucus*), is not British at all, but Primitive Irish. Secular Irish settlements of one sort and another on the western British mainland between the late fourth and seventh centuries form a topic we cannot here pursue in detail, but it is a movement for which a number of independent lines of evidence can be adduced. In almost every case, secular settlement was followed by a secondary wave of ecclesiastical activity, as we saw in the second chapter in the case of monasticism spreading from Ireland to the Scottish coast and thence to

[1] *CIIC* i. 440, no. 462; *LHEB* 140–1, 171–2, 296 n. 2.

Northumbria. Such activity must account for the appearance of this new inscriptional form, in Wales and the south-west.

J. D. Bu'lock's useful analysis of early inscriptions in Wales[1] shows a clear divergence between the two distributions (Fig. 52). The earlier tombstones, bearing the formula HIC IACIT and the lines of horizontal lettering, have a considerable focus on the organized sub-Roman church in north-west Wales; and the later tradition, with vertically lettered epitaphs containing FILI or FILIUS and of course a number of inscriptions actually in ogam, shows a pattern which is concentrated on the modern counties of Pembroke, Carmarthen, and Cardigan.

Side by side with this late sixth- and seventh-century habit of including a small initial cross on a tombstone's inscription there arose a different custom; that of using, to mark a grave, a smaller stone (pillar, slab, or boulder) bearing only a plain cross and no inscription whatever, either in ogam or Latin letters. There is again a small overlap, in that such stones *can* bear one or two words above, or below, the simple cross—examples are mainly northern, and one might cite the Barnakill (mid-Argyll) slab, with an incised linear cross and an illegible name beneath,[2] or the peculiar little slab from Iona with an outline expanded-arm cross with chi-rho upper hook, and two words read (by Professor Kenneth Jackson) as LAPIS ECHODI ('the stone of Echodius' (Irish *Echoid*)) incised along the top edge.[3] Both these are of the seventh, rather than the sixth, century (Fig. 53; see also Pl. V).

The very much larger groups of purely uninscribed stones with simple crosses are not likely to date much before the end of the sixth century. The forms of cross which they contain can be called 'primary', undeveloped and unornamented, and we can divide the stones, functionally, into small slabs or pillars which presumably stood upright at one end of a grave ('primary cross-slabs') and smaller stones, sometimes little more than large flat pebbles, which were laid by the head of the burial, probably even

---

[1] Bu'lock 1956.

[2] Campbell and Sandeman 1964, 74, no. 475.

[3] Unpublished; I am grateful to Professor Kenneth Jackson for allowing me to quote his reading.

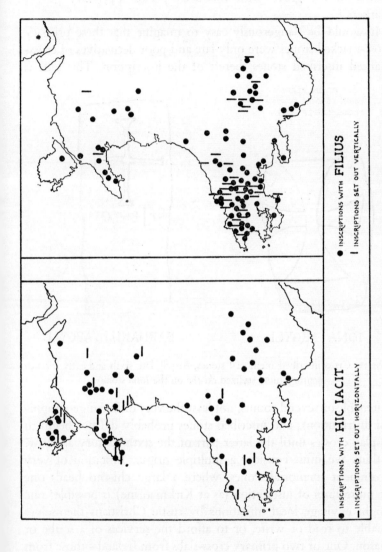

FIG. 52. Distributions of early inscribed memorial stones in Wales (after J. D. Bu'lock).

• INSCRIPTIONS WITH FILIUS

| INSCRIPTIONS SET OUT VERTICALLY

• INSCRIPTIONS WITH HIC IACIT

— INSCRIPTIONS SET OUT HORIZONTALLY

buried in the grave with the dead person ('primary grave-markers').

It would be dangerously easy to imagine that these primary cross-marked stones were only late and poor derivatives of cross-marked inscribed stones, bereft of the inscription. This idea is

INSCRIPTION READS
'LAPIS ECHODI'
ALONG UPPER EDGE

IONA., ARGYLL   BARNAKILL, ARGYLL

FIG. 53. Cross-inscribed memorial stones, Argyll, late sixth and early seventh century (note stylized *chi-rho* on the Iona stone).

untenable on several counts, not least the very different geographical distributions; and inscribed stones probably did not begin to display crosses until the latter part of the sixth century anyhow. I think we must consider a multiple origin. Imitation of very prominent memorial stones, where a large chi-rho heads one or more lines of inscription (as at Kirkmadrine) *is* possible; one might envisage local imitations by rustic Christians themselves unable to read or write, or to afford the services of a scribe or mason. One or two primary cross-slabs from Ireland—those from Cloonlaur and Doomakeon, co. Mayo,[1] come to mind—show solitary ringed crosses based on encircled chi-rho forms; a rather simpler ringed cross occurs on a little slab at Iona.

[1] Henry 1947, 35–6, pl. ix. 1 and ix. 2.

There is also a potential source of inspiration in the various objects of Christian use, other than tombstones, current by the late sixth century (and afterwards) in Britain and Ireland. Mlle Henry has drawn attention[1] to a resemblance (Fig. 54) between a primary slab at Kildreenagh, Loher, co. Kerry, which bears an incised double-outline cross with stylized Greek letters alpha and

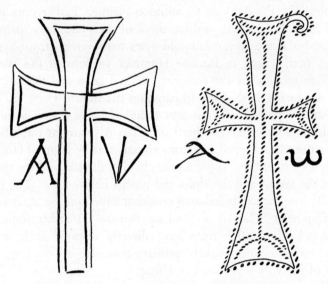

FIG. 54. Crosses with pendant letters; (left), stone pillar, Loher, co. Kerry—(right), *Codex Usserianus Primus* (MS. Trinity College, Dublin)—from photographs (F. Henry 1968).

omega below the side arms; and a cross with an upper chi-rho hook similarly accompanied which appears in a very early seventh-century manuscript (the *Codex Usserianus Primus*, T.C.D. 55, a gospel book). While, as she writes, 'it would be dangerous to insist on what may be a fortuitous coincidence', the appearance of small initial crosses at the beginning of inscriptions on late sixth-century tombstones is another innovation, for which the model of illuminated initials in manuscript style,[2] glimpsed in gospel books and service books, still forms the most likely inspiration.

[1] Henry 1965, 62, pls. 58–9; add also Harrison 1963, 132, pl. xl. a (Karabel no. 10—*circa* 530).   [2] Henry 1964, pl. 12.

One cannot rule out, either, the distinct possibility that individual shapes and forms of simple crosses on these primary stones were copied directly off imported Christian objects. 'Open-work book-covers', the bronze, gilt-bronze, or silver fretwork or open-work plaques affixed to the front of books or book-satchels, are generally represented in the Irish record by somewhat later examples, like the Athlone Crucifixion plaque.[1] Earlier ones may well have disappeared, and we think of such unusually splendid specimens as the Byzantine gold open-work cover (from Syria? about 600?), now in Berlin.[2] Humbler versions of this would provide models for the elongated central cross and the circular chi-rho forms, both easily imitated on flat stones. There are also imports of pottery. A fragment found at Dinas Emrys in north Wales is not, I think, a sherd of 'Class A' ware, as published,[3] but a roundel, chipped out from a small pottery lamp of familiar early Christian type, showing the chi-rho, the sun and the moon over the arms,[4] and the alpha and omega below them. The little double-outline expanded-arm crosses stamped on the inner bases of imported 'Class A i' (= Late Roman C) dishes found at Tintagel, Cornwall,[5] may have directly inspired such stones as an early-looking (broken) primary cross-slab in slate (Fig. 55), one of the very few found at Tintagel.[6]

The excavation (1964–5) of the enclosed developed cemetery on Ardwall Isle provided an interesting group of primary stones.[7] Associated with burials in phase 2 (that of the small timber oratory with its aligned graves) were some extremely simple little pieces, the designs executed in knife-cut grooves. One such, probably buried at the head end of a dug grave, is a small (9 inches by 16 inches) slab of rough stone with a linear cross—two knife-grooves at right-angles; another was found reused in the phase 3 altar; and there are two others (museum nos. C 1, C 18) with tiny linear crosses on large beach pebbles at Whithorn Museum,

[1] Henry 1963, pl. 46; Henry 1964, pl. 46.
[2] Berlin-Dahlem, Staatliche Museum (measures 14 by 19 cm.).
[3] Savory 1960, 61, fig. 7, no. 36, and pl. viii. b.
[4] Nash-Williams 1950, 76 n. 1.   [5] Radford 1956, pl. vi. b.
[6] Radford 1935a, pl. lix.
[7] Thomas 1967b (drawing by Mr. T. D. McArdle).

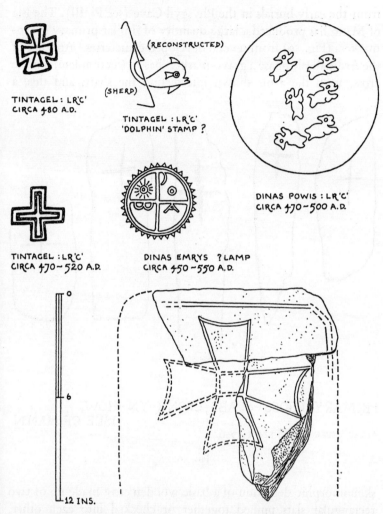

TINTAGEL: LR'C'
CIRCA 480 A.D.

(RECONSTRUCTED)

(SHERD)

TINTAGEL : LR'C'
'DOLPHIN' STAMP ?

DINAS POWIS : LR'C'
CIRCA 470-500 A.D.

TINTAGEL : LR'C'
CIRCA 470-520 A.D.

DINAS EMRYS ?LAMP
CIRCA 450-550 A.D.

0
6
12 INS.

TINTAGEL : FRAGMENTS OF SLATE HEADSTONE
RADFORD, ANT. J XV (1935) 414, PL LIX

FIG. 55. Art on imported Mediterranean pottery (class A) as a possible source
for motifs on 'primary' cross-slabs.

from the early burials in the Physgyll Cave (see Pl. III). The Isle of Mann has produced a large quantity of similar primary grave-markers (Fig. 56) from several developed cemeteries.[1] Another of the Ardwall Isle phase 2 grave-markers has an (incomplete) outline cross, with the arms shown intersecting the shaft; and this, a

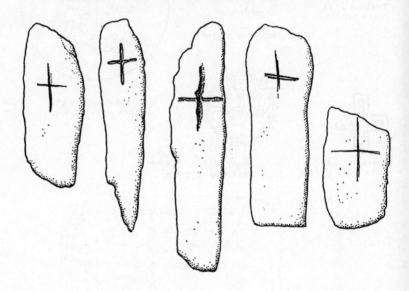

PRIMARY CROSS–SLABS, CRONK–YN–HOW,
                                    ISLE OF MANN
AFTER BRUCE AND CUBBON, 1930

FIG. 56.

skeuomorphic depiction of a basic wooden cross made up of two rectangular slats pinned together or checked into each other, occurs elsewhere in North Britain (Fig. 57). I have noted it, for instance, on a tiny grave-marker from Holm of Noss, Shetland, in Lerwick Museum (Pl. IV); and it is seen on a small boulder from Staplegorton, Dumfries.[2]

[1] Listed in Thomas 1967b, 159 n. 32.
[2] Staplegorton—Radford 1955a, 179, fig. 1; Holm of Noss, unpublished, Lerwick Museum (by courtesy of Mr. Tom Henderson).

Alongside the primary cross tradition we find a simple pictorial element, the origins of which could be as diverse as those of the isolated cross (Fig. 58). There is a small slab from Ardwall Isle with an extraordinary knife-point graffito scene showing a stylized human holding a crozier; it recalls the not dissimilar tiny figure

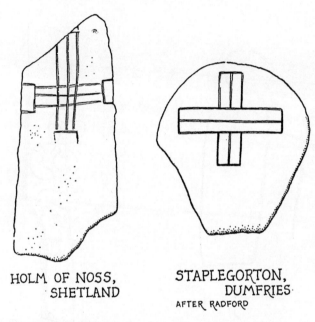

HOLM OF NOSS,
SHETLAND

STAPLEGORTON,
DUMFRIES
AFTER RADFORD

FIG. 57. Skeuomorphic depictions of wooden crosses on primary cross-slabs.

surmounting a ringed cross on a seventh-century slab at St. Gob-net's, co. Cork; and another on a slab from Burness Point, Orkney.[1] A most peculiar stone from Ardwall Isle, a long thin piece which narrows to a basal tang and thus must have been intended to stand upright in the ground, shows (in incised outline) a tiny human figure, three small ringed saltire crosses piled together in a triangle, and some form of quadruped (perhaps meant to be the *Agnus Dei* or Lamb of God, a symbol otherwise known in North Britain, though at a slightly later period). This stone raises a suggestion of

[1] RCAMS Orkney and Shetland 1946, i, no. 347; cf. also *CIIC* ii. 191, no. 1068 (Isle of Man).

peripheral Pictish influence, since humans, animals, and all forms of crosses are combined on the Class II (Christian) symbol-stones of Pictland.

Apart from the various forms of cross, a widespread Christian motif is the hexafoil or 'marigold pattern'. In itself, it is found in

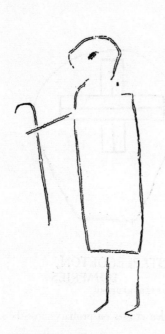 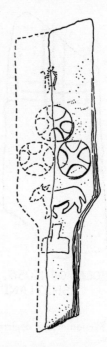

[ARDWALL NO. 11]
GRAFFITO FIGURE, ENLARGED

[ARDWALL NO. 17]
CONJECTURAL RESTORATION
OF LEFT HALF OF STONE

ARDWALL ISLE : PICTORIAL 'PRIMARY' STONES

FIG. 58.

secular Late Roman ornament but, in Christian use, it immediately recalls the six-armed linear cross which, as we saw in the Rhineland sequence, can quite easily arise from a simplification of the six-armed (Constantinian) chi-rho. Ringed or encircled hexafoils are not uncommon in the seventh century, and should be seen, as

Fr. Padraig Lionard has rightly pointed out,[1] as special manifestations of a wider class—crosses constructed from compass-drawn arcs. Again, there is a link with early insular manuscript illumination.[2]

A particularly interesting problem, relevant to the primary cross-marked stones and the few inscribed memorials of North Britain, is that of their connection (if any) with the much more regularly shaped series favoured by the early church in Northumbria, and found in the regions dominated by Northumbrian religious art and episcopal rule in the later seventh and eighth centuries. This problem has exercised many minds, including those of Baldwin Brown and W. G. Collingwood;[3] are the little 'name-stones' (once called 'pillow-stones') of Northumbria[4] quite independent of the Irish church, or not? What about the other development so closely associated with Northumbria, the rise of the free-standing cross, where the stone itself is shaped and sculptured to the cross outline?

In phase 3 at Ardwall Isle burials associated with the eighth-century stone chapel[5] would have been those of Christians who, whatever they spoke in life, would have been under the cure of an Anglian Northumbrian see at Whithorn, not many miles away. The cross-slabs belonging to these phase 3 graves are not only executed in a new technique—unlike those of phase 2, with its knife-grooved pieces, the execution is now all in broad 'pocked' or chisel-punched lines—but are shaped, are 'free-standing crosses' rather than just cross-decorated slabs, and must each have stood upright at one end of a grave (Fig. 59). The shape of these crosses shows what W. G. Collingwood labelled 'semi-circular arm-pits', and there are greatly expanded, almost T-ended, terminals. The latter feature is Northumbrian in feeling, observable (for instance) on two much bigger, and flattish, shaped crosses from Whitby, Yorks., which could be older than about 750.[6] The idea that 'pocked-line technique' is in broad terms later than 'incised-line

[1] Kendrick 1939, 18–19, pl. vi; Lionard 1961, 110.
[2] Henry 1965, pl. 58.   [3] Collingwood, W. G. 1927.
[4] Ibid. 12–13; 'name-stone' is now preferred.
[5] Thomas 1967b, 132, fig. 23.
[6] Peers and Radford 1943, figs. 6 and 7.

FIG. 59. Ardwall Isle, shaped stone cross (height, 16½ inches) drawn by Mr. T. D. McArdle.

technique', at any rate in south-west Scotland, is borne out by the series of stones from Whithorn; here, later stones with pocked designs combine the ring element from the older encircled chi-rho with the expanded-terminal 'arm-pit' cross shape of Northumbria.[1]

My belief, that the phase 3 Ardwall stones are not only free-standing crosses of the eighth century (albeit on a small scale) but must also, like the larger Whitby ones, be some of the earliest examples of this innovation, is likely to provoke controversy. The origin of the free-standing shaped cross, whether in function it be funerary, or dedicatory, or merely commemorative, is still a major puzzle. How and when did the cross escape from its rôle as a two-dimensional outline depiction on a flat surface, and become a three-dimensional object with a height of 10, 12, or 14 feet, an open-work ring head, and relief ornament on all possible surfaces? Collingwood argued[2] that the 'staff rood', a sort of large early Christian totem-pole (in wood) with a little shaped cross as its summit—a type whose former existence can be safely inferred from stone counterparts with abundant

[1] Collingwood, W. G. 1927.   [2] Ibid. 5–9.

skeuomorphic traces of the timber original—was modified to become a free-standing shaped cross; and that this most probably occurred during the eighth century, at Hexham, in the hands of a school of stone-carvers of great skill and inventiveness.

This ingenious thesis somewhat overlooks the fact that free-standing wooden crosses may have been current, widely, before the eighth century. These are mentioned in lives of Eastern saints;[1] Adomnán refers to what must presumably have been such on Iona in the seventh, if not the late sixth, century;[2] a cleric is depicted carrying one, with arc-struts making up a ring head, on a late seventh-century Irish cross-base;[3] and Oswald, so Bede tells us, erected a wooden cross of some size at Heavenfield in 633 or so.[4] The late Sean P. Ó Ríordáin argued that such crosses, having either small straight struts in the four angles of the arms, or four arc-struts together forming a ring head, were translated directly from wood into stone in eighth-century Ireland. He further adduced,[5] from normal stone cross-slabs in outline or relief, what he claimed were skeuomorphic depictions of just such carpentry prototypes, nail-heads and all.

I would only add here that I think Ó Ríordáin's date could be a century earlier, that the free-standing cross *did* originate in timber and was directly copied in stone, and that in view of the fact that there are several types of large free-standing stone crosses we must assume an equal variety of wooden prototypes (and more than one place where this transition could have been effected). I think it possible that very small shaped wooden crosses may have been placed on, in, or at graves from the early seventh century, that small primary stones like those from Ardwall Isle and Holm of Noss depict these, and that the little Ardwall Isle phase 3 free-standing crosses of Anglian appearance may be copies in stone of lost wooden fore-runners, specifically adapted to a Northumbrian shape.

[1] St. Theodore of Sykeon (*circa* 600)—*Life*, caps. 45 and 52 (ed. Dawes and Baynes 1948, 121, 126). See also Adomnán's *De Locis Sanctis* (ed. Meehan 1958, 86–7), ii. 16.

[2] Adomnán, *Vita Columbae* i. 45, iii. 23 (Anderson and Anderson 1961, 307, 523).

[3] Henry 1940, 105, fig. 39 (Ahenny, North Cross).

[4] *H.E.* iii. 2. [5] Ó Ríordáin 1947b.

We will now revert to primary cross-marked stones, the earliest uninscribed Christian memorials, as a generalized class, in order to examine three further problems; distribution, exact function, and

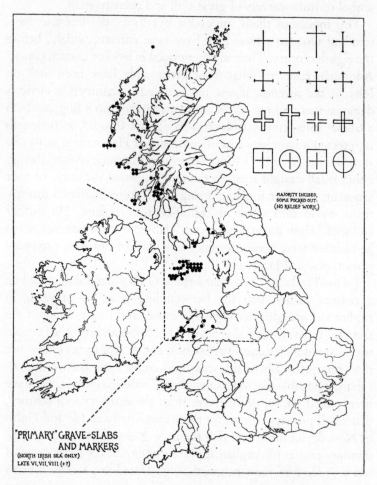

FIG. 60. Distribution of primary cross-marked stones, North Britain and North Wales.

degree of continuity from pre-Christian times. Though primary stones, as I shall for brevity's sake describe them, are widely distributed, they are by no means uniformly distributed (Fig. 60). Their range in North Britain is, I believe, a rough index of missionary activities associable with the northwards spread of Irish-based monasticism, mainly in the seventh and eight centuries. This is a spread which takes us, by the eighth century, to the Northern Isles; and even, by the ninth or tenth, to the Faeroes, where such stones occur at Skúvøy and Kirkjubøur.[1] Nor is the map really vitiated by the fact that primary cross-slabs or little cross-marked pillars may have been continuously made, and used, in places like the Outer Isles right up to the medieval period.

Primary stones *are* found in the southern half of Wales, as they are occasionally in southern and south-west Ireland (for instance, at Church Island, co. Kerry);[2] though in Ireland they appear to have a northern emphasis. In Cornwall, curiously, there seem to be very few examples from sites of this period.[3] One wonders whether there was not an unintentional geographical distinction, between the use of Christian ogam epitaphs in the south of Ireland and in those mainland Irish colonies derived mostly from the south and east of Ireland, on the one hand; and the use of primary stones in the north and west of Ireland and the northern (Manx and Scottish) Irish colonies on the other. Apart from rare and scattered instances, and the very much later 'Pictish' ogams of the far north, ogam-inscribed stones are hardly found at all in the north.

I have deliberately avoided any categorical statements about *where*, in relation to a grave, any primary cross-slab (or for that matter any inscribed tombstone) originally stood. It might be thought that, as in our own day, all such stones stood at the head or west end, with the inscribed or figured face facing eastward. The evidence on this point in the early Christian period is distinctly weak. Smaller stones, wedged into the ground at the time of burial, cannot have stood upright for long, and almost all recorded stones, if not first noticed in museums or on church window-sills, have been found in disturbed positions. The few undisturbed settings that we can indicate sometimes show us *two* stones, at head and feet, only one stone being figured. This was

[1] Kermode 1930. [2] Ó'Kelly 1958, fig. 8 and pl. xiv. a.
[3] Thomas 1966b.

the case at 'Eithne's Grave' on Eileach an Naoimh, and in the circular enclosure at Derrygarrane South (Fig. 27). Edouard Salin drew attention to another pair, from a sixth- or seventh-century grave at Kaiser-Augst,[1] at the head and feet of the grave; the head-stone, which is substantially the larger, has an outline cross of primary character on its east face.

The most important, documented, North British instance is that of the grave of Acca, bishop of Hexham, who died at Hexham in 740.[2] Symeon of Durham's twelfth-century account[3]—and I see no reason to disbelieve him—is that there were *two* stone crosses, decorated with wonderful carving, one at the head and one at the foot of the grave; and that the cross at the head end was inscribed with a statement saying that Acca was buried there. This epitaph may have been something like one from a Whitby cross,[4] broken, but restorable so that it would have read HIC REQUIESCIT IN HOC SEPULCHRO . . . 'Here lies at rest in this grave'.

The idea of some very tenuous link going back from the free-standing cross, through cross-marked or ogam-inscribed pillars, to the plain stone pillars ('menhirs' or longstones) of British prehistory cannot be entirely dismissed. Cremations in short cists at the feet of large granite menhirs (the cists lie on the east, north, west, or south sides impartially) are common in Bronze Age Cornwall,[5] and this rite is also known from Wales, Ireland, and Brittany. There are cases in both Cornwall and Brittany where finds of wheel-made pottery and coins at the bases of menhirs point to ritual (perhaps cenotaphic) depositions as late as the Roman period. The upright stone, as a subsidiary aspect of the prehistoric 'sacred circle' complex, is no less likely to have im-pressed its importance on the popular mind than the circle itself.

It can be questioned, however, whether any such pagan aspect could lie behind the introduction of an entirely different form of gravestone, one we have not yet mentioned, the recumbent slab. Just as today most of our graveyard memorials assume one or

---

[1] Salin 1950–9, ii. 37, 81.   [2] Collingwood, W. G. 1927, 29–30.
[3] *Sub anno* 740 (*Rolls Series*, vol. 75, ii. 33).
[4] Peers and Radford 1943, 44–5, fig. 6.   [5] Russell and Pool 1964.

other of two forms—the upright stone, or the full-length slab lying prone over the grave itself—so too in western Britain the recumbent cross-slab[1] eventually appeared as an alternative to vertical memorials. Fr. Lionard's study of these monuments, in Ireland and in areas of Irish settlement, is of special interest in showing that hardly any categories of recumbent slab were in use before the eighth century. The earliest of those few which can be approximately dated, with reference to the chronicled obits of the persons supposedly named in the inscriptions, would belong to the periods 709–12, 783–6, and 787–91. A small slab (2 feet by 3 feet) from Tullylease, co. Cork,[2] which names the Saxon priest *Berechtuire* (Berichter or Berchert), employs a design which, from its close similarity to ornament in the very late seventh-century Lindisfarne Gospels, was presumably copied straight out of some Hiberno-Northumbrian manuscript. Even if this slab was executed in the early eighth century, it is in many ways an isolated object.

Lionard shows how the recumbent slab designs exhibit much the same development as do the designs—mostly crosses—on primary cross-marked stones, and on some later tombstones with minuscule lettering and very evolved ornament. The recumbent slabs also increase in size, from small irregular flags to regular body-length rectangles. By the later eighth century the art of the recumbent slabs, an art which had at first drawn upon the simpler vocabulary of the primary stone group, began to develop its own style. The equal-armed cross with square centre and enlarged square terminals, the cross potent, and various crosses with hollowed angles, all betray the substantial artistic intercourse between a number of major Irish monastic houses, and those of Northumbria, if not beyond. The recumbent slabs become a lithic reflection of that give-and-take in differing media, whose highest expression can be seen in the series of great insular manuscripts. This is most clearly visible in the very large group of late Irish slabs bearing 'expansional crosses', crosses whose arm-terminals are circular or semi-circular expansions, surrounded by (or enclosed within) developed ornament of spirals, plaitwork, and step-patterns.

The suggestion that the recumbent slab might have been inspired

---

[1] Lionard 1961.   [2] Ibid. 154–5, pl. xxxi. 1.

by the visible lid of an otherwise buried sarcophagus (in, say, Merovingian Gaul) lacks force. The development of the decorated sarcophagus lid, and (as we shall see) of the lids of composite or solid stone shrines, involves a long median ridge and bilateral ornament, intended to be viewed from one or both long sides. Recumbent slabs bear unified ornamental schemes and are meant to be viewed from the head, or more probably the feet, end. I believe that, as Lionard's survey strongly implies, the recumbent slab is just an extended development of the recumbent grave-marker, whether a primary west British grave-marker or a Northumbrian name-stone. The larger, finer, surfaces of so many recumbent slabs, which could have been placed on trestles or a bench for the mason to work upon, would inevitably lead in a period of great artistic experiment in all conceivable media to the final static perfection of the tenth- and eleventh-century slabs at Clonmacnois.[1]

As I do not intend, if possible, to progress beyond 800, we shall not be considering the numerous schools of 'high crosses'—in Pictland, in the west of Scotland, in Northumbria, in north-west England, in Man, in Ireland, in Wales, and in Cornwall. These take us up to the twelfth and thirteenth centuries, and though a few of them do appear to be funerary monuments, the great majority were clearly erected as dedicatory and commemorative monuments; this also places them firmly outwith the scope of the present chapter. Perhaps I may conclude by drawing attention to a small but unusual class of early cross-slabs, the so-called 'face-cross' group, since the joint lesson of cultural transmission and iconographic devolution that can be drawn from studying these slabs is well worth bearing in mind, if only as a corrective to loose thoughts about the development of Christian monuments in general (Fig. 61).

These cross-slabs are known as 'face crosses' because the upper-most arm of the cross consists, not of a vertical bar, but stylized front-view head representing either God or Christ. The proto-types are certainly from the East Mediterranean. In the art of the Coptic Church in Egypt, there is a special form of the cross motif,

[1] Macalister 1909.

in which the lateral arms and the long lower arm are terminally flared or expanded, and the uppermost arm is depicted as an annulus or double circle; this is called the 'crux ansata', from its resemblance to the hieroglyphic Egyptian sign *ānkh*, 'life'.

Crosses headed with this circular element are seen on Coptic grave-slabs, some of the better known being the sixth-century

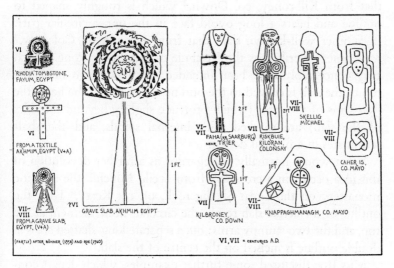

FIG. 61. Examples of the 'face cross' group.

tombstone of *Rhodia*, from the Fayyum, now in Berlin[1] (the circle contains five pellets, and the outline letters *alpha* and *omega* are pendent from the side arms), and a rather simpler funerary stele from Akhmim, in which the circle is a multiple laureate ring surrounding a youthful face with a scalloped nimbus.[2] In discussing some later Irish versions of this cross form, Miss Helen Roe[3] has illustrated a detail from a Coptic textile (also from Akhmim; Victoria and Albert Museum, regarded as sixth-century) showing a long-shafted cross surmounted by a studded annulus containing a face (of Christ?). The close resemblance between these long-shafted crosses headed by encircled faces, and straight-forward

---

[1] Beckwith 1963, 54, fig. 114; Wessel 1965, 10, pl. 4.
[2] Böhner 1958, i. 247, abb. 16.   [3] Roe 1960, 201, fig. 6b.

K

depictions of Our Lord crucified, is clear when one looks at objects like the small gold plaque, again from Akhmim and of this period, figured by Nash-Williams (after C. F. Kaufmann).[1]

That the idea of the 'face-cross' was known in western Europe, including the British Isles, by the seventh century now seems clear if we turn to some British and Irish slabs. The most striking is that from Kilbroney, co. Down,[2] which is roughly shaped to outline and bears a long ovoid face in the upper circular part. In another well-known slab, that from Kiloran, on Colonsay,[3] sometimes described as the Riskbuie or Reaskbuie stone (which may conceivably have been intended as a recumbent one), the top of the slab is curved to the outline of the top of the head, the side-arms of the cross (which protrude slightly beyond the sides of the slab) are marked with internal spirals, and the shaft terminates in a fish-tail design.

What would normally be regarded as a further devolution of this idea occurs in a cross-slab from Sceilg Mhichíl, the eremitic monastery on the Great Skellig rock, off co. Kerry.[4] Here the outline of the actual slab recalls the circular 'head' element at the top, and the two stumpy arms; but a separate long-shafted cross in double outline is incised on the centre of the slab.

Miss Roe discussed some further examples, which depart considerably from the suggested prototype and involve another motif altogether, the 'breast-plate' form, that cannot now concern us. Recently Richard Bailey has noted[5] (from Brigham, Cumberland) a final echo of the 'face-cross' tradition in the tenth century. We are concerned, however, with the manner in which a Coptic (or as Miss Roe would have it, equally, Syro-Palestinian) cross-form, combining a *crux ansata*, an encircled face upper element, and a stylized Crucifixion, could appear in the far north-west at a date which may well be in the seventh or early eighth century.

Her suggestion that it may have been copied from such objects

---

[1] Nash-Williams 1950, 191, fig. 211.
[2] Roe 1960, 193, fig. 1a; ASNI Down 1966, 303 (cross no. 2, there regarded—to my mind, most improbably—as being 'post-medieval').
[3] *ECMS* III. 396, fig. 413; Roe 1960, 193, fig. 1d.
[4] Roe 1960, 193, fig. 1b.
[5] Bailey 1963.

as the Palestinian pilgrim-flask which she figures,[1] examples of
which are known from Bobbio, in Italy, a monastic foundation of
circa 613 associated with St. Columbanus and with Irish brethren
who were unquestionably in touch with their homeland, is a
compelling one, though I think that the transmission by way of
imported Mediterranean textiles (also suggested by Miss Roe) is
even better. We cannot exclude the high probability that, by the
late seventh century, oriental textiles had appeared in many of the
major houses of the church in Northumbria; something like these,
together with contemporary ivories, inspired (I believe) many of
the so-called 'narrative scenes' or 'hunting scenes' on Class II
Pictish stones. We should therefore expect that certain other areas
of western Europe, in which the church, or local courts, are
otherwise known to have been in receipt of Mediterranean
imports, might reveal, in local tombstone series, similar localized
versions inspired by the 'face-cross' concept. This is now indeed
the case. Kurt Böhner has published[2] a large slab, nearly 7 feet
long, from a burial-ground at Faha, in the Trier area. On this,
the elongated cross has an upper pear-shaped head which has in its
centre a simplified oval face, and the very bottom of the shaft has
a forked termination symbolizing separate short legs or feet. This
could, on the strength of the finds from Faha, perhaps be of
seventh-century date.

There remains, none the less, the alternative explanation; that
the British and Irish 'face-crosses' represent no more than independent, clumsy, attempts to combine the idea of the Cross *per se*
with the depiction of the crucified Christ. We cannot be sure. This
is admittedly less likely than the idea that they were inspired by
Mediterranean models, in view of the facts (*a*) that contact with
the Mediterranean at this period is independently inferred, and
(*b*) that there exists at least one similar derivative in Germany.
We must always take care lest, in pressing such exotic and attractive resemblances between objects from widely separated parts
of the Old World, we forget that nearly all these arguments are
not based on certainties—only upon inferences.

---

[1] Roe 1960, 200, fig. 5.   [2] Böhner 1958, i. 246–8; ii, taf. 71.

5. The Cult of Relics

ONE OF THE GREAT HEROES of early Northumbria was the Bernician prince, Oswald. As a young man in political exile he had been converted to Christianity by the Irish, probably on Iona.[1] Regarded as, at any rate, the secular founder of the monastic church in Northumbria, he was an intimate of the saintly Bishop Aidan, spoke Irish in addition to English, and was reputed to be generous to the poor, of noble disposition, and formidable in battle. He was killed in 642 at the battle of *Maserfelth*; the pagan victor cut off Oswald's head and arms and fixed them on upright stakes.[2]

Bede's *History* is our primary source for Oswald's life, and the subsequent events connected with Oswald. The latter may be concisely summarized. The exact place of his death became a sacred spot. A girl who had some form of paralysis was cured at the moment she was taken to this spot, even though she was asleep.[3] Earth taken from the ground here, when mixed with water, cured some sick people who swallowed the mixture;[4] and when some of the same earth, wrapped in a little bag, was hung up on a house-beam, that beam was preserved intact when the house itself was burnt down.[5] Oswald's decapitated head was taken to Lindisfarne;[6] and his right hand and arm to Bamburgh, to be encased in silver;[7] his remaining bones were taken eventually to Bardney, in Lincolnshire. At Bardney they were reverently washed, the water used to wash them was by chance poured away in a certain corner of the cemetery there, and earth taken from this corner (again mixed up in water, we assume) was used to cure

[1] Contrary to popular belief, and some scholarly writings (cf. Duke 1932, 82; Knight 1933, ii. 111), Iona is *not* expressly mentioned by Bede; *H.E.* iii. 1, iii. 3.
[2] *H.E.* iii. 9.　　　　[3] Ibid.　　　　[4] Ibid.　　　　[5] *H.E.* iii. 10.
[6] *H.E.* iii. 12.　　　　[7] *H.E.* iii. 7.

those possessed of devils—probably a reference to epileptics.[1] Some of the water had, however, been spilled on a pavement at Bardney; when the pavement was swept, some of the dust was collected, tied up in a cloth, and put in a little box. Quite by chance this box was taken into a house in which there was an epileptic sufferer, who as a result was cured.[2] The stake on which Oswald's head had been originally set up became venerated as a holy object; years later, St. Willibrord, who possessed a chip of wood off this stake, cured an Irish friend of plague by making him drink some water in which this chip had floated.[3] A wooden cross, which Oswald had set up with his own hands at Heavenfield, on the Wall, in 633 to commemorate his victory,[4] was also regarded as sacred; the drinking of water in which splinters from this cross had been soaked cured both men and beasts, and a monk of Hexham, called Bothelm, healed his arm (which he apparently fractured while walking on ice) by laying upon it some moss taken from this cross.[5]

I have selected these cases, some of which involve no less than five steps from the original (e.g. Oswald—Oswald's posthumous bones—water in which bones are washed—pavement on which water spills—dust swept from pavement put in box—box taken into house cures epileptic) mainly from one writer's account of one person. They could be repeated in essence, in the British Isles alone, from Bede's work and from other sources in connection with Aidan, Alban, Brigid, Chad, Columcille, Cuthbert, Germanus, and dozens of minor figures. A host of similar examples could be garnered from early European and Mediterranean hagiography. What unifying belief lies behind this catalogue of wonders?

We can best illuminate this question by considering two short passages. In the Gospel according to St. Luke, chapter 9, at verse 44, we have the miracle of the woman with an issue of blood, who

. . . came behind him and touched the border of his garment, and immediately her issue of blood staunched. And Jesus said, 'Who

---

[1] *H.E.* iii. 11.   [2] Ibid.   [3] *H.E.* iii. 13.
[4] *H.E.* iii. 3.   [5] Ibid.

touched me?' When all denied, Peter and they that were with him said, 'Master, the multitude throng thee and press thee, and sayest thou, Who touched me?' And Jesus said, '*Somebody* hath touched me; for I perceive that virtue has gone out of me' (*nam ego novi virtutem de me exiisse*).

The second passage I take from a study by Mircea Eliade.[1]

When a sorceress burns a wax doll containing a lock of her victim's hair she does not have in mind the entire theory underlying that bit of magic—but this fact does not affect our understanding of sympathetic magic. What *does* matter to our understanding is to know that such an action could only have happened after people had satisfied themselves by experiment, or established theoretically, that nails, hair, or anything a person has worn preserve an intimate relation with their owner even when separated from him. This belief is based on the notion of a 'space connection' between the most distant things whereby they are linked by means of a kind of sympathy governed by its own specific laws . . .

Now the compilers of early Lives of saints, and this certainly holds good for the British Isles, attribute a variety of powers to holy persons. One, with which we are not here concerned, is sheer *potestas* of a magical kind—the power to quell rough seas, to make winds cease, to subdue raging beasts, and (this is particularly common)[2] to halt or to deflect fire, even from a distance. Another, usually pictured as having been manifested through direct personal contact, is the power of healing, and whatever the medical or psychological rationale of this may be, it is quite clear that a few people like St. Cuthbert, and St. John of Beverley, did possess this gift, just as some people do today. The third capacity is something which is normally revealed only after the subject's death, or is regarded as having existed independently of the person from whom it was derived. This we may call (following the Gospel story) 'virtue'. It is an arcane power, a kind of spiritual radioactivity, which resides in both exanimate and inanimate things and is transferred by contact. It can be used for many ends —for the control of natural events, for the deflection of evil, even

---

[1] Eliade 1958, 9–10.   [2] *H.E.* i. 19, ii. 7, iii. 16.

for the just punishment of the profane, but its main employment is for the cure of the sick, and in this respect it might be argued to be an enlargement of the power of healing.

The concept of 'virtue', in this sense, is what forms the link between St. Luke's miracle-story and Eliade's definition of sympathetic magic. The cult of relics we can define as being all those material reflections which flow from a firm belief in the existence and power of virtue. These include the acquisition and the manufacture of relics, which are objects in which virtue resides; their display, their external adornment, the associated symbolism and mythology, and the worldly consequences of possessing them. It offers material for a fascinating analysis because, as I explained in the first chapter, we can in Britain and Ireland now claim to have a good measure of both the literary and the archaeological evidence of this cult, and these two categories of evidence, as we shall find, constantly explain and expound each other.

In the brief account of the relics of St. Oswald and their properties, we can at once see that they fall into two groups. There are *corporeal* or physical relics, such as his head and his bones; and *incorporeal* or representative ones, things which had at any time touched any part of him, like the cross which he had personally erected or the stake on which his head was fixed.

Incorporeal relics can, naturally, arise from fortuitous association. We cannot suppose that any Northumbrian intended that Oswald should be conquered, slain, and decapitated; it was a tragic and accidental event. A good example of this occurs in the shape of a bound manuscript gospel book of the mid-eighth century, the so-called Ragyndrudis Codex preserved at the Landesbibliothek, Fulda.[1] The cover bears some deep sword-cuts which also mark the contents, and the book can, convincingly, be regarded as the very object which St. Boniface held above his head on 9 June 754 when he and his companions were martyred by pagan Frisians at the mound of Dokkum. As the *Vita Secunda* tells us[2] 'When he was about to be struck by a sword, he put the Book of the Holy Gospels on his head, that under it he might be saved

---

[1] Halbertsma 1961, 438 and afb. 31; for description, Sherer 1905.
[2] Halbertsma 1961, 33 (in Latin); Levison's edn. (Levison 1905), 73.

from the force of the blow, and might thus have the protection in death of that which he had delighted to read in life.'

Most incorporeal relics were however manufactured; we have seen how splinters, chips, and moss were removed from wooden relics associated with Oswald. A widespread custom was to allow small objects, usually little strips of cloth or silk, called *brandea*, to touch the bones of a saint, or even of an Apostle. If obtained from Rome, as many of the outstanding specimens were, the *brandea* or their containers should bear a wax papal seal. Thus in the early Life of (Pope) Gregory the Great, written soon after 700 by an unnamed monk at Whitby,[1] there is a story of some men, possibly from the church in Gaul, who were sent to Rome to obtain relics and were given sealed boxes by Gregory to take back with them. On the return journey the men opened the boxes to peep inside, and finding only some grubby bits of cloth (*viles . . . pannorum sectiones*) they went back to Rome to ask for something better. The point of this tale is that they had been given incorporeal relics—perhaps strips of something alleged to be an Apostolic garment, perhaps *brandea*—because the dismemberment of the corporeal remains would then (late sixth? early seventh? century) have been regarded as sacrilegious. The relics, mostly of the Apostles Peter and Paul, taken to Britain by Germanus in the fifth century[2] and by Mellitus in 601,[3] sent to Northumbria by Vitalian in 655,[4] and imported on a large scale by Benedict Biscop, Wilfrid, and Acca, would almost certainly have been incorporeal relics of this kind. In most of these instances, the purpose of obtaining the relics was the sanctification and consecration of newly built churches in outlying provinces of the Christian West, and in the next chapter we shall see how this was carried out. As with Willibrord's mission in Frisia in 692, each church was supposed to be dedicated to God in honour of the appropriate saint.[5]

As actual *brandea* hardly ever survive it is worth noticing a medieval instance from Switzerland.[6] This involves an 18-inch high 'bust reliquary', carved wood covered with silver sheet,

---

[1] Ed. Colgrave 1968 (ibid. 108–11, 153).   [2] *H.E.* i. 18.
[3] *H.E.* i. 29.   [4] *H.E.* iii. 29.   [5] Cf. *H.E.* i. 30, v. 11, v. 20.
[6] Zschokke 1963.

which comes from Bourg St. Pierre and possibly refers to a saint called Candidus; it seems to be workmanship of the mid-twelfth century. Investigation at the University of Basle revealed, through X-rays, a rectangular cavity within the apparently solid head, and some small holes were found on the underside, the flat base of the neck. Using a medical cystoscope and special forceps, three small bundles of cloth were identified within this cavity, and one of these was extracted. It proved to be a piece of silk, with traces of a mauve wax (probably a papal seal), wrapped in muslin, and then contained in a finger-length canvas bag.

The principal corporeal relic is, naturally, the whole body, preferably incorrupt with the bones still in place and the outer integument somehow preserved, and failing that, the disarticulated but nevertheless complete skeleton. In the Church of western Britain and Ireland between the sixth and eighth centuries, possession of the founder's body was desirable—one might almost add, essential. The presence of a notable saint and famous monastic founder would attract a constant stream of pilgrims, endless prayers, and gifts of land and money, to say nothing of prestige, or status as the mother-house of a monastic *paruchia*. When St. Cuthbert was dying on the Great Farne, he explained to the brethren[1] that he wished to be buried there, not at Lindisfarne, because (as he told them) 'the presence of my remains will prove very irksome', and he explained that, apart from the normal rush of pilgrims, they could expect 'the influx of fugitives and every other kind of malefactor. They will flee for refuge to my body'. The brothers persuaded him, however, to allow the transfer to Lindisfarne, and at this period of time they could hardly have done otherwise.

In less fully documented cases, and I think in almost all those cases where obscure and purely local saints are involved, certain place-name elements which we have already mentioned (like *andóit* and *merther*)[2] may serve to identify those particular churches and developed cemeteries which possessed, or claimed to possess, the body of the relevant saint and founder. This is, by its nature, a problem which is not really susceptible to archaeological

---

[1] *H.E.* iv. 29; Bede, *Prose Life of Cuthbert* (ed. Colgrave 1940), cap. 37.
[2] See p. 89.

solution. It is also one which is exacerbated by the fact that we cannot assume that such bodies are necessarily still in their original graves.

From the fifth century onwards in the British Isles, we have evidence that the body was prepared for veneration as an accessible corporeal relic—the preparation involves an action which, in Latin, is called *translatio* or *commutatio*. At a period after death which could be anything from a few days to a century, but was not infrequently of the order of five to ten years, the original grave was opened and the remains of the body uplifted. If the body was 'incorrupt', which implies that it was found in a desiccated or partly mummified condition, as with St. Cuthbert, it would then need a full-length container to house it. Generally we must suppose that the skeleton became disarticulated in removal and was reduced to the skull and a mere jumble of bones, requiring a rather smaller container. The corporeal remains were first washed, and were then enclosed in some form of box, or structure, which was not reinterred below ground, but was designedly visible, and may then have been placed above the original, filled-in, grave. These remains were enclosed in such a way that, either by removing a lid, or by gaining access through some aperture in the end of the side of the container, the bones could be seen and venerated. They could also be touched with the bare hand, or with some such object as a *brandea* which, through this direct contact, would itself now acquire virtue and become a relic of the incorporeal or representative kind.

In the Mediterranean, where the cult of relics began with the Christian martyrs of the pre-Constantinian age, years of careful and intensive research (with which we associate the names of R. Egger, Ejnar Dyggve, André Grabar, and Richard Krautheimer[1]) have established beyond doubt that this cult is central to the development of most early church architecture. Crudely expressed, the sequence runs, Early Christian cemetery—special tombs of martyrs in a cemetery, with access to relics—little yards of buildings enclosing such special tombs—full basilican churches

---

[1] Egger—see Dyggve 1951, xii (bibliog.); Dyggve 1951; Grabar 1946; Krautheimer 1965—all with refs. to earlier works.

encapsulating such little yards or buildings. Though the *locus classicus* for the demonstration of this sequence remains Salona or Salonae, on the Adriatic coast of Yugoslavia (the modern *Solin*, north of Split), we can point to some early instances in the west.

There is, firstly, a suggestive passage in Sulpicius Severus' life of St. Martin of Tours,[1] which mentions (this should be about 380 or so) a cemetery near Tours with the grave of a supposed martyr, over which a previous bishop had erected an altar. From Bonn[2] we have two such specially marked tombs dating from about 260, and enclosed in a little rectangular yard (roughly 9 by 11 feet); around 400 this became incorporated in a chapel. From Xanten there is an elaborate succession of structures,[3] where a double burial of 360s was enclosed in a small wooden surround about 390 (this was burnt down, and replaced after 400) which in Frankish times attracted a surrounding cemetery. About 450 or so, the focus was enclosed in a larger stone-built chapel, and by the eighth century, in the first of a series of full churches.

The initial, and most important, structural elaboration of the martyrial relic-tomb, one found widely in the Mediterranean by the fourth and fifth centuries, is the little unroofed or partly roofed rectangular yard or surround;[4] its erection denotes not only privacy, but the actual possession of the tomb by devotees or relatives, and it provides a place for funerary feasts and commemorative gatherings (Fig. 62). Analogous surrounds do, of course, occur in connection with wealthy graves in pagan Roman cemeteries. There is a curious later-day Scottish counterpart in the form of the unroofed 'lairs' or walled private burial-plots, some with formal classical frontages, to be seen in the older Edinburgh cemeteries (Calton Hill and Greyfriars). In a rather grotesque way the substantial Scottish 'death-houses', above-ground vaults erected to defeat the activities of Burke and Hare or earlier resurrectionists,[5] are the partial counterparts of the next stage, the martyrial chapels within cemeteries. In the Warriston cemetery

---

[1] Cap. 11 (ed. Hoare 1954, 256).   [2] Radford 1968, 33–4, with refs.
[3] Ibid. 32–3, with refs.   [4] Dyggve 1951, chap. iv and figs. therein.
[5] This is one tradition; the structures are really part of a much wider fashion in funerary architecture.

in Edinburgh there is even a Gothic tomb-chapel of 1858, with red-glass roof and with pre-Raphaelite marble effigies over the internal tombs.

The surround of the martyrial tomb was called the *cella memoriae*, the cell or enclosure of the *memoria* (the accessible tomb with its corporeal relic). Some of the best examples are those at

FIG. 62. *Cella memoria*, Kaplijuč (Yugoslavia), fifth century A.D. (after Dyggve).

Salonae, where Dyggve's exposition of these vast martyrial cemeteries remains a landmark in Christian archaeology.[1] Where the British Isles are concerned, I think we can now detect evidence that the visible aspect of the Mediterranean, and western European, cult of relics was introduced at two slightly different stages in the general sequence we have discussed.

The first is that of the *cella memoriae* itself, the accessible burial in an open-air surround. The second stage corresponds to that point or those points in the continental development where the martyrial tomb is found to be *inside* a church—either because the

[1] Cf. Dyggve 1951, esp. figs. iv. 10, iv. 11, iv. 12.

church itself came first, and the burial and subsequent *translatio* of a saint (one or both events) took place within an existing structure; or because a church had (as at Xanten, Cologne,[1] and elsewhere) been built over an earlier open-air grave or had incorporated some still older chapel which had been so placed. In the special context of North Britain, our later discussion will centre around the interesting forms assumed in both timber and stone by the actual containers of relics—reliquary-coffins and shrines —some of which have no immediate parallels outside the British Isles.

It is perfectly possible that there may have been a *cella memoriae* of St. Alban in the fourth century, over which the original predecessor of St. Albans Abbey was erected;[2] and Gildas, in the sixth century, may be alluding to open-air martyrial shrines as well as to those in churches.[3] I believe the oldest surviving examples to be those in south-west Ireland. They are connected with a little-known group of special burials which I call 'slab-shrines' (Fig. 63). In these, the exhumed skeletons appear to have been bundled into quite a small space—certainly not body-length, but only some 3 feet 6 inches, or 4 feet, long—just long enough to accommodate all the bones. These spaces are rectangular cavities, dug in the ground, and roofed with slabs. The complete monuments resemble little ridge-tents in stone, with the two long-side slabs forming a sharp ridge, and with two triangular-shaped end-pieces as gables.

One of these, at Killabuonia, co. Kerry,[4] has an end-piece with a hole 6 inches across through it, and a small cross of primary type incised on the end-piece just above this hole. In two others, at Killoluaig and at Kilpeacan, both of which have now collapsed, similarly perforated slabs occur.[5] Bones and a skull are visible inside the Killoluaig slab-shrine.

These features, which are of course easily destroyed and easily overlooked in field-work, occur sparsely in Ireland. Two very large and fine examples, in one of which I myself observed a

---

[1] Cologne—Radford 1968, 34–5, with plan. [2] Morris 1968a.
[3] *De Excidio*, cap. 10. [4] Henry 1957, 101, fig. 18, pl. xxxix. b.
[5] Ibid. 98, fig. 17, pl. xxxix. a; and 82, fig. 11.

moss-covered skull and some long-bones in December of 1966, stand beside a small and early church, Teampull Chronain, sited in the limestone hills of co. Clare (pl. vii).[1] The only instance so far encountered outside Ireland, and it is by no means a certain one, is the little rock-cut hollow of phase 1 at Ardwall Isle, overlain

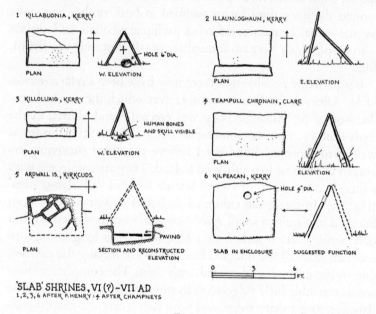

'SLAB' SHRINES, VI (?)–VII AD
1,2,3,6 AFTER F. HENRY : 4 AFTER CHAMPNEYS

FIG. 63.

by the phase 2 timber oratory.[2] It is the right size and form for the below-ground part of a slab-shrine and it is hard to think of a better explanation for it at the moment.

Five of these slab-shrines in co. Kerry, all of which occur in enclosed and partly or wholly developed cemeteries, are either contained within or directly associated with small rectangular enclosures.[3] These enclosures (Fig. 64; pl. vi) are defined by low walls or by fences of vertically set stone slabs. The few slab-shrines

[1] Fergusson 1886.   [2] Thomas 1967b.
[3] Henry 1957 (Caherbarnagh, Illaunloughan, Killabuonia, Killoluaig, and Kilpeacan).

known elsewhere (Fig. 68) in Ireland, in the north and east, do
not exhibit these surrounds, and the use of the slab-shrine alone
may perhaps have been borrowed from the south-west area. Just
as the perforated slabs of the actual shrines, which allow access to
the corporeal remains inside, are the equivalent of the much more

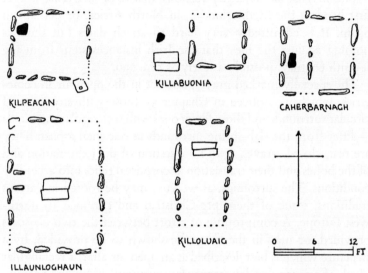

RECTILINEAR GRAVE ENCLOSURES, CO. KERRY
AFTER F. HENRY.

FIG. 64.

elaborate access-apertures found in Mediterranean martyrial
graves,[1] known (in the singular) as *fenestella, fenestella confessionis,*
or *confessio,* so I would suppose that the Irish rectangular grave-
surrounds are directly imitated from the *cella memoriae.* This is
relevant to a point discussed earlier,[2] the uncertain manner by
which the Old Irish *cell,* later *cill,* may have successively been used
to name, firstly an enclosed cemetery with one or more special
graves in it, and secondly a developed cemetery with its church.
Bearing in mind that south-west Ireland and the southern Irish
littoral, a long stretch about whose earliest Christian archaeology

[1] Dyggve 1951, chap. v and figs. therein.   [2] See p. 88.

we still know comparatively little,[1] reveals other traces of external contacts—imported pottery,[2] the use of the term ANM in Christian ogam epitaphs,[3] and instances of the hooked or looped chi-rho motif on tombstones[4]—I do not think we need dismiss the idea that these slab-shrine surrounds were inspired by Mediterranean *cellae memoriae*; by versions, that is, of such *cellae* seen at first hand in the Mediterranean, in North Africa, or perhaps in Spain. It is admittedly very hard to attach dates but there is nothing against the idea that the Irish instances stem from the seventh century, possibly as early as *circa* 600.

The specially marked graves, also set in the open air in cemeteries, which we noticed in Chapter 3—those with any form of circular surround, and those fewer ones with rectangular surrounds—differ from the slab-shrine surrounds in one vital aspect. They are real, closed, graves, with no question of the exhumation and of the bones and their translation as corporeal relics into accessible conditions. The surrounds, as we saw, may be rooted in various traditions, some of them pre-Christian and confined to northwest Europe. A compromise of a sort between the two classes is provided, or may in the future be shown to be provided, by a structure which is best described as an open-air altar, a rectangular block of masonry or dry stone, often surmounted by one or more cross-marked slabs. This is known to archaeology by its Irish name, *leacht* (Old Irish *lecht*: Latin *lectus*, 'bed, grave'), and does occur outside Ireland, mainly in areas of Irish settlement. Though I would argue that the *leacht*, also, has an ultimate origin in Mediterranean Christianity, the fact remains that no example known to me anywhere has yet been shown to cover a grave; because of this, we must regard it as a special sort of altar, and relegate further mention of it to Chapter 6.

The second potential introduction into the British Isles of aspects of the cult of relics, the martyrial tomb within a church, is a topic fraught with uncertainty. The shrine or reliquary-coffin within a church is, in Ireland and in North Britain, very

---

[1] Henry 1957, an honourable exception, is in many ways an isolated and pioneer field-study.

[2] See p. 23.   [3] See p. 106.   [4] See p. 100.

V. Inscribed memorial pillar, 1·25 m. high, from Ardwall Isle (mid 8th century?); the name of the deceased, CUDGAR, is possibly repeated in the smaller, incised, lettering (reading HUTHGAR) below the large 'R' and near the right edge

VI. (*Above*) Inscribed memorial pillar, granite, from Beacon Hill cemetery, Lundy (late 6th or early 7th century); ringed cross and POTITI ('The stone of Potitus'). (*Below*) Beacon Hill, Lundy: outer W. face of a rectangular *cella memoriae* walled with granite slabs, containing three graves. Slightly later (7th century?) graves, seen in the foreground, abut this much a feature of the seventh century, reaching greater elaboration in the eighth. It appears, therefore, at a time when both the continental martyr-burial sequence and the British and Irish traditions of church construction are far developed. The extensive literature referring directly or obliquely to this topic allows us to suppose that such shrines were in almost all cases added to existing churches, and were not, as in earlier centuries in Europe and the

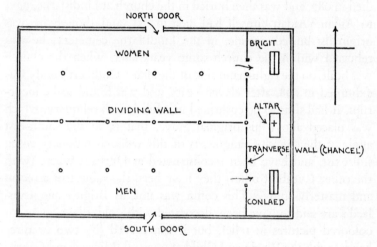

TIMBER CHURCH AT KILDARE, CIRCA 700 :
CONJECTURAL PLAN, AFTER DESCRIPTION BY COGITOSUS

Fig. 65.

Mediterranean, focal points around which churches eventually grew.

In the British Isles we are initially concerned with constructions in wood, the favoured position within a church being at the east end, alongside the altar. The *Life of St. Brigit*, by Cogitosus, a tangled production[1] which is none the less a source for the Christian archaeology of Leinster in the seventh century, describes how in a great timber church at Kildare[2] the richly decorated sarcophagi, if we can call them that, of Bishop Conlaed and of Brigit herself stood on the right and the left of the altar (Fig. 65).

[1] Kenney 1929, 356–60; and see p. 206.   [2] See p. 208.

They were certainly visible, probably wooden, and were said to be surmounted by crowns of gold and silver; an interesting detail, since this can hardly fail to recall the *regna* or votive hanging crowns like those connected with the Visigothic rulers of seventh-century Spain,[1] and this reminds us of the Iberian connections to which Hillgarth and others have devoted much argument.[2]

We get many further references from Northumbria. Cuthbert died in 687, and was then buried in the church at Lindisfarne, next to Aidan.[3] Aidan himself had died in 651, and though he was originally buried outside, in the Lindisfarne cemetery, he was reburied within the church some years later, when the church was built, on the right-hand side of the altar.[4] Cuthbert's body was exhumed in 698, after eleven years, and was found to be incorrupt. It had thus to be enshrined in a full-length reliquary, which was placed above his original grave, that is, in the south-east angle of the church.[5] Fragments of this wooden reliquary-coffin still exist, and have been reconstructed at Durham where (with the other Cuthbert relics) they have been the subject of a recent and masterly study.[6] This coffin was not, as Brigit's and Conlaed's are said to have been, decorated with gold, silver, gems, or coloured pictures in relief, but it *was* carved (by two or three hands) with the Virgin and Child at one end, Michael and Gabriel at the other, five archangels along one side, the Twelve Apostles along the other, and Christ, with the four evangelical symbols, on the lid. It was a flat-topped wooden coffin, about 5 feet 6 inches long, 1 foot 6 inches high, and tapering in width from 16 inches at one end to 15 inches at the other. It appears to have contained an inner lid or tray just above the body-space, on which small associated incorporeal relics could be exhibited, and it may just possibly have stood at Lindisfarne within some rougher or plainer outer casing.

The wooden coffin-reliquary, of which this is a case, was known in Merovingian Gaul, and the idea may have come thence to Northumbria during the later seventh century, quite indepen-

---

[1] Illustrated in Culican 1965, 180–1.
[2] Hillgarth 1961; Hillgarth 1962.   [3] *H.E.* iv. 29.
[4] *H.E.* iii. 17.   [5] *H.E.* iv. 30.   [6] Battiscombe 1956.

dently of events in Ireland. The tapered shape of Cuthbert's coffin, something not derivable from Roman wooden coffins in Britain, must recall the distinct tapering seen in Merovingian stone sarcophagi of late classical tradition. Much more of a problem is posed by Bede's description of what happened to the remains of Ceadda or 'Chad'. Chad was buried in 672, at Lichfield, in Mercia, next to St. Mary's Church, and was later exhumed and translated into the church of St. Peter. Bede's words[1] are mistranslated in all English versions that I have encountered, and I translate them afresh, literally. 'Moreover the place of his burial' (that is, of the reburial of Chad's bones) 'is covered with a wooden coffin[2] made in the shape of a little house, having a hole in one side through which those who go thither out of devotion may insert their hands and take some of the dust . . .' (to mix with water to cure ailments, etc.).

Apart from its interest as a direct account of the operations of 'virtue' in regard to a relic-tomb, this is a very clear statement, as Bede's statements always are when they describe aspects of Christianity visible in his own day. Chad's second grave was *open*, it was covered only by some wooden structure, and there was a hole in this structure admitting direct contact with the sacred dust.

This arrangement recalls those in the Kerry slab-shrines, which also allow similar direct access, but in the instances of Chad's shrine the material is wood, not stone, and the upper element resembles not just a ridged roof, but 'a little house', implying both roof and walls. Now such structures *are* known, but not as yet in Britain. A very clear case (Fig. 66) is grave no. 764, a male burial, in the large Reihengräberfeld (cemetery with graves set in rows) at München-Aubing on the outskirts of Munich.[3] This grave has four shallow post-sockets, one at each corner of, and immediately adjacent to, the roughly rectangular grave-pit, and Dannheimer's reconstruction of the superstructure as a wooden *Totenmemoria*, a shrine for the dead, is quite legitimate. These tiny little 'houses' above graves are inferred from other German cemeteries, and though in the case of München-Aubing we may have a Christian one, the origins of this group could be rather mixed

[1] *H.E.* iv. 3.   [2] *tumba lignea.*   [3] Dannheimer 1967.

—wooden copies of the ridged-lid sarcophagus of a martyr-burial
on the one hand, late miniature versions of the prehistoric 'mor-
tuary house' above a cremation or inhumation on the other. Nor
do we get much specific guidance in the case of Lichfield. Chad
was himself a Northumbrian, which means that a house-shaped

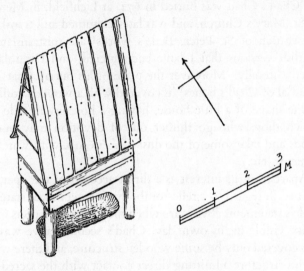

'TOTENMEMORIA', MUNCHEN–AUBING, GRAVE 764
DANNHEIMER'S RECONSTRUCTION, "CUT AWAY" TO SHOW
GRAVE UNDERNEATH WOODEN STRUCTURE

FIG. 66.

wooden superstructure could have been copied in or through
Northumbria by people who had seen such on the Continent; he
had also been a pupil of St. Aidan at Lindisfarne, had spent some
time in Ireland, and quite probably had some Irish monks (any of
whom could have known of the slab-shrine as a burial monument) with him at Lichfield.

Just as we saw earlier[1] how, over the later seventh and eighth
centuries, the timber chapel was replaced in popularity by the
stone-built one, and hypothetical crosses made of wood gave way
to free-standing crosses in stone, so (in the period centred on 700)

[1] See p. 78.

the wooden reliquary-coffin was apparently superseded by composite shrines made entirely of stone. This last remark is particularly true of North Britain; these eighth-century northern stone shrines constitute a rich and varied class, their distribution extending from Mercia to the Shetland Isles. I have little doubt that, behind this north-eastern emphasis, we should see the greatly

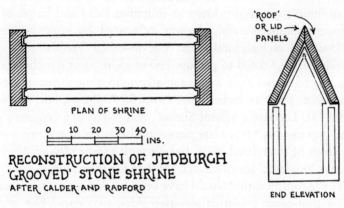

PLAN OF SHRINE

0 10 20 30 40
└──┴──┴──┴──┘ INS.

RECONSTRUCTION OF JEDBURGH
'GROOVED' STONE SHRINE
AFTER CALDER AND RADFORD

'ROOF'
OR LID →
PANELS

END ELEVATION

FIG. 67.

intensified religious and technological intercourse (after 715) between the church in Northumbria and the church among the Picts—two areas of social vitality and advanced artistic experiment at this period.

Dr. Radford's plausible reconstruction[1] of certain sculptured fragments at Jedburgh into a house-shaped stone shrine, which he would date to about 700, and link with St. Boisil of Old Melrose, shows the first step in the wood-to-stone transition (Fig. 67). This shrine is, in fact, a translation from wood-working. The long sides, their ends set in grooves in the slightly overlapping end panels, are (in a necessarily coarser fashion) reminiscent of the constructional details of Cuthbert's coffin; the latter also has rebated vertical corner-joints, and a tongue-and-groove joint between the bottom-board and the end-pieces.[2]

---

[1] Radford 1955b, 44; cf. RCAMS Roxburgh 1956, i. 207, figs. 258–9.
[2] Battiscombe 1956, 212–18, and pls. vi–xi.

The subsequent history of this stone version of the ridge-roofed reliquary-coffin may be briefly sketched. It seems eventually to have become a solid monolith, designed to stand above a (not necessarily accessible) grave, but still with occasional features skeuomorphic of its wooden prototype. The undatable (eighth? ninth? tenth century?) solid stone shrine from Clones, co. Monaghan, which we noted in connection with gable-finials,[1] is a monolithic copy, right down to imitation locks and hasps, of a wooden reliquary-coffin, slightly influenced by contemporary ecclesiastical architectural style. The so-called 'Hedda stone' at Peterborough,[2] dated to perhaps 800 or so, is 3 feet 6 inches long and 2 feet 6 inches high, and is a smaller solid stone shrine; so, too, is another, 3 feet 10 inches long, from St. Andrews, Fife, known as the 'St. Leonard's School Shrine', and found in a cemetery of long cists in 1895.[3] It is a late piece—probably ninth century—and the form of its stylized 'roof' links it with a large class of Anglo-Danish 'hogback' tomb-covers, too late for discussion here.

The Jedburgh shrine would have been (excluding the two-piece lid) a four-piece construction—two sides, two ends. The other composite stone shrines we must now examine are (again, lids or roofs excluded) eight-piece and, if 'double shrines', thirteen-piece. The new element is the separate vertical corner-member, into which the end or long-side panels are fitted; and this fact allows us to describe all these as 'corner-post shrines' (in contrast to, say, slab-shrines and the apparently isolated Jedburgh monument).

The corner-post shrine distribution is North British (Fig. 68). The only known Irish examples are very developed, and one of the two is apparently of fully medieval date.[4] There is a further distinction between the corner-post shrines, and the coffin-reliquary type (including the Jedburgh shrine and its later solid relatives); corner-post shrines possessed, not two-piece ridged roofs, but single piece lids which were either flat or only slightly coped.

---

[1] See p. 77. [2] Radford 1955b, 58–9 with refs.
[3] Cruden, S. E., note in Radford 1955b, 59–60 and pl. vii. b.
[4] Henry 1957, 90, fig. 13 (Kildrenagh, Valentia Is.); and O'Kelly 1958, 87–90, fig. 6, pl. xiv. d (Church Island).

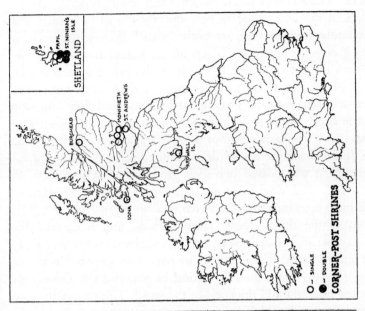

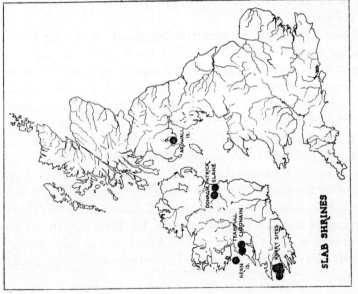

FIG. 68.

The actual corner-posts, which range from roughly shaped pillars of the local stone to near upright blocks of regular and rectangular cross-section, are easily spotted, because they exhibit long grooves, an inch or so deep and an inch or more wide. The grooves do not run the full length of the posts; they stop well short of the bottoms, as the bottoms of these posts must have been socketed into the ground for stability, and they also stop a little short of the tops, implying that the summits of corner-posts rose a few inches clear of the side and end-panels and of the lids (individual schemes of decoration confirm this). A normal corner-post will possess two such grooves on adjacent faces. In what are called 'double shrines', the longer sides of the originals will have been interrupted by two median posts, each with *three* grooves—the third groove faces inwards, and is to take the median partition panel. The panels themselves, which are simply flat shaped slabs of stone, tend to have two opposed sides cut down slightly from the full vertical height, and also thinned or rebated from the full thickness of the panel. This creates the two lateral 'tongues', which engage in the appropriate grooves in the corner-posts.

A panel so fashioned is seen from Burghead,[1] with a low-relief hunting scene typical of the Pictish Class II (Christian) art; it is part of a long-side panel, and with it must go a roughly squared corner-post with two grooves, and a zone of crude relief interlace on an outer face[2]—this is no older than the eighth century. Both were found in an old cemetery at Burghead. Another finer corner-post, which has for years stood on the main stairway in the National Museum of Antiquities, Edinburgh, without anyone remarking upon its true character, is a Pictish Class II relief cross-slab, a tombstone, in fact, from Monifieth, Angus, where it was found built into the former church.[3] This stone, first carved (at a guess) in the earlier eighth century, has been converted into a corner-post (Fig. 69). The grooves have been carefully cut, but in such a way that when used, the face with the relief cross would

---

[1] *ECMS* III. 137, fig. 138 (= Burghead no. 7).
[2] Ibid. 139–40, fig. 141 (= Burghead no. 11).
[3] Ibid. 228–9, fig. 241 (= Monifieth no. 1).

face outwards, and the reverse face, with the Pictish symbols, inwards.

There are two small, plain, two-grooved corner-posts from Iona (Fig. 70), neither of them found in any significant context,[1] but by far the finest assemblage comes from Shetland. In field-work there during the summer of 1967, I formed the impression

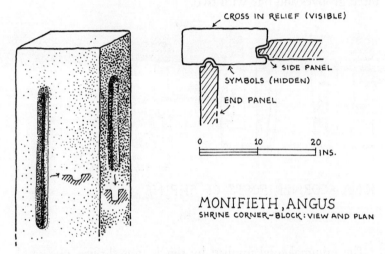

MONIFIETH, ANGUS
SHRINE CORNER-BLOCK: VIEW AND PLAN

FIG. 69. A Class II Pictish symbol-stone converted into a shrine 'corner-block' (or rectangular corner-post); the relief decoration is omitted from the drawing for the sake of clarity.

that the church and churchyard of Papil (Fig. 71), on East Burra,[2] may have been the principal monastery for the southern half of Shetland, and that the site on St. Ninian's Isle, where the famous silver hoard was found, was a contemporary developed ceme-tery.[3] There are two sites which have produced the shrines. Surviving shrine-components, now displayed in the fine new museum at Lerwick, form an impressive series. From Papil there is a complete side-panel, and there is an acceptable record of three more short panels (all lost); two corner-posts with three grooves

---

[1] Unpublished; found in 1958 and 1960.
[2] RCAMS Orkney and Shetland 1946, iii. 74–5 (no. 1266).
[3] O'Dell *et al.* 1959; O'Dell 1960.

each, and apparently a third similar post (also lost); two corner-posts with two grooves each, and the top of another corner-post. From St. Ninian's Isle there are three fragments of a side- or end-panel, showing the chamfered tongue; five corner-posts, all with knobbed tops and chamfered angles, two with three grooves each and three with two; and two plainer corner-posts, one with three grooves and one with two.

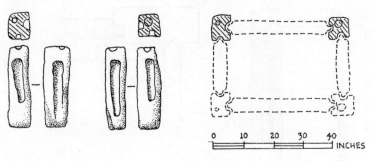

IONA : CORNER POSTS OF SHRINE

FIG. 70.

The minimal total implied by this is four shrines, one single and one double from Papil, and two double from St. Ninian's Isle. The double shrines are curious, but there is a prototype. Bede tells us[1] how, in August of 716, abbot Huetbert of Monkwearmouth exhumed the skeletons of his predecessors, Easterwine and Sigfrid, who had died respectively in 684 and 689, and placed both lots of remains in one coffin, separated by a partition in the middle (*sed medio pariete divisa*); this was then laid in St. Peter's Church, close to the altar. Bede uses the word *theca*, and we can suppose that a double reliquary-coffin in wood is meant.

Though it is highly probable that the first Christians in Orkney and Shetland were Irishmen, who approached the Northern Isles from the monastic foundations on the west coast of Scotland, these Shetland shrines (none of which, I feel, is necessarily older

[1] Bede, *Historia Abbatum*, in Plummer 1896 (text; i. 364–87) (notes; ii. 355–70), cap. 20.

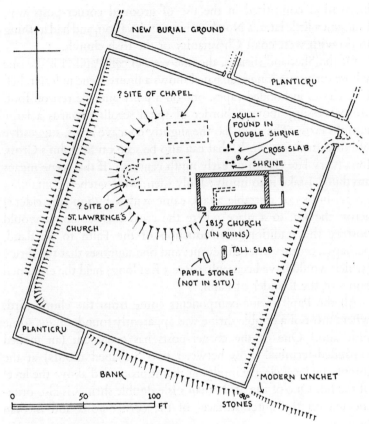

NEW BURIAL GROUND

PLANTICRU

? SITE OF CHAPEL

SKULL:
(FOUND IN
DOUBLE SHRINE

CROSS SLAB

SHRINE

? SITE OF
ST. LAWRENCE'S
CHURCH

1815 CHURCH
(IN RUINS)

TALL SLAB

'PAPIL STONE'
(NOT IN SITU)

PLANTICRU

BANK

MODERN LYNCHET

STONES

0   50   100
├──────┼──────┤ FT

PAPIL, BURRA, SHETLAND

FIG. 71.

than the middle of the eighth century) look rather towards Northumbria. Such Christian art as there is in pre-Norse Orkney and
Shetland suggests a relation with the east coast Pictish art styles
of the Christian era. The character of some of the metalwork in
the St. Ninian's Isle hoard, and the primary cross-slab found
inverted over this hoard which is incised with a hollow-angle
'armpit' cross, also point to Northumbrian artistic and ecclesiastical influences, of a character detectable from the early eighth
century in Pictland. This is important, because the constructional

innovation comprised in the use of grooved corner-posts was,
I suggest a little later, a Northumbrian innovation, and had nothing
to do with west coast Christianity or the Irish church.

Of the Shetland shrines, the one we can call Papil *A* is the one
whose surviving long-side panel shows a figure scene in low relief.
Five clerics in hooded capes, one on a pony and the rest on foot,
are processing above a border of spiral scrolls towards a large
upright cross. The cross has the slightly concave arms, suggestive
of Northumbrian work, that can also be seen on St. John's Cross,
Iona (very late eighth or early ninth century). If this scene means
anything, I take it to imply: Holy men, with satchels containing
gospel-books or portable altars, came with a bishop (the rider?)
across the sea, to a place where the cross was set up. It would
portray the traditional introduction of the Faith to Shetland,
perhaps a century after the event; and one supposes that the shrine
(which would have been only some 3 feet long) held the exhumed
bones of the founder of Papil.

All the Papil shrine-components come from the churchyard,
where most of a double shrine was apparently found, *in situ*, some
time ago.[1] One of the corner-posts has ornament (an incised
expanded-terminal cross between two S-shaped motifs) at the
top of one face, clearly implying that it protruded above the level
of the lid. One of the St. Ninian's Isle double shrines is also ornamented on the outer surfaces of the corner-posts and median
posts.

The most ornate example of any composite stone shrine is that
from St. Andrew's Fife, reconstructed in the museum there, recently
published in detail[2] by Dr. Radford, and perhaps intended to hold
the relics of the local saint, Regulus or Rule (Fig. 72). There is
room for discussion on the exact form of the lid—I would myself
argue that a flat lid is just as probable as a roof-shaped one—and
we cannot exclude the suggestion that the present reconstruction
uses part of the lid as a side-member. Stylistically and typologically
this shrine should be late, and while avoiding here the unresolved
arguments as to its precise date[3]—arguments which tend to be

    ¹ Moar 1944.   ² Radford 1955b.
    ³ Henderson 1967, 88, 149–57, refs. and pls.

based on art-historical aspects—I would point out that the later dating (ninth century) is the most probable.

Where were these corner-post shrines intended to stand? True, the St. Ninian's Isle corner-posts (five from shrine *A*, two from shrine *B*) were found in a kind of walled surround, outside the

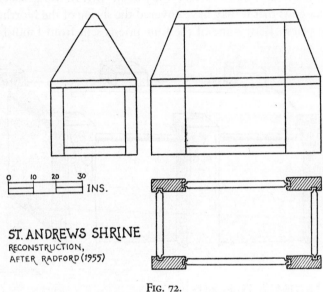

0 10 20 30 INS.

ST. ANDREWS SHRINE
RECONSTRUCTION,
AFTER RADFORD (1955)

FIG. 72.

south-east corner of the medieval chapel, but this mixture alone suggests that this was a secondary, and muddled, attempt to re-erect a shrine in the Middle Ages. Those shrines whose ornament, when there is any, demands a unilateral viewpoint—like Papil *A*, with its decorated panel, and St. Ninian's Isle *A*, only one long side of which bears (Fig. 73) a unified ornamental scheme— must have stood within a church or chapel, like the wooden structures associated with St. Cuthbert and St. Chad, and moreover, they must have stood against a wall. Even with all the posts set in the ground, I doubt if any shrine would have remained stable for long without some lateral support. If there were room, a shrine might have stood against the inner east wall, to the right of (south of) the altar, the favoured position for burial; the alternative would have been against the south wall, close to the inner south-east corner. The arguments for some such positioning are strengthened by a study of one of the very few remaining shrine-lids, the magnificent slab from Wirksworth, Derbyshire. This, slightly coped, originally about 6 feet 8 inches long, may date from the late seventh century. In his careful study of it,[1] Mr. R. W. P. Cockerton suggests that it may have covered the shrine of the Northumbrian priest, Betti—one of the four priests sent from Lindisfarne

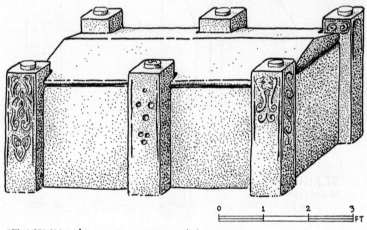

ST. NINIAN'S ISLE, SHRINE 'A'
ISOMETRIC SKETCH

FIG. 73.

to Mercia in 653. The iconography of the slab comprises ten scenes, from the Nativity (unfortunately missing) through the Crucifixion to the Ascension, ending with the Mission to the Gentiles. As Dr. Kurth comments,[2] 'The fact that the two rows of figures are arranged in the same sense implies that the sarcophagus was intended to stand against a wall and to be seen from above, from the level of the spectator'—and, we may argue, from one side only.

Shrines which were oriented, or covered an oriented grave of any kind, would present their gable-ends to a viewer entering

[1] Cockerton 1962.   [2] Kurth 1945.

a church and walking towards the altar. Dr. Radford has shown[1] that a passage in the twelfth-century life of St. Indract may reflect this. A boy visits the Old Church at Glastonbury, falls asleep, and in a dream sees two men coming to him, one from each of the pyramids which are on either side of the altar. It could indeed be argued that the end view of a shrine with a hipped or ridged roof might lie behind such a late description.

An interesting recent discovery, the counterpart of which might well be found in Britain or Ireland, occurred during Günther Fehring's excavation of the Dionysius-kirche at Esslingen am Neckar, near Stuttgart.[2] The primary structure, perhaps of the period 725–750, was a small stone chapel, 21 feet by 20 feet, to which a western enlargement containing seventeen Alemannic (lay) graves was added. Fehring describes this as a nave, but it seems possible that it was more like a small enclosed burial-yard. Against the centre of the inner east wall of the primary chapel, and thus in a position where it would be under the (missing) altar, there was a stone-lined grave, oriented east-west. We can regard this as a reliquary grave, and the original burial (which would have been exhumed, and translated into this reliquary grave) may have been made in another grave found just outside and partly below the east wall. The reliquary grave was covered with a single-piece stone lid, coped, like the Wirksworth slab,[3] having an access-hole through this lid, closed with a removable conical stone plug.

If we return now to the constructional technique of the composite, corner-post, stone shrines, we must realize that (with the exception of the 'grooved' Jedburgh shrine) the techniques and details involved are not borrowed from carpentry; nor is it at all likely that corner-post shrines in wood ever existed in the British Isles. The basic device, the insertion of the lateral tongues of panels (Fig. 74) into corresponding vertical grooves in posts, is copied from that used to construct (among other things) low multi-piece chancel-screens in early churches in the Mediterranean. Here it is a survival from classical architecture, and its later deflection to a funerary context appears to be entirely a British phenomenon.

[1] Radford 1955b, 57, n. 2.   [2] Fehring 1967.   [3] See p. 158.

The Mediterranean chancel-screen (Fig. 75) was generally composed of small, square-section, pillars, often with decorative knobs or terminals, between which and into which were slotted the square screen panels, *cancelli* or *transennae*; these last are often richly ornamented with relief carvings or with geometric open-work.[1]

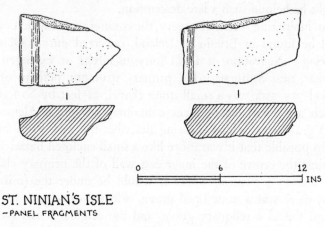

ST. NINIAN'S ISLE
– PANEL FRAGMENTS

Fig. 74.

There is a complication here, in that it seems probable that the basic idea of the chancel-screen, as an internal church division, may have reached Ireland during the seventh century, conceivably through the intermediacy of ecclesiastical fashions in Spain or as part of the general sea-borne contact with the Mediterranean. The description which Cogitosus gives[2] of a large wooden church, in the seventh century at Kildare (Fig. 65), implies a partition of this kind, in wood, probably unbroken across the centre, but with two gaps or entrances near the side walls, not unlike the surviving arrangements in late Visigothic churches in Asturias.[3] In Cormac's

[1] e.g. Dyggve 1951, figs. iv. 32, iv. 33, iv. 34 ('fretwork screen plates'); Stojkovic 1957, figs. 3 and 4; Van der Meer and Mohrmann 1958, figs. 231, 262, 264, 430; Volbach 1961, pl. 80 (shows groove); Barruol 1964 (with details of assembly); De Palol 1967, 253, fig. 89, and lam. lvi. 1.

[2] Cf. Bieler 1963b, 28 (translation).

[3] e.g. S. Cristina de Leon—Culican 1965, fig. 37; see also *Ars Hispaniae* (Madrid) vol. ii, 1947, fig. 386.

II. Teampull Chronain (St. Cronan's church), Termon, Co. Clare; small limestone church of (?) 9th/10th century, with some reconstruction in 12th, and two 'slab shrines' of rather earlier date. (*Above*) View from west, showing partial remains of enclosure; (*Below*) View from south-east, showing shrine

VIII. Central area of large Romanesque altar mensa, Whithorn, showing recess for consecrated super-altar (Whithorn Priory)

Glossary of around 900, the word *caincell* is glossed as *a cancella.i. cliath* ('from (Latin) *cancella*, that is, a hurdle').[1] As early as the eleventh century, and doubtless before then, 'chancel-screen' is translated by *crann chaingil*, 'the piece of woodwork of the chancel'.[2]

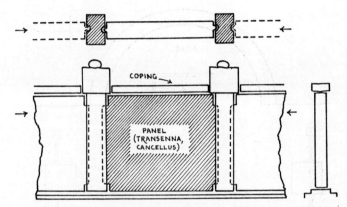

SKETCH DIAGRAMS : EARLY CHANCEL SCREENS IN SLOTTED POST AND PANEL TECHNIQUE

FIG. 75.

In the context of the shrines, we are, however, concerned with screens in stone, and for this reason I would look to an independent transmission of the idea into late seventh-century Northumbria. The techniques, and probably the work of actual continental masons and carvers, introduced by Benedict Biscop, provide the explanation.[3] Definite pieces of stone chancel-screens, whether as grooved posts or as likely panels, have yet to be noted from Hexham and Jarrow, but a curious group of eighth-century fragments which, artistically, must be called 'Northumbrian', from South Kyme, Lincs., are best explained as *cancelli*;[4] and there is a thick

---

[1] Kuno Meyer, in *Anecdota* iii (1910), s.v.; cf. Petrie 1845, 206, and Stokes 1887 ii. 645 (*cro-chaingel*).

[2] I owe this note to the kindness of Professor Kenneth Jackson.

[3] Bede, *Historia Abbatum*, cap. 5 (Plummer 1896, i. 368).

[4] Taylor and Taylor 1965, 365–6, with refs.

slab which may be the central part of a double panel, in this case a provincial outlier, from Bradford-on-Avon, Wilts.[1]

The adaptation of the post-and-panel screen to a shrine may involve only two steps; in the first, a shrine of some kind stands within a chancel-screen (Fig. 76), which may bend through four

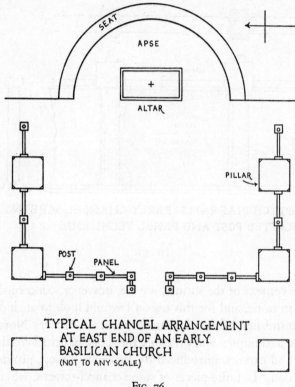

TYPICAL CHANCEL ARRANGEMENT
AT EAST END OF AN EARLY
BASILICAN CHURCH
(NOT TO ANY SCALE)

Fig. 76.

right-angles to enclose it, and in the second, the enclosing screen is itself detached to form the shrine and is given a lid. With this sequence in mind, the remarkable knobs on the top of the St. Ninian's Isle Shrine *A* corner-posts could directly recall the more prominent knobs which surmount so many chancel posts. The resemblance between one of the St. Ninian's Isle corner-posts with

[1] Taylor and Taylor 1963, 250–1 and fig. 3.

its scroll ornament, and a slotted chancel post with similar small knob and vertical S-scrolls from a sixth-century Byzantine church at Doclea in Illyria,[1] is not as far-fetched as it might seem.

It now remains for us to deal briefly with the related, but very much smaller, portable reliquaries. These, sometimes known as 'house-shaped shrines',[2] are essentially boxes with ridged or hipped-gabled lids, and can be closer in form to the external shapes of contemporary churches than many of the full-size stone shrines. The skeuomorphism is not direct, because this shape is only partly derived from that of a church, and is also indebted ultimately to a long series of tombs or sarcophagi which are themselves based on the outline of the earliest Christian (in the classical world, sometimes non-Christian) temples.

The house-shaped shrine, which can fairly be described as a pan-European type, contained small corporeal relics (like a finger-bone), representative relics, or a collection of relics. A famous sixth-century Byzantine ivory, now preserved at Trier,[3] shows two metropolitans carrying such a shrine, on their triumphal carriage, in a procession to a basilica with an attached *martyrion*. In the British Isles the use of the reliquary may have been introduced directly through Ireland or, perhaps more probably, into seventh-century Northumbria. Two of the most interesting examples are now preserved in Edinburgh. The so-called 'Monymusk Reliquary', which Joseph Anderson showed[4] must be identified as the historical *Brecbennoch* of St. Columba named in land-grants of about 1210 and 1315, and which is said to have been carried at Bannockburn, is about 4 inches long. The box and the hinged lid are carved from solid wood, the casing being bronze sheet with hollow-moulded angle-strips, and the front-plate delicate engraved silver. Hinged strap-terminals on both shorter ends (one of which still remains) would have taken a strap for suspension around the carrier's neck. The (stylistic) date of the reliquary is open to some discussion, but it could conceivably have

[1] Stojkovic 1957, fig. 5.
[2] List, for British Isles, in Swarzenski 1954.
[3] Van der Meer and Mohrmann 1958, 153-4, fig. 509.
[4] Anderson J. 1880; Anderson J. 1881, i. 242, fig. 93.

been made at the period when Columba, buried at Iona in 597, was exhumed and translated (about 700). What it contained we do not know.

FIG. 77. The Andenne Reliquary (actual size).

The other incomplete reliquary at Edinburgh is a less elaborate version of the *Brecbennoch*[1]—it has only three square gem-settings, and lacks the three roundels of the latter. It comes from the river Shannon. The three roundels do appear on two other reliquaries of this type, that from Lough Erne, now in Dublin,[2] and the so-called Copenhagen reliquary. This was found in Norway, has a secondary runic inscription scratched on the base

---

[1] Anderson J. 1881, i. 246, fig. 90.   [2] Coffey 1909, 42–3, fig. 50.

('Ranvaig owns this casket'), and is generally regarded[1] as Viking
loot, probably from Ireland. The pronounced roof-ridge which
so strongly recalls the church-like form is also seen (Fig. 77) on a
little-known bronze reliquary, early eighth century in date and
quite possibly made in Britain, preserved at Andenne in Belgium.[2]

We must not here overlook the extraordinary 'Shrine of St.
Manchan', which is kept at Boher church, co. Offaly. This[3] is
a gabled structure 19 inches high, covering a rectangular floor-
space 2 feet by 16 inches. It is made from yew wood, with gilt,
bronze, and enamelled fittings, and it contains some fragmentary
bones, one part of a femur, presumably those of the saint who
traditionally died in 664. Sir Thomas Kendrick's careful study,
and the late Miss Senior's comments on the art styles, leave little
doubt that all visible embellishments are twelfth century. None
the less I suspect that, even if the woodwork core is also of this
Romanesque date and is not appreciably older, this may be a
twelfth-century reproduction—suitably elaborated—of a much
plainer original in nothing but wood, made in (say) the late
seventh or early eighth centuries. The construction (Fig. 78) is
simple, involving little more than rebated jointing. Two feet is a
greater length than that of portable reliquaries, but would allow
the inclusion of such (unbroken) long bones as a femur. The shape
is bound to suggest the upper half of a coffin-reliquary of the
ridged-roof class, the postulated super-structure of St. Chad's
shrine at Lichfield, and the co. Kerry slab-shrines; and one is
disposed to see this as basically a medieval copy of some earlier
wooden shrine that sat directly over a grave—made in the post-
Roman era, decaying away over four centuries, and religiously
copied for inclusion in some rebuilt church.

The numerous instances of *self-shaped shrines*, where the external
casing form is dictated by the original shape of whatever is enshrined—gospel books, little bells of hammered and bronze-
coated iron, crozier-heads, or corporeal relics like arms and feet

---

[1] Anderson J. 1881, i. 248 n. 1, fig. 92.

[2] *Karl der Grosse: Werk und Wirkung* (= Charlemagne Exhibition Catalogue),
Aachen 1965, 135 and abb. 23.

[3] Kendrick and Senior 1937. This has recently been restored at the British
Museum, and is now well displayed in Boher church.

—are generally later than anything we have been discussing. An instance would be the twelfth-century Shrine of St. Lachtin's Arm, from co. Cork,[1] which does in fact contain within it a much older wooden hand-reliquary. Some of the most interesting

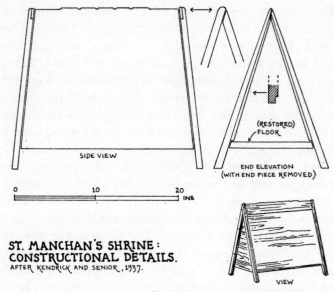

SIDE VIEW

(RESTORED) FLOOR

END ELEVATION
(WITH END PIECE REMOVED)

VIEW

ST. MANCHAN'S SHRINE:
CONSTRUCTIONAL DETAILS.
AFTER KENDRICK AND SENIOR, 1937.

FIG. 78.

portable shrines are those which contain or surround portable altars, a complex topic which will be examined in the next chapter. We might conclude by reminding ourselves that, despite the lapse of centuries, major corporeal relics of unquestioned authenticity are still shown and venerated. The mummified head of Blessed Oliver Plunket, martyred on the scaffold in 1681, today rests grimly in its glass-fronted niche in Drogheda Cathedral, on the Boyne.

[1] Coffey 1909, 53–4, pl. xii.

6. *The Altar*

WHAT DISTINGUISHES a Christian church or chapel, seen as a ruined foundation or as an excavated monument, from contemporary secular structures? The answer must exclude some elements (the rectilinear plan, entrances on the west or south, an east-west longer axis, and even the modular proportions of three to two, or two to one) which can and do occur in both secular and Christian buildings in the protohistoric period. Clearly, context can be a partial guide—the presence of associated burials, the relationship with any form of enclosed cemetery, or the vicinity of prominent crosses. The most distinctive, and the surest, clue to Christian character is, however, the presence of an altar; and this is despite the archaeological drawback that altars, unlike wall-footings or graves, tend to commence only at ground-level and seldom survive intact.

An altar, as the focal point of a church, can be defined as something which provides a flat, raised surface, ritually consecrated, on which a symbolic sacrifice can take place during an act of worship. Our definition cannot go beyond this, since such factors as shape, material, size, and exact position, are all subject to variation. The resemblance (in phenomenological terms) of the Christian altar to any other altar of pagan or pre-Christian type will be obvious, and it is widely recognized that the very word 'altar' (Latin *altare*, from *altus*, 'high, raised-up') is in deliberate contrast to the Latin word *ara*, meaning a pagan altar. There are certain elements, for instance those of sacrifice, of the central position, of symbolic ornament, perhaps of such secondary functions as oath-taking, which Christianity may have adopted from pagan practice; though as far as the British Isles are concerned this is likely to have taken place in the Mediterranean and on the Continent rather than here. In this chapter we deal exclusively with the

Christian structure, and I use the word 'structure' intentionally, because the Christian altar has very seldom been (as the pagan altar nearly always was) a single, unitary, piece of stone or of any other material.

We saw in the last chapter[1] how one particular line of development of the Christian Church could follow the sequence of; martyr's grave in a cemetery—*cella memoriae* around that grave— funerary chapel enclosing the *cella*—basilican church enclosing one or more such chapels. It is thus essential to realize that, in the Mediterranean from as far back as the fourth century, the main or subsidiary altars in such eventual churches could have begun, not only as altars erected *de novo* when the last and greatest church was built, but as the surfaces or superstructures of martyrs' tombs in unroofed *cellae*, continuously adapted to altar-like use from a period long before the last church took shape. In his long analysis[2] of this particular arrangement at Salonae, Dyggve has shown that the purpose of such an early altar-table directly above a martyr's relics (whether as an addition to the accessible tomb, or as the top or lid of the tomb itself treated as such) was a complex one. It would involve such aspects as the pouring of libations, some of which would trickle through access-holes in the surface or tomb-lid to the grave below; the ritual meal shared by the living with the dead, including (on appropriate feasts) the Eucharistic meal as well; the deposition of gifts; and mere veneration. The excesses of this form of martyr-cult, which could extend to (in Dyggve's words)[3] 'great common meals, food orgies, and cultic dances', need hardly bother us. Our concern is whether anything of the basic idea, the use of the upper surface of a martyr's tomb or special grave as an altar table, reached the British Isles. In view of the transmission of such other features as the *cella memoriae*, the jars of Eucharistic wine and the cross-marked table wares, monasticism, and so many minor aspects in the field of art and letters, this must be regarded as, at the least, a possibility. I believe that it does appear, in the shape of the odd little structure known by the modern Irish word, *leacht*.

---

[1] See p. 138.   [2] Dyggve 1951, chap. v.
[3] Ibid. p. 113.

The leacht (plural, *leachta*) can be described as a small square or rectangular construction of stones or boulders or slabs, a neat rough-masonry block, with a flat top on which a variety of decorated stones or slabs may stand affixed. None, as far as I know, has ever been excavated, and we are thus in the awkward position of not knowing whether *leachta* contain, or cover, burials. In remoter parts of Ireland they sometimes serve today as stations in localized penitential cults, an involvement in living religion which means that, far from being allowed to become ruinous, they are maintained, occasionally repaired, and can even have been rebuilt. The *locus classicus* is undoubtedly the island of Inismurray, or Inishmurray, whose small monastery, enclosed in its thick cashel wall, we noted in the second chapter.[1]

Inismurray is about a mile long. There are, today, eleven leachta of one sort or another, placed in an irregular circuit around the island. Nine have specific individual names, but as they include the inevitable ascriptions to Blessed Mary, Patrick, and Columcille, one would be cautious in attaching much weight to this aspect. There are three more leachta actually within the monastic cashel, and one adjacent to the outer face of the cashel wall, making a total of fifteen.

As a specimen, we can take the one called *Altoir beg*, 'the little altar', inside the cashel[2] (Fig. 79). This is a neatly built (or rebuilt) solid mass of dry-stone masonry, 3 feet by 5 feet 6 inches in plan, and 3 feet high, aligned on the cardinal compass-points. A single slab, with a ring cross and a linear cross below it, stands upright in the middle of the flat upper surface of this leacht. The surface is today covered with a number of pebbles, which possess some votive and folkloristic significance.[3] Very similar is the 'Eastern altar', also within the cashel enclosure; 8 feet by 6 feet, and 4 feet high, with a smaller, square-headed, cross slab on it.[4] The third leacht within the cashel is the one called *Clocha-breaca*, similar to the first two. The two slabs which now stand upon it are not *in situ*, and were placed there by the former Board of Works. What may, however, be an original accessory (Fig. 80) is a curious

---

[1] See p. 33.
[2] Wakeman 1893, 45, 71–2, fig. 34.
[3] Mitchell 1884; Evans 1957, pl. xv.
[4] Wakeman 1893, 72–3, fig. 35.

tanged stone block, some 2 feet high,[1] on the upper end of which there is a cylindrical hollow, closed with a round stone lid or cap whose downward-projecting boss fits into this hollow.

If we seek to classify these leachta in terms of other, more widely recognized, Christian monuments, their altar-like character is suggested by at least three features. Least important is the application of the word *altoir*, which may be very recent. The normal

INISHMURRAY :
THE 'ALTOIR BEG' LEACHT
(AFTER WAKEMAN, 1893)

Fig. 79.

height of the surface of a leacht above the ground, between 3 and 4 feet, is an appropriate height for the surface of an altar but too high for most graves, tombs, or shrines. Some, though not all, of the cross-slabs which surmount the Inismurray leachta are of a peculiar design in which the central cross is flanked by (or surrounded by) four smaller crosses (Fig. 81). This appears on the slab on *Leacht Choluimcille*,[2] and on several others;[3] the disposition of five crosses together is bound to recall the five crosses on an altar mensa.

Continuing the hypothetical connection with the altar-graves of early Mediterranean Christianity, the funerary aspect of the

[1] Wakeman 1893, 59, fig. 26; 68–71, fig. 32.
[2] Ibid. 146–9, figs. 78 and 79.   [3] Ibid. 140, fig. 72; 152, fig. 84.

leachta resides in another group of features. The word *leacht*, if it could be shown to be a continuously used term, takes us to Old Irish *lecht* and Latin *lectus*, 'bed', in the Early Christian sense of 'grave'. Four of the outlying Inismurray leachta (Fig. 82) stand

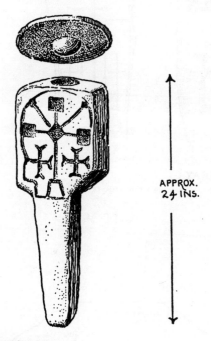

APPROX. 24 INS.

INISHMURRAY :
STONE RELIQUARY AND LID-STOPPER FROM THE 'CLOCHA BREACA' LEACHT
(AFTER WAKEMAN, 1893)

FIG. 80.

within small walled enclosures—two circular,[1] two rectilinear[2]— which remind us, for the circular ones, of all those specially marked graves with circular surrounds,[3] and for the other two, of such things as the co. Kerry rectangular yards around the slab-shrines which I suggested[4] could be local versions of

[1] Ibid. 127–8 (Olla Muire), 132–4 (Crois Mor).
[2] Ibid. 128–32 (Trathan na righ fhear); 141 (Trionid Beg).
[3] See p. 62.   [4] See p. 143

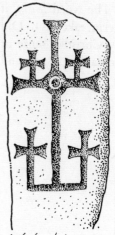 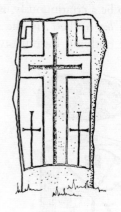 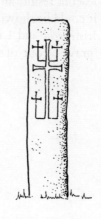

(TRÍONÍD MÓR) (LEACHTA CHOLUIMCILLE) (REILIC ODHRAIN)

INISHMURRAY :
CROSS-SLABS, WITH CENTRAL CROSS AND FOUR CROSSLETS
(AFTER WAKEMAN, 1893)

FIG. 81.

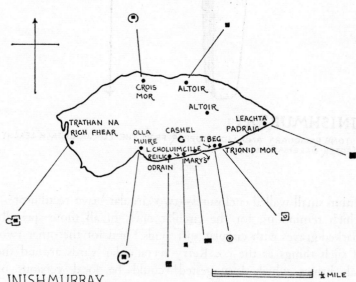

INISHMURRAY
POSITION AND SHAPE OF THE
LEACHTA AND ALTARS, WITH SURROUNDS

FIG. 82.

Mediterranean *cellae*. Lastly, the object on the Clocha-Breaca leacht is of course a small stone reliquary.

I emphasize again, most strongly, that one would have to excavate a fair sample of all the known leachta before coming to any valid conclusions. The type has a restricted distribution. There are (or were) three (Fig. 83) within the cashel on Illauntannig, or St. Senach's Isle, off the Kerry coast;[1] a large group of small ones both inside and outside the cashel enclosure of an eremitic monastery on Caher Island, co. Mayo, reported by Mlle Henry;[2] and an unspecified number on the so-called 'Station Island' in Lough Derg, co. Donegal, a strictly controlled centre of the present-day cult of St. Patrick. No survey of leachta in Britain and Ireland has been made, and short of one it is uncertain how widely they occur, particularly as ruined examples are liable to be overlooked. In the Irish settlements the best-known instance (Fig. 84) is probably St. Patrick's Chair, Marown, in the Isle of Mann. This[3] isolated leacht is rectangular, measured about 4 feet by 7 feet, is now a bare 18 inches high, and has two cross-incised slabs still standing on it. In 1964 I noticed two collapsed structures about a hundred yards from the developed cemetery on Ardwall Isle, which looked very like the remains of leachta, of the order of 6 feet square. The early cemetery at Cladh a'Bhile[4] in the west of Argyll contains, besides a large group of early cross-slabs, what I would regard as several obvious leachta, built up around natural boulders.

Dr. Radford has drawn attention[5] to what he considers may be the base of a leacht in the cemetery of the little monastery at Birsay, in Orkney. Slightly more convincing is his report[6] of a square base (about 6 feet) from the earliest phase of the monastery at Tintagel. There are also references in Nicholas Roscarrock's manuscript hagiography (of about 1590), and in the twelfth-century *Life of St. Illtud*, to what sound like leachta in Cornwall and in south Wales respectively. The latter (in Wade-Evans's

---

[1] Dunraven 1875, i. 37–42, with plan.
[2] Henry 1947. [3] Kermode 1907, 102–3, fig. 46.
[4] Campbell and Sandeman 1964, 65, no. 422, with refs. (seen, 1967).
[5] Radford 1959, 18. [6] Radford 1935a, 413.

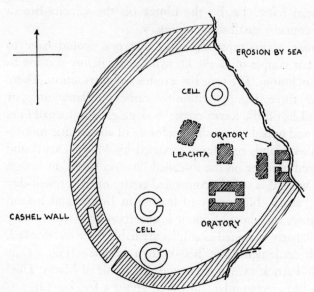

OILEN TSENAIG, ILLAUNTANNIG OR ST. SENACH'S ISLE
MAGHAREES, CO. KERRY
AFTER DUNRAVEN, I.38

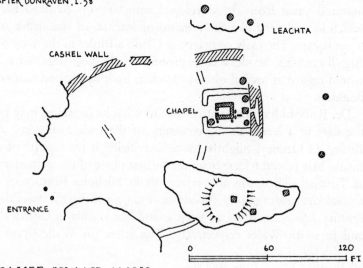

CAHER ISLAND, MAYO
AFTER F. HENRY

FIG. 83.

translation)[1] tells us that 'the body (of Samson) was taken and honourably carried by the clergy and buried in the midst of quadrangular stones (*in medio quadrangularium lapidum*) standing upright in the cemetery, a stone cross being placed above and the insignia of a bishop inscribed below . . .'.

Do we then assume that leachta began as special graves whose superstructures came to be treated as open-air altars, or merely as

'ST. PATRICK'S CHAIR', MAROWN, IN 1906
AFTER KERMODE, 1907

Fig. 84. Ruined leacht, 'St. Patrick's Chair', Marown, Isle of Mann.

open-air altars, in themselves copying other and older forms which once did stand directly above graves? Are the leachta in any sense parallel to the Mediterranean altar-graves? This is a puzzle to which, in the absence of excavation, I can give no answer.

We turn now to the typology of the altar within the church, and it is convenient to treat this under three headings; fixed altars, their altar frontals, and portable altars.

The classic study of the fixed altar is the two-volume *Der Christliche Altar,*[2] by Fr. Joseph Braun, S.J.—a monumental and essential work. Braun distinguished four kinds of fixed altar. These are *Tischaltar* (table altar); *Kastenaltar,* best rendered as 'hollow altar'; *Blockaltar,* or solid altar; and lastly *Sarcophagaltar,* which is the equivalent of our medieval and post-medieval

---

[1] Wade-Evans 1944, 217.   [2] Publ.: Munich, 1924.

altar-tomb and thus falls outwith the scope of this book. Early Christian Britain and Ireland provide some evidence for the table altar, and rather more for a type which would fall between Braun's *Kasten-altar* (a completely hollow stone chest) and *Blockaltar* (a solid masonry altar which can possess a small internal hollow for relics). I propose to call this insular form 'cavity altar'.

Virtually nothing is known, directly, of the forms assumed by altars in fourth-, fifth-, and sixth-century Britain and Ireland. That there were altars is hardly in doubt, both by analogy with the Church elsewhere, or from such references as those contained[1] in Patrick's writings. If any kind of legacy from Roman times be considered, the most simple form of table altar is that (Fig. 85) with a single, central, leg or prop, like a small pedestal table.[2] Some of the fifth/sixth-century stone table altars of the Marseilles region[3] were of this kind, and it is a design which could have reached western Britain by the early sixth century. Is it possible that an odd passage in Cogitosus' *Life of Brigit* refers to one such, albeit in wood?

I translate from the Bollandists' text;[4] the passage describes Brigit's escape from a betrothal arranged by her parents, and her subsequent vows made before a bishop.

She, in the presence of God and the bishop, kneeling humbly at the altar and offering her virginal self to the Almighty Lord, touched the wooden base (*fundamentum*) on which the altar was supported. This piece of wood, as if in memory of this former act of virtue, remains still green and undecayed up to the present day, as if it had never been cut down and stripped of its bark, but might still be flourishing, fixed in its roots; and to this day it drives out the languors and the ills of the faithful.

Apart from the passing reference to *virtue*, made inherent in the wood by Brigit's touch, we must note that the altar had a wider fame. In the medieval Notes, attached to the late eighth-century

---

[1] e.g. *Confessio*, cap. 59; 'Canons', sect. 5.
[2] Braun's *mit einzigen Stütze* group.
[3] Ward Perkins 1938, 80–2, fig. 1, pl. xxix.
[4] *Acta Sanctorum*, tom. Feb. i (1658), *Vita II*, cap. i (p. 136).

Félire Óengus[1] under 2 February, we are told that 'Thus was
Brigit, with the foot of the altar in her hand,[2] and seven churches
were burnt with that foot in one of them, and it was not burnt,
sed servata est per gratiam Brigidae'. In plain English, this means that
the 'foot' (*cos*) of the altar was subsequently housed in no less than
seven churches, one after another; all of them were burnt down,

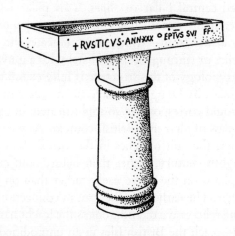

NARBONNE : 'RUSTICUS' ALTAR (A.D. 456)
AFTER HÉLÉNA, AND WARD PERKINS.

FIG. 85.

but the 'foot', preserved through Brigit's grace, survived on every
occasion.

We can dismiss this supposed miracle as a plagiarism from some
such source as Bede's account[3] of the reused and incombustible
beam against which Aidan had leant when he was dying; but the
single wooden pillar, as I think we must interpret it, of the altar
at which Brigit made her vows was clearly a famous relic, perhaps
a short length of stripped tree-trunk originally fixed into a hole
in the ground.

On a much smaller scale it might be suggested that in the phase
2 timber oratory on Ardwall Isle, an intermediate post-socket[4]

[1] Stokes 1905, 66-7.   [2] *ocus cos na haltoire ina laim.*
[3] H.E. iii. 17.   [4] Cf. plan, Thomas 1967b, fig. 26 (post-hole *D*).

half-way along the line of the putative east wall, and just inside the line of this wall, could also indicate a single-prop wooden altar on these lines.

In the Mediterranean, half-way between the table altar and the hollow altar (*Kastenaltar*), there can be found a form which, regardless of whether or not it has four corner-legs, possesses a greatly enlarged central pillar or *stipes*. This pillar is square in plan, hollow, contains various relics, and has an opening (*confessio*)—normally at the front—which communicates directly with the enclosed relics or (through a short shaft) with a grave beneath the altar.[1] The typology of this structure is fully examined, in the context of Salonae, by Dyggve.[2] I have never encountered anything which would correspond to so sophisticated, but essentially transitional, a class of altar in a British context. As we saw in the previous chapter, the cult of relics in the British Isles attains its peak in the eighth century, rather than before, and exhibits an occidental emphasis on the grave itself, rather than on the grave as part of an altar. The earlier Mediterranean connection between the altar and the relic-grave did not, unless the leacht has anything to do with this, reach the British Isles in an unmodified form. In Britain the rite of burial *beside* the altar, a practice overwhelmingly witnessed by the surviving literary sources, takes the place of burial *beneath* the altar in the central provinces of the late Empire.

The insular version of the altar-cum-grave is what I have labelled 'the cavity altar'. Some of Braun's *Kastenaltar* examples show, by way of the vestigial legs or columns which are skeuomorphically modelled at the four vertical corners, that one line of development must have involved expansion of the hollow central pillar to fill the entire area below the *mensa*, or altar surface, engulfing any remaining legs at the four corners. One then has an altar with an internal hollow (for relics), the hollow being accessible from the front, the back, the sides, or even via the upper surface.

Owing to the ravages of time and man, very few relic-cavities in British or Irish altars have been published, or even noticed.

---

[1] Dyggve 1951, figs. v. 6, v. 13, v. 36, v. 38.   [2] Ibid., chap. v.

This is partly because such cavities, which are small (containing only representative relics) and are normally in the uppermost part of the altar, can hardly be discussed in relation to a type of structure of which one expects, today, to find only the base.

W. F. Wakeman, when visiting Inismurray in 1844, cleared out the top of the altar in Teach Molaise (one of the little churches within the monastic cashel). He found, so he writes,[1] 'a cist-like hollow within the centre of the altar', which contained a sliver of yew-wood, two inches long, but as the church was then still in use by the islanders, the bare existence of the cavity (as it was in 1844) is all one can cite.

St. Ninian's Isle (or Point), on Bute, a small developed cemetery at the end of a long sandy spit, is a developed cemetery with a chapel which, when excavated,[2] proved to possess quite a complicated altar. An extruding slab was found on the south side, perhaps acting as a 'kneeler' for pilgrims engaged in veneration. Despite its ruined state it seems likely that this altar held a box-like cavity, below the upper surface, on this south side (Fig. 86).

There is a similar example from the other end of Britain—at St. Helen's in the Isles of Scilly (Fig. 16). Here, in the tiny eighth-century chapel of St. Ilid or *Elidius*, a little three-sided relic cavity, defined by small granite slabs, can be seen inserted in the south side of the altar.[3]

Our fourth instance comes again from Ardwall Isle, this time from the stone chapel of phase 3 (eighth century). The altar (Fig. 87) was first encountered, below the turf, as a patch of local shell-sand, which proved to have been the filling of the upper part of a hollow altar.[4] Total excavation revealed some interesting constructional facets. Though one might describe the altar as a composite, hollow, masonry structure, it had originally four long thin stone corner-posts, flanking the corners of the main body, helping to support the (missing) *mensa*, and thus only partly vestigial.[5] The cavity, which was central rather than lateral, cannot have been easily accessible, as one supposes the cavities to have been in the cases of St. Ninian's (Bute) and St. Helen's (Scilly).

[1] Wakeman 1893, 42.   [2] Aitken 1955.   [3] O'Neil 1964.
[4] Thomas 1967b, pl. xv, 136–8.   [5] Ibid. fig. 25.

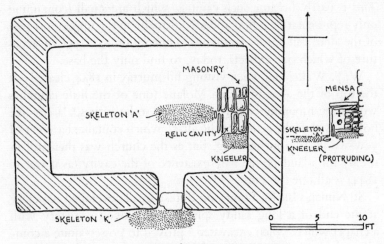

CHAPEL AT ST. NINIAN'S POINT, BUTE
PLAN AND SUGGESTED RECONSTRUCTION (SOUTH ELEVATION)
AFTER W.G. AITKEN TRANS. BUTE N.H.S XIV (1955)

FIG. 86.

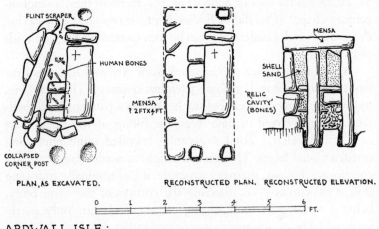

ARDWALL ISLE:
ALTAR OF PHASE III STONE CHAPEL (8TH CENTURY)

FIG. 87.

It was backed by a thick flat slab forming part of the altar's back wall,[1] on whose surface a tiny primary cross was incised, and this slab may have been a phase 1 or phase 2 grave-marker reused in this new role in phase 3. The cavity contained a jumble of very fragmentary bones; though at first it was thought, with some likelihood, that these would refer to a single individual, expert examination by the late Dr. W. R. M. Morton of Belfast[2] showed that portions of no less than five skeletons were present, the remains of two being darker in colour than the rest and therefore from an earlier burial-phase than the others. The most economical explanation is that these are all parts of disturbed burials—a male and female from phase 1 (the primary Ardwall Isle cemetery) and three males from phase 2 (that of the timber oratory and its aligned graves)—which the builders of the phase 3 stone chapel had turned up in making the foundations, and which (treated as early Christian *sancti*) they chose to enshrine in the new altar.

We may just dispose here of Father Braun's other early class, the *Blockaltar*, the altar made from a single stone. Such are not common anywhere, and it may well be that Christians regarded them as having pagan connotations, the Roman *ara* being of course of this form. One does, in Britain, encounter Roman sculptural material and worked stone reused in early churches.[3] There are fonts of this sort; the font in St. Andrew's, Wroxeter, is a large Roman capital,[4] and at St. John's Lee, by Hexham, Bede's 'cemetery of St. Michael',[5] there is a rather primitive and shallow font made from a Roman *ara*. Not surprisingly, there seems to be no British instance of a Roman altar having been converted to, or incorporated in, a Christian one.

The *mensa*, the ordinary Latin word for a table, is the universal label for the consecrated flat upper surface of the altar, which must cover the whole area of the altar and any relics enshrined below or within, and which (following a series of early councils and decrees) was generally of stone by the seventh and eighth

---

[1] Thomas 1967b, 158, fig. 32 (no. 14).   [2] Ibid. 184–5.
[3] Cf. St. Andrew, Corbridge—Taylor and Taylor 1965, i. 172–6.
[4] Ibid. ii. 694–5, with refs.
[5] See p. 83.

centuries.[1] Both the absolute size, and the relative proportions, of altars in first-millenium Britain are topics of great complexity, and it seems improbable that size and length/breadth ratio can be employed as any kind of chronological guide before the eleventh century.[2] A very preliminary search through plans showing early Christian altars in the British Isles implies that absolute length is not really dependent upon the internal breadth of a church or chapel, and that a length/breadth ratio, in plan, of two to one was relatively common. This is notably so in the Isle of Mann, where the altars of the majority of keeill chapels average out at 4 feet by 2 feet; and also in pre-Norman Cornwall, where the chapels themselves follow a localized module which, unlike that found in early Christian Ireland, is based on the double-square.[3] To what extent this may have been influenced by popular literary models is of course a matter of opinion, but one recalls that in Adomnán's guide to the Holy Land, *De Locis Sanctis* (composed about 680), the great golden altar of Hagia Sophia in Byzantium is described as being two cubits in length and one in breadth.[4]

Similarly, the question of the five consecration crosses incised on the surface of the mensa—one in the centre, one at each corner —is one which really deserves much longer analysis that we can give here. The crosses, the physical witness of that episcopal consecration also requisite in the case of early cemeteries and churches, appear in one guise or another at a primary stage of Christian architecture; and again there were numerous edicts, decisions, and pontificals regulating them. The absence of any such crosses from what might otherwise be regarded, from context or position, as a certain instance of a mensa could mean that one is dealing with the top of a subsidiary altar, on which a consecrated portable altar, or smaller slab with the five crosses, would rest centrally during any celebration of the Mass. Again, if the top of an altar has any form of central hollow or recess, and lacks consecration

---

[1] Cf. *H.E.* ii. 14 (stone altar in timber church at *Campodonum*, an unlocated place in the Dewsbury area).

[2] Thomas 1967a, chap. 7.   [3] Thomas 1968b.

[4] iii. 3 (ed. Meehan 1958, 111).

crosses, it can be regarded as a surface with a cavity for relics, sealed by a *cippus* or duly consecrated slab, like a portable altar, which fits into this recess flush with the surrounding surface. These are, however, both later developments, which one would be surprised to encounter at all in British churches of the pre-Viking age.

The vertical, front, aspect of an altar can assume a number of forms; in the case of table altars there may be no tangible 'front element' at all. From aesthetic motives, and perhaps by analogy with richer domestic furnishing, a textile screen is found covering the front of many early altars—notably table altars—in paintings and mosaics.[1] This could be independently fixed to some vertical frame, or it could be a continuation, hanging down to the floor, of a cloth laid upon the mensa. In medieval usage this gave rise to the term *antependium* ('front hanging'), but the older word 'frontal', Latin *frontale*, can be employed here regardless of the material.

It is probable that by the seventh century a number of Irish and North British churches possessed linen frontals, even though this can only be inferred. Benedict Biscop and Wilfrid, fitting out their late seventh-century Northumbrian churches, could have introduced such. The Irish *Penitential of Cummean*,[2] which stems from a late seventh-century original, cites penalties for those who spill wine from the chalice on to the altar linen. The letters of St Boniface, full of incidental and revealing detail, include one written about 720 to a friend who was abbess of the Minster at Thanet;[3] 'By the same messenger, I send you (a sum of money) and an altar cloth . . .'.

By about 700, it is feasible on the Continent to detect the two major classes into which the ornaments of altar frontals tend to fall—the central Cross, with stylized flanking panels, and Christ in Majesty (sometimes superimposed on a vestigial or subordinate cross-motif). Both these designs find analogies in the decoration of the longer sides of sarcophagi of late Classical type, and the

---

[1] Cf. Van der Meer and Mohrmann 1958, fig. 446 (S. Vitale, Ravenna).
[2] Bieler 1963a, 5–7 (date), 130.
[3] Talbot 1954, 70.

predominance of one or other in any area must be in part due to local taste, or to the influence of some very notable model.

The major European stone frontals are all comparatively late. The magnificent panel now in S. Martino, Cividale del Friuli, commissioned by the Lombard king Ratchis in memory of his father Pemmo, is closely dated to the years 734–7.[1] Nearly 5 feet long, and a single slab, it must be regarded as the work of a Lombardic craftsman. Christ, the cross confined to His halo, is flanked by seraphs with eye-studded wings, and is shown in a mandorla (or oval frame), surrounded by four angels; the composition may be copied from an ivory. The most striking instance of the other series, the central Cross, is the massive gold repoussé-work frontal in Sant' Ambrogio, Milan, made by the goldsmith Volvinio in the period 824–59.[2] A little over 7 feet long, the composition is best appreciated in diagram form,[3] which emphasizes the three important elements combined here by the first half of the ninth century. These are: one, the central enlarged cross (here incorporated in an oval mandorla-like frame, of the kind so often found in connection with the other Christ-in-Majesty series); two, the division of the field into three panels, a central one and symmetrical flankers; and three, but still important, the clear rectilinear borders which stress the divisions between these three constituent panels.

The British Isles contain seven possible stone frontals, only two of which have ever been discussed in this context at all. Two of them are of the central Christ series, and the other five of the central equal-armed Cross series. Despite their comparatively crude execution, all are worthy of note, and without prejudice as to their absolute dates, all are pre-Norman (one, which will be omitted here, only just so).[4]

The most widely known is the so-called 'Calf of Man Crucifixion', found many years on the Calf, the islet off the foot of the

[1] Schaffran 1941, 104–6; for the type of ivory, Beckwith 1963, pls. 96 and 109.

[2] Bibliography—*Karl der Grosse: Werk und Wirkung* (Charlemagne Exhibition catalogue), Aachen, 1965, 377–9.

[3] Ibid. 378.

[4] The *Leuuit* stone, Camborne; *CIIC* ii. 177, no. 1044, and Thomas 1967a, 71–2, 81–5, 90, 101–9.

Isle of Mann, and assumed to be from a lost chapel site.[1] Carved on slate in low relief, the design, when drawn out, permits a reconstructed panel about 17 inches across and about 30 inches high. Now the normal height of an altar (from the ground level to the surface of the mensa) is between 36 and 39 inches—this is, I think, ultimately related to the level at which the human forearm, bent horizontally, can best function—and if one allows a few inches for the footing and for the thickness of a slate mensa, 30 inches is an acceptable height for an altar frontal panel. In dating this piece, whose true nature was pointed out by Dr. Ralegh Radford,[2] attention has naturally been focused on the openwork plaque from Athlone, probably a book cover, which is generally agreed to belong to the eighth century.[3] In fact some details—the hair, the posture of the lower left-hand figure, and Christ's forked beard—are better matched by the unlocated and similar gilt-bronze plaque in the National Museum of Ireland, Dublin (often called 'the N.M.D. plaque'),[4] which is also eighth or early ninth century in date. I would, however, look closely at the curious 'lobate' treatment of Christ's lower robes, a striking instance of a convention recently discussed by Werckmeister,[5] and adequately represented also in the St. Matthew figure from the Northumbrian Echternach Gospels of around 700.[6] A date in the first half of the eighth century is thus a possibility.

The other centralized Christ frontal is even closer to the crucifixion scene, and probably a little later in date, but occurs in an area where some measure of Irish influence is possible. It comes from Phillack, in west Cornwall, is made from local granite, and is now terribly worn;[7] associable perhaps with some pre-Norman chapel within the developed cemetery now occupied by Phillack parish church,[8] it is today built into a modern lych-gate (Fig. 88). In publishing this stone, details of which were first revealed by flashlight photography, I argued that Christ is depicted in a tunic and that this, with the disposition of the figure, is best matched by

[1] Kermode 1907, pl. xvi (no. 50); Megaw 1958.
[2] Megaw 1958, 237.
[3] Henry 1940, 122, 138, 188; Henry 1963, pl. 46.
[4] Henry 1964, pl. 8. [5] Werckmeister 1963. [6] Ibid., pl. xxvii.
[7] Thomas 1961. [8] Thomas 1962.

the relief figure on the lintel from some lost church, found at Dunshaughlin, co. Meath, and vaguely assigned to the eighth century.[1] It would not surprise me if the Phillack stone was somewhat later. It is reconstructable as being 31 inches high and 24 inches

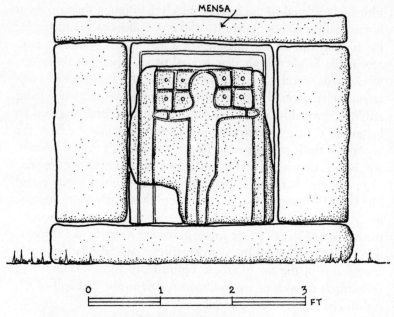

PHILLACK, CORNWALL
RECONSTRUCTION OF ALTAR, SHOWING FRONTAL PANEL

Fig. 88. The Phillack crucifixion panel: stippled area indicates surviving stone, now built into modern lych-gate.

wide, which (as with the Calf of Man panel) argues the original existence of two separate blind flanking-panels to constitute the whole frontal.

The frontals with central crosses begin with a large panel from Flotta, in Orkney.[2] This is 5 feet 5 inches long, 32 inches high, and 3 inches thick. The (undressed) reverse face has two deep

---

[1] Henry 1940, 92; but see *Lagore Report* (*PRIA* 53 C (1950), 16).
[2] *ECMS* III. 23, fig. 19.

vertical grooves, set 3 inches in from the lateral edges, which must have received the forward ends of missing sidepieces in Orkney flag (Fig. 89). The technique is loosely akin to that of the Jedburgh 'grooved shrine',[1] and does not resemble that of the Shetland corner-post shrines at all; it is so simple a device that not much

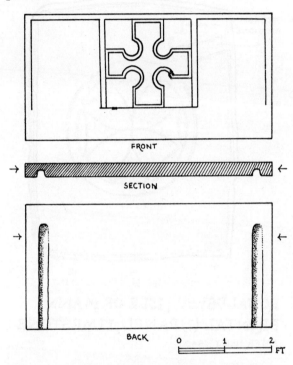

FRONT

SECTION

BACK

0 1 2 FT

FRONTAL PANEL, FLOTTA, ORKNEY

FIG. 89.

typological weight can be attached to it, and it does not suffice in my view to indicate that the Flotta stone is a shrine-panel. On the ornamented face the central 'arm-pit' cross is also found on a small slab from the Broch of Burrian, Orkney, with an ogam inscription unlikely to be any older than the eighth century;[2] and the interlace ornament has an exact counterpart on a ninth-century

---

[1] See p. 149.   [2] *ECMS* III, 24, fig. 20.

cross at Ireton in Cumberland.[1] A date in the later eighth century would therefore fit the Flotta frontal.

There are no less than three panels in the Isle of Mann, in addition to the Calf of Man crucifixion panel. Two of them—one from

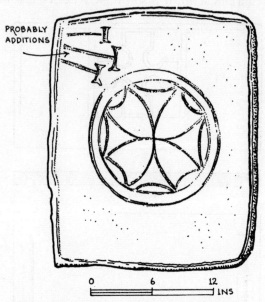

PROBABLY
ADDITIONS

0   6   12
|_____|_____| INS

RONALDSWAY, ISLE OF MANN
FRONTAL (?) PANEL, LIMESTONE
AFTER NEELY, 1940.

FIG. 90.

Kirk Maughold,[2] and the other (Fig. 90) from Ronaldsway[3]—are rough or fragmentary and need not detain us, although they are indeed best explained as the remains of central frontal panels with centralized cross ornament. The last (Fig. 91) is of considerable interest. It is also broken, and was found in the keeill called Ballavarkish, in the parish of Bride.[4] It is only $1\frac{1}{2}$ inches

---

[1] Collingwood, W. G. 1927, 83, 111, 119.
[2] Kermode 1907, 110, pl. ix (no. 23).   [3] *MAS* vi. 29–30.
[4] Kermode 1912, 69–74, figs. 15 and 16; *MAS* iii. 32–5, figs. 30 and 31.

thick, and can be reconstructed as 26½ inches wide and 30 inches high, with the rectilinear bordering so common on these frontals. The type of cross—the arm-pits have become inserted discs, and there is a ring-head between the parallel-sided arms—is consistent with a date centred on 800 or so.

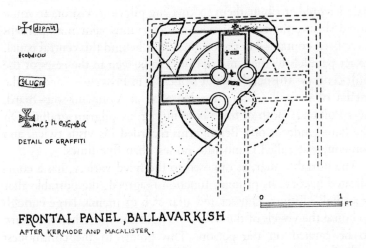

DETAIL OF GRAFFITI

FRONTAL PANEL, BALLAVARKISH
AFTER KERMODE AND MACALISTER.

FIG. 91.

Unique in the British series is the group of names and tiny graffiti scratched on this panel; they are clustered around the upper part, suggesting that the slab stood upright. The names, in insular minuscule and written by various hands, have been variously read by Kermode[1] and Macalister.[2] They include LUGNI, or LUGRI; DIPRUI; CONDILICI; a name beginning with M, followed by the word SCRIBA ('scribe'); and a name starting BRE-. Macalister thought he could read an ogam LAGUBERI. Kermode could offer no parallel to the appearance of the names as such, and Macalister, for once at a loss, wrote 'These look like the work of ancient schoolboys'. These are, however, mostly personal names in Old Irish, two of them (Lugn- and Condilic-) being elsewhere

[1] Kermode 1907, Kermode 1912 (as previous note).
[2] *CIIC* ii. 191, no. 1068.

attested;[1] all are preceded on the stone by tiny little initial or superscript crosses; and all seem to end in Old Irish o-stem genitives or, more probably, Latinized genitives or datives (final -i). The names thus imply, through this case-ending and through the initial crosses, 'Pray for . . .' or 'Pray for the soul of . . .'; and as they have clearly been scratched at intervals, near the top of the slab, I would attribute them to kneeling pilgrims, visitors to some noted shrine, the relics of whose anonymous saint may perhaps have been contained in the original altar behind this central panel. Exact parallels to these inscriptions can be seen in the cases of the fifth-century 'Rusticus' altar at Minerve, in Provence;[2] and on the mensa of a sixth-century marble altar at Vouneuil-sous-Biard, near Poitiers.[3] Both of these bear numerous pilgrim graffiti. On the latter, indeed, one Berengarius recorded his visits twice, and someone else called Gunbaldus no less than five times.

The portable altar, as opposed to the fixed variety, has a complicated history. Its primary function is agreed; the portable altar is a small, distinct, consecrated altar-slab or mensa, large enough to house the vessels of the Mass, and light enough when necessary to be carried on the person. This points to the commonest early function, the provision of a mensa for the service of the Mass in those places not possessing fixed consecrated altars of their own.

Since portable altars *are* both small and portable, and (unlike full-size fixed altars) could come to be regarded as the property of individual clerics, it is inevitable that among the few surviving instances from the earliest days of Christianity the majority prove to have become relics, by association, of their first owners. As relics, these little altars—in wood, in base or precious stone— were enclosed in ornamental cases, on the analogy of the larger self-shaped shrines we mentioned earlier.[4] Such cases might enclose, next to the original altar, some other representative relic

[1] *Lugne*—Anderson and Anderson 1961, index (573), s.n.; *Lugna*—Stokes 1905, 431; *CIIC* ii, nos. 588 and 944; *Conduilig*, as gen. of *Cu-Duilig* ('Hound of Duilech'), Stokes 1905, 243.

[2] De Fleury 1883, pl. xliii; Ward Perkins 1938, fig. 1; Durliat 1957, fig. 1.

[3] De Fleury 1883, pl. xliv.

[4] See p. 165.

of a major saint or apostle, whose name or symbol could then be displayed on the container.

It is reasonable to think that this elaboration took place after the death of the first owner, and perhaps later, after his corporeal enshrinement, if the portable altar was first interred with its owner. There is some evidence on this score. The altar-shrines, or encased portable altars, exhibit one or both faces of the actual altar, in part or wholly, so that pilgrims could see and touch the actual altar; conceivably, too, *brandea* could be infused with sanctity if they were brought into contact with such a peculiarly sacred, if non-corporeal, relic. What we do not know—and I see no easy way to ascertain this—is whether portable altars when first in use by their original possessors could somehow have incorporated *brandea* as well—stuck to the underside, or, with wooden portable altars, inserted in some lateral slot.

Bede's accounts[1] of the rural ministries of such men as Aidan and Cuthbert offer many instances of pastoral duties carried out in hill-country, or recently converted areas, where permanent chapels with fixed altars can hardly then have been established. The square satchels or wallets shown hanging around the necks of clerics on (for instance) the decorated panel from the Papil shrine[2] are usually interpreted as book-satchels, but we should not over-look the chance that they really held portable altars. A panel on the ninth-century cross-shaft at Old Kilcullen, co. Clare,[3] portrays a cleric surrounded by what we might call 'the tools of the trade' (Fig. 92); we can recognize his bell, an umbrella-like crozier, and a square object by his head which may represent his portable altar.

The oldest British portable altar—one of the most famous any-where—is the small oak rectangle[4] which once belonged to St. Cuthbert (Fig. 93). It was encased in silver as an associated relic, probably at the first *translatio* of 698. It was seen in 1104 and 1827, is now on display at Durham, and has been very fully studied.[5] One face of the original altar bears five little crosses, elongated

---

[1] Aidan—*H.E.* iii. 5, iii. 17; Cuthbert—Bede's *Prose Life of Cuthbert* (ed. Colgrave 1940), caps. 9 to 14.

[2] See p. 156.   [3] Henry 1965, pl. 73.

[4] It measures $4\frac{3}{4}$ in. by $5\frac{1}{4}$ in., and is $\frac{3}{4}$ in. thick.

[5] Radford, in Battiscombe 1956, 326–35.

FIG. 92. Ornamented relief panel on shaft of high cross at Old Kilcullen, co. Kildare; the square object between the man's head and the crozier handle may represent a portable altar.

ones of a kind certainly current in seventh-century Ireland, and, on a band, the words IN HONOREM S PETRV; the cult of the principal Apostle was widespread in Northumbria at this time. The silver shrine-case can be restored to show, on one side, the Apostle seated and holding a scroll, with the words S[AN]C[TV]S PETROS APOSTOLOS. The other face is incomplete; as restored, it has a silver roundel (set off-centre) which, stylistically, should be rather later than 698. Dr. Radford has made the interesting suggestion that it dates from about 875 to 900, when the community at Lindisfarne had migrated, carrying their relics, to Chester-le-Street in Durham.

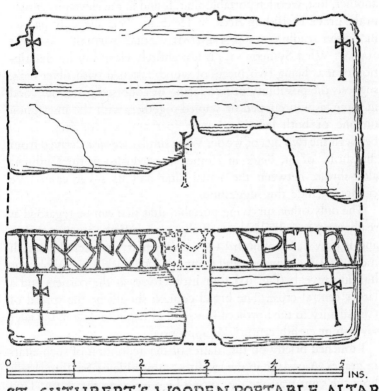

ST. CUTHBERT'S WOODEN PORTABLE ALTAR

AFTER RADFORD, 1956

FIG. 93.

What is not quite clear is whether this roundel can really be described as 'a repair', and whether the face to which it was added, now called 'the back', was originally an unbroken and imperforate face, like the present front with the picture of St. Peter. I would argue that this second face was, in a sense, the *front*; that it possessed an original circular aperture, a little off-centre, to allow physical contact with the relic[1] inside; and that it was later decided to seal this face entirely, perhaps to prevent pilgrims from trying to remove splinters from the wooden altar.

We can here compare Symeon of Durham's account[2] of another, lost, wooden portable altar, found in the eleventh century in the grave of Bishop Acca, at Hexham. This allegedly had an incription reading ALMAE TRINITATI . AGIAE SOPHIAE . SANCTAE MARIAE. What Symeon says is not entirely clear, but his description of it as being two pieces of wood, fastened with silver nails, suggests the possibility of two facing or addorsed plates of wood in some fashion clipped or stapled together, with the inscription on one or both faces, and with (perhaps) appropriate *brandea* between the two bits of wood. Were similar *brandea*, derived from the shrine of St. Peter in Rome, inserted also in the Cuthbert altar-shrine, between the actual altar and its silver case? We cannot exclude this suggestion.

The only other surviving portable altar that can be regarded as really early was dredged up off-shore near Wick some years ago, and is now in Edinburgh.[3] Of a sedimentary or altered stone, it measures 4 by $3\frac{1}{2}$ inches, and is about $\frac{3}{4}$ inch thick. Careful oblique lighting reveals (Fig. 94) four little crosses at the corners and a larger central cross. The broad context should be the spread of Christianity to the northern Isles, and I imagine a date in the later seventh or eighth centuries is appropriate.

I touched briefly on the matter of the deposition of such altars in graves. A passage in the twelfth-century life of St. Illtud[4] tells how the saint was one day sitting by a cave, on the shore. Two men arrived in a boat, and arranged with Illtud to bury, within the cave, the body of another saint which they had brought with them. This duly happens, and the altar (by means of which various wonders are later performed) remains, in some mysterious fashion, suspended over the burial.

Now just as the many-coloured altars of a number of other

---

[1] Radford, loc. cit. 333, fig. 3.
[2] *Historia Regum*, s.a. 740 (*Rolls Series*, vol. 75, ii. 33).
[3] Nat. Mus. of Antiquities of Scotland, register no. KG 91.
[4] Wade-Evans 1944, 224-7.

Cornish and Welsh saints in medieval lives may truly represent memories of portable altars made from porphyry, or variegated limestones (these are not uncommon on the Continent), so this confused episode may hark back to a time when portable altars *were* customarily buried with their possessors. We cannot now

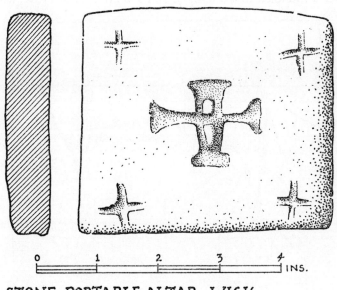

STONE PORTABLE ALTAR, WICK.

FIG. 94.

be sure whether, in the cases of Acca and Cuthbert, this took place, or whether the altars were separately preserved and added to the main group of relics at the time of enshrinement. An instance of altar-burial was, however, found in 1965 at Ardwall Isle.

The skeleton of an elderly and arthritic man was found lying on its side; the burial[1] belonged to phase 2, that of the seventh-century timber structure. By the side of the skeleton was a large piece of local slate, which appeared to have been displaced from an original position on the chest or rib-cage, and two or three

---

[1] Thomas 1967b, fig. 26, grave xxii.

other fragments, which joined the first, were found within a few inches. The pieces can be reconstructed (Fig. 95) to give a thin slate slab, about 1 foot square, with knife-point inscribing of the kind seen on the various little grave-markers of phase 2.[1] There are four outline crosses, one in each corner (one has been recut over a muddled first attempt), and a central linear cross, with a

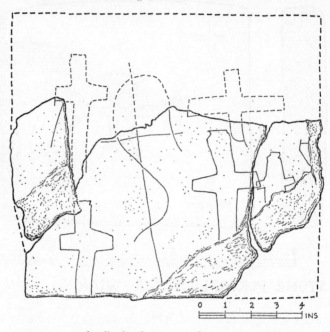

FIG. 95. Ardwall Isle: fragments of a stone portable altar.

kind of capital 'S' superimposed. On a small grave-marker,[2] found near the foot of this grave, there is another incised outline cross, in all respects identical to those in the four corners of the slate plaque.

I would not regard this as an actual portable altar, used in life by this person (probably a local cleric) and buried with him; it is a little too large and much too hastily worked. The identity in shape of its corner crosses and the cross on his grave-marker shows, I think, that both stone were *ad hoc* carvings made specifically for his burial. This is a 'burial' portable altar; the analogies

[1] Thomas 1967b, 161–3, fig. 34.   [2] Ibid. 161, fig. 33 (no. 19).

are surely with the finds from the medieval burials at Whithorn, of the successive bishops interred below the east end of the Priory church. These graves contained objects of great value and interest, but also—and this occurs elsewhere—worthless 'burial' chalices made of lead.[1]

There are many other portable altars recorded in the British Isles, and despite oft-repeated statements about their great rarity,

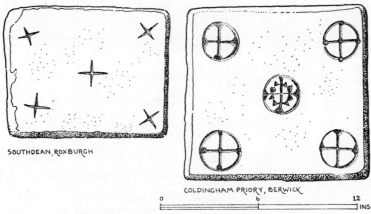

SOUTHDEAN, ROXBURGH

COLDINGHAM PRIORY, BERWICK

0   6   12 INS

MEDIAEVAL PORTABLE ALTARS FROM SCOTLAND

FIG. 96.

it is hard to escape the conclusion that there may be anything up to a hundred or more of them—some in private hands, the vast majority in ecclesiastical ownership, occasionally replaced in the centres of modern altars or communion-tables. The average size of these would be about 10 by 14 inches, and none is anywhere near as small as St. Cuthbert's, or the little stone altar from Wick. In some cases the form of the five crosses—cross crosslets, crosses patées, crosses as rosettes—betrays the medieval date; in others the context, for example recovery in the ruins of a church known to have been founded in the twelfth century, tells us this (Fig. 96). These altars have two functions; as portable altars, the objects for which we find indults noted in episcopal registers, and as the

[1] For medieval funerary chalices, see Westlake 1921.

sigillae, or 'fixed' portable altars, which (having been consecrated) are placed in the centre of a large unconsecrated altar-top, sealing a shallow cavity (Fig. 97) in which representative relics lie. Both these usages refer to medieval rather than Early Christian practice.

I conclude with a word about the associated communion vessels. Setting aside for the moment the attractive contention, advanced

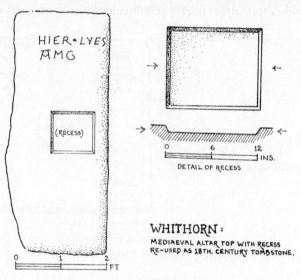

HIER•LYES
ÆMG

(RECESS)

0   6   12
￼ INS.
DETAIL OF RECESS

WHITHORN:
MEDIAEVAL ALTAR TOP WITH RECESS
RE-USED AS 18TH. CENTURY TOMBSTONE.

0   1   2
￼ FT

FIG. 97.

(See also Pl. VIII.)

by Mgr. David McRoberts,[1] that the silver bowls found in the St. Ninian's Isle (Shetland) hoard are some form of eighth-century communion vessel, we have only a very few early insular chalices. The series begins with the tiny gilt-bronze chalice, a bare 2½ inches high, found in the last century at Hexham.[2] This (Fig. 98) could well be seventh-century Northumbrian workmanship, and is the kind of thing we suppose Cuthbert would have carried, its base easily accommodated on his little portable altar. Typologically this is related, at some remove, to the great Tassilokelch,[3] an

[1] McRoberts 1961.
[2] Cripps 1893; Wilson, D. M., and Blunt 1961, pl. xxviii. a.
[3] Haseloff 1951.

elaborate piece 10½ inches high, made between 777 and 778 at the order of Duke Tassilo, and presented to the monastery at Kremsmunster in Austria, still its home; its maker was, it is now thought, either a Briton or someone trained in a British workshop. Not entirely dissimilar, though plainer, is the fine silver chalice found (with a hoard of largely ecclesiastical objects) at Trewhiddle, in

FIG. 98. The little Hexham chalice (actual size).

Cornwall, preserved in the British Museum, and dateable to about 872–5. It is 5 inches high and, as Mr. David Wilson's analysis shows,[1] of composite form.

The greatest of all insular chalices, and one of the great treasures of insular craftsmanship, is the famous chalice from Ardagh, co. Limerick.[2] It was found quite by chance, in 1868, in a rath or little fort, by a peasant digging potatoes, and was part of a hoard which also contained a much simpler bronze vessel (perhaps a form of chalice) and four silver brooches.

[1] Wilson, D. M., and Blunt 1961; diagram, 89, fig. 3.
[2] Henry 1965, 107–8.

The Ardagh Chalice, which is regarded as early eighth century in date, is 7 inches high, composed of a near-hemispherical bowl whose rim is surmounted by a hollow moulding. Two ornate semi-circular handles are riveted on. The foot is a domed plate with a flat sole-plate, padded with lead, and joined to the bowl through a short cylindrical stem with upper and lower expansions, which contains the iron joining-bolt. A round gilt-bronze cap hides the top of the bolt, and its bottom is concealed by an elaborately mounted crystal. Basically, this is a silver chalice, with gold (solid and filigree) and enamel embellishments.

This bald description cannot conceal the mastery of highly detailed workmanship and design, or the sheer visual impact, of this magnificent ritual object. The nature of most of the archaeological material that we have been considering in this book, however novel or interesting to the student of the Christian past, has not been particularly exciting from an aesthetic viewpoint; it is no bad thing to remind ourselves that from the mud and uncertainty of rustic Christianity in those early days, such jewels as the Ardagh Chalice could arise.

7. *The Relevance of Literary Sources*

IN THE EARLY SUMMER OF 1862, my great-great-grandfather Charles Thomas, who was by then the leading figure in the Cornish mining world, was in Norway; he was making a tour of inspection of certain mining ventures for the Scandinavian government. Writing to his wife from Trondhjeim on 20 May, he describes a carriage-trip of the previous day, which had taken him over a mountain road well above 3,000 feet. He remarks:

The fir will not grow here, a few stunted birch are to be seen, but the little unpretending juniper, apparently too delicate to endure exposure, is found here by the millions—not growing so luxuriantly as in the valleys but existing and, it seems, bearing some fruit in this wild region. How can this be? The juniper never raises his head very high, and here not more than two or three feet; and just before the piercing winds begin to blow at the approach of winter, God, the Father of All, casts a thick mantle of snow over these delicate ones. So this lowly plant is kept alive in the midst of winter, when the more aspiring fir withers and dies.

After this piece of factual botanical reportage we get the exegesis.

So have I often seen that the humble follower of Christ, who makes no show in the Church, and who so far esteems others better than himself as to make him diffident and reserved in making professions, lives and bears fruit in the time of trial, persecution, and death; while the bold professor, who is ever striving to rear his head above his fellow-Christians, and to make a show in this world—such have I often seen to wither and quail before the wintry blast of trial, opposition, affliction, and temptation.

I choose this passage because it illustrates, in essence, the same pitfalls that beset us if we take most early religious writings at their face value, and attempt from them to construct the same view of the past that we can obtain from archaeology, or epigraphy, or numismatics. In the first place, though my great-great-grandfather was a prominent Methodist and a local preacher, I am sure he did not talk like this. His letter is not a letter in the sense in which words like 'Dear Mother, Please send my football boots; it snowed yesterday; love from John' constitute direct inter-personal correspondence. It is an artificial literary production, perhaps the source of a later sermon or so, and indeed a very similar letter written from Prussia has a note at the end, 'Tell Alice to put this in my desk, when all have seen it'. In the second place, the exegesis is a piece of metaphorical writing, equating the humble juniper with the meek of this world, and the aspiring fir with the bold and proud; it could be based on other types of vegetation in other natural circumstances, and it tells us more about the writer than it does about winter conditions and their consequences. In the third place—and this is important—neither the literary flourishes, nor the Christian moral, conceal the straightforward existence (in May of 1862, at a place called Gumdal, and at about 3,500 feet O.D.) of this particular botanical eco-system, which may, for all I know, have since disappeared under a state forest or a hydro-electric scheme.

How much, then, of the early religious literature of the British Isles can we safely regard as bearing any direct relationship to the material circumstances at the time of writing; that is, to real people who did or said real things, and to what we would like to think of as history? What *is* this literature?

Apart from Bede's *Ecclesiastical History of the English Nation*, completed in 731, and in a class by itself, any light we might wish to shed on the development of Christianity (or on those manifold Christian details which we otherwise seek to recover through archaeological exercises) must be drawn almost wholly from the surviving literature of the Church itself. Since both literacy, and Latin, the most common medium of expression, are at this period virtually the prerogatives of the Church, nearly all the literature that has come down to us is directly or indirectly ecclesiastical. The only important exceptions, which are in Old Irish, Old

Welsh, and Old English, are the fragments of 'heroic' secular literature like the *Táin bó Cúalnge*, the *Gododdin*, and the oldest Anglo-Saxon poetry. On the religious side, there are, it is true, various Rules, Penitentials, Canons, Martyrologies, and specialized works like Adomnán's *De Locis Sanctis*, but the majority of the sources, for our purpose, fall within a specific literary form, the 'Life' or *Vita* of a given saint. In the preceding chapters we have had occasion to draw upon such Lives, and even more upon Bede's great history, to illuminate obscure material points, and to help define certain problems of interpretation which present, or future, archaeological research may solve. On what principles, if any, should we approach this literature?

This is and always will be an exceptionally difficult mode of inquiry, though the progress of contemporary scholarship does make it easier for each new generation of students. Of course it is perfectly true, if trite, to point out that the strict canons of historical research must, at all times, be observed. The original text, the *ipsissima verba* of the writer, whether in Latin or one of the Celtic languages, must be sought—by comparison of all surviving redactions, by palaeographic inquiries, and by linguistic analysis. Not the least of our debts to Professor Bieler is that which we owe him for establishing a reliable Patrician corpus. This is the first stage. Any translation of (say) a Latin text must take account, not of what a word may have meant to Cicero, or in William the Conqueror's time, but of what it meant to the writer and his readers. Was the author thinking in Latin, and if so, what sort of Latin? or was he (like Adomnán) probably thinking in archaic Irish and translating into Latin as he wrote? In the case of a Life, we ask ourselves, not only what it is about, but when was it written? How much is from first-hand knowledge, or second-hand, or just hearsay? How much has been plagiarized (and this bears no pejorative sense in this context) from other or older Lives, or from the Bible, and under what circumstances? Finally we get to the crux; what portions can safely be regarded as factual descriptions of real things or actual events, at a given place and at a fixed time, and is there independent confirmation from archaeological work or some other, secular, historical source?

Beyond this (possibly rather discouraging) list of obstacles between the early Christian writer and the modern reader, there is yet another problem; that of *function*. Just as the letter from Norway which we read a little earlier is not a straightforward letter in the modern sense, so the Life of a saint is not a biography, in the sense in which we would apply this label to Harold Nicolson's *George V*, or Philip Magnus's *Kitchener*. The hagiographer's aims, often very fully stated in a prologue, may embrace the justification of the subject's sainthood, the listing of as many miracles as possible including post-mortem ones (as an advertisement for the efficacy of a shrine), the comparison of miracles in the subject's life with miracles in the Gospels, and the establishment of the spiritual supremacy of a given church or diocese or monastic foundation. Only a few advanced literary productions, like Eddius's Life of Bishop Wilfrid, which tries to provide an apologia for a stormy career that had a political as well as a religious side, begin to offer the flavour of modern biography.

In using any Life, then, as a source of evidence for the material culture of its locality and period, one must first adjust one's mind to all these points. I would add another, which is far more subjective. It is necessary to assess the personality of the writer, if the style permits this, in order to detect whether he is obsessed with any particular aspect of his subject's career, whether he acknowledges sources, whether or not he bothers to disguise plagiarisms by altering minor details, and the manner in which he keeps glancing over his shoulder at his potential readers. Very few people indeed—Bede is a noteworthy exception, once one gets to know his works intimately—survive this kind of investigation of their roles as reliable purveyors of fact.

Every student of this period will have a slightly different approach to this problem.[1] The criteria which I have found helpful as an archaeologist, and which (I believe) minimize the risks inherent in using these particular sources to support or to confirm archaeological inferences, are roughly as follows. In the age of developed monasticism, Bede's writings, and all Lives written

---

[1] There are very few useful works on pure interpretation as such; but cf. Grosjean 1945, Delehaye 1955, Morris 1966, Morris 1968a.

before about 800, must always outweigh any Lives of pre-ninth-century saints written at a later date, even if such later Lives may incorporate lost material of the 'period of incomprehension', which we will look at below. In cases where more than one Life exists of a given saint, the one written by a contemporary, or failing that, by a member of the saint's own foundation, is in general to be preferred. On this score, the anonymous Life of Cuthbert should, as factual evidence for Cuthbert's material background, be preferred to Bede's rather more polished Prose Life; and apart from the eye-witness account of Cuthbert's death which Bede alone includes, this is a perfectly tenable position. The anonymous writer was almost certainly a pious Lindisfarne brother; Bede wrote (rather as one might engage Sir Arthur Bryant to write the life of Mahatma Gandhi) at the request of the Lindisfarne community, who wanted a stylish production to accompany the post-698 shrine of the saint.

Again, whether or not one chooses privately to credit all or any of the miracles recounted in these Lives, it must be realized that miracles which obviously imitate those occurring in known earlier Lives (especially of leading monastic founders), or miracles of the New Testament 'water into wine' class, all have to be excluded as irrelevant to history. Other miracles—and this falls within the scope of the religious phenomenologist like Eliade rather than the historian's field—probably reflect local, non-Christian, folk-lore; or (if more subtle) can contain a symbolism derived from local pagan beliefs. O. G. S. Crawford many years ago isolated[1] some aspects of Adomnán's *Life of Columba* as falling within this class. One must also be careful not to confuse *miracles*, which involve the participation or the cure or the confusion of humans, with *visions*, which are events requiring no more than a human observer. We realize now that such accounts of celestial visions, of fire in the skies, or of bands of angels, accompanying a birth, a death, or some tremendous event, cannot be dismissed as pious embroidery. These are garbled descriptions, sometimes surprisingly circumstantial, of such phenomena as meteoric showers, comets, and (this is particularly relevant in

[1] Crawford 1934b.

North Britain) auroral displays. Dr. Justin Schove's study[1] shows how the ascertainable chronology of such celestial events (which follow approximately the eleven-year sunspot cycle) can be correlated, tentatively, with visions reported on such occasions as the birth of Columba in 521/522.

When these reservations have been made, the most important residue in the early Lives, for the archaeologist, is the whole range of incidental details. A saint, on his way to visit a sick chieftain, is delayed when the wheel of his chariot falls off; the lynch-pin is lost, with no substitute anywhere available, but the wheel is replaced and stays put until the party reaches the chieftain's stronghold (where a few miraculous words effect a speedy cure of some otherwise terminal ailment). This is an imaginary episode put together from three or four existing ones. If a Life, containing this, were written within half a century or so of the subject's death, it would in no sense constitute evidence for a miraculous cure—the chieftain might have been ill-wished, or in the grip of hysterical paralysis—but it *would* be evidence, and the more unusual the detail the stronger the likelihood of this being so, for the use at that time of a vehicle whose wheels were free-turning on a fixed axis. Only vehicles of this kind employ lynch-pins and only someone familiar with this device would mention one. There is no reason for the hagiographer to invent the purely incidental detail. The settings of most incidents and miracles can, with near-contemporary Lives, be taken to reflect settings familiar to the writer and his audience, or their immediate forebears. Unfamiliar and imaginary settings would detract from the probability of stories which in themselves, even to an audience of unlettered rustics, are bound to demand a certain suspension of disbelief. Members of agricultural communities know very well that bulls do not normally give milk, that cows which have been butchered and disjointed do not reassemble themselves and walk around, and that once a haystack is alight it takes more than a shower of rain to quench it.

Let us now illustrate these principles from one of the earliest Lives, that of St. Brigit or Brigid, of Kildare, thought to have been

[1] Schove 1950.

written about 650 to 675 by someone whose name, or perhaps nickname, was *Cogitosus*.[1] It is a medium-length life in passable Latin; there is no modern critical text as yet, and I shall work here from the so-called *Vita Secunda*, or second version of the Life, published by the Society of Bollandists in 1658.[2] Oddly, there is also no modern English translation. This hurdle—and the belief (expressed most fully by R. A. S. Macalister)[3] that 'Brigit' was a pagan fire-goddess with a sacred oak (the *daur* of Cell Daro, Kildare) tended by a band of vestal virgins, the community being transformed into a Christian convent in the sixth century, with the abbess as a personification of Brigit—has not on the whole encouraged either archaeologists or historians to take a deeper interest in the Life. As a picture of central Irish material culture in the mid-seventh century, it constitutes a greatly underrated record.

The only passage which is quite often cited, most recently by Professor Bieler,[4] is that which describes a large timber church at Kildare, either in Brigit's time or more feasibly in the time of Cogitosus. Here I have to join issue with certain historians, notably Professor Donald Bullough;[5] I do not agree that the description is an imaginary one, or that the substance has been plagiarized from Adomnán's slightly earlier account[6] of the Holy Sepulchre church at Jerusalem (if so, the phraseology of Cogitosus may well owe something to *De Locis Sanctis* at this point). The great church is not, in itself, either improbable or beyond the technological resources of the period. The successive timber halls at Castle Dore,[7] and at Doon Hill, Dunbar,[8] the variety of structures at Yeavering,[9] to say nothing of slightly smaller communal buildings on Iona,[10] all bear this out. The most cogent evidence, to me, of its existence is to be found in the following passage. It

[1] Kenney 1929, 359–60, with refs.

[2] *Acta Sanctorum*, tom. Feb. I (1658).

[3] e.g. in his *The Archaeology of Ireland* (2nd (rev.) edn., 1949), 365–6, and in other minor writings.

[4] Bieler 1963b, 28.   [5] Bullough 1965, 31–3.

[6] *De Locis Sanctis*, i. 2, i. 3. Is this really earlier than *Vita Brigidae*?

[7] Radford 1951b.   [8] See note, *Med. Arch.* 10 (1966), 175–6.

[9] See note, *Med. Arch.* 1 (1957), 148–9.

[10] These are defined by large sill-beam trenches and post-sockets.

refers to some alterations being carried out in this supposedly
fictitious church, and I give a carefully literal translation.[1]

When the workmen were hanging the old door on its pivots, in the
north doorway—the one through which St. Brigit herself used to
enter the church—it transpired that it was now impossible to close up
the whole of this new, restored, doorway. About a quarter of the area
yawned open. If an additional piece, equal in size to this quarter, had
been fastened to the top of the new door, it would, then, have been
possible to fill the new doorway properly.

While the workmen were standing around arguing whether to make
an entirely new, and larger door, or whether to fit a plank on to the
top of the old door (which would then fill its frame completely), that
clever old man we mentioned before, who was the outstanding craftsman of all the Irish, said: 'We ought really to pray to the Lord, as well
as to St. Brigit, during this coming night, so that she herself may tell
us what we should do tomorrow about this business'. So he himself
passed the whole of that night next to the shrine of St. Brigit, praying.
And the next morning, all these prayers have been offered, the old
door was shoved into position in its pivot, and it filled the whole of
the door-frame! The frame was in no way smaller than it had previously
been, nor could anyone detect any addition to the door itself. Thus
St. Brigit in person must have somehow increased the height of the
old door, so that it would now fit the doorway without leaving any
extra space at all (except, of course, when this door was opened,
inwards, so as to give access into the church). This was acclaimed as
a miracle brought about by Divine Providence in the eyes of everyone,
the very doorway and the door obviously making this clear.

Now it is impossible to regard this story, all the details of which
(including the men standing around arguing) breathe verisimili-
tude, as having anything to do with an imaginary church. The
mention of a north doorway, one of several doorways, would
alone imply something very much more substantial than the
normal seventh-century church (even a *tech mór*), in which a
single west door would be the rule.[2] The door was a planking
door, and it was hung by having two vertical extensions on the
'hinge' side which fitted into, and then turned in, corresponding

---

[1] *Vita Secunda*, cap. 8.   [2] Cf. plans in Leask 1955.

pivot-holes in the lintel and sill.[1] An advanced version of this might involve special socketed pivot-stones, set into the lintel and sill to minimize uneven wear.[2] I get the impression that, whether or not St. Brigit ever used this particular doorway, Cogitosus is not only describing something he has seen, and can see, but something which is pointed out to pilgrims as a witness to Brigit's sanctity.

Contrast this doorway story with the following, which relates to St. Brigit's childhood.[3]

For instance, as she grew older, she was sent by her mother to the dairy, in order to make butter from the churned milk of the cows. As all the other women normally undertook this task, Brigit herself could just as well do it, too; and, like the others, see to this produce of the cows when times were slack. But this generous-hearted and lovely-souled girl, wanting to obey God's prompting rather than human commands, gave the milk, and distributed the butter, to beggars and passers-by. So, when the time came, as usual, for the girls to hand over what they had produced in the dairy, Brigit's turn arrived. Her fellow dairymaids showed what they had done; and then Brigit was asked if she, too, had carried out her work. She, trembling with fear of her mother (because she had nothing to show, having given everything away to the beggars) and indeed expecting no mercy, none the less opened her heart to God, the inextinguishable flame of whose faith had been kindled for ever in her heart. In a split second, God, hearing the voice and the prayers of the girl, came to her rescue, through the power of His Divine kindliness (because He is the judge of what is appropriate in such cases); and, because of His Divine trust in this girl, He caused all the butter to be restored in abundance. So, wonderful as this may seem, in the moment after her prayer, the most holy virgin was able to reveal that her task *had* been completed. Not only was there nothing left for her to do, but she had apparently done far more than all the other girls.

And when this miracle (of all the work she had done) had been duly noticed by everybody, they gave praise to God, who had brought it about; and they were awestruck that such a power of faith had been implanted in her young heart.

[1] Peate 1940, 210–12.   [2] Mitchell 1880, 126–8, figs. 94 to 96.
[3] *Vita Secunda*, cap. 1.

In this second story, we find a motif (the miraculous restoration *in toto* of something which has been consumed, lost, or removed, in order to save the hero from disgrace) which is common to a number of Lives.[1] All it tells us about real circumstances is that in early Irish society the women churned milk into butter, which is something we know already.

I want to give just one more extract[2] from this Life of Brigit, one which does have a lot of meaning for the archaeologist, and one on which no comment appears to have been passed.

Now the prior (*praepositus*) of this most great and famous monastery of St. Brigit . . . sent the workmen and masons to look for a rock, from which they could hack out a millstone, in a certain area where they ought to be able to find something suitable. The men, without any previous knowledge of the route, and climbing up a difficult path, pressed onwards to the peak of a rocky mountain; and there they chose a great stone, on the very top of the highest point. Hacking away at it from all sides to produce a circular shape, they converted this rock into a perforated millstone. But when the prior of the monastery (for whom these workmen now sent) arrived at the foot of the mount with a team of oxen, he could neither push nor pull the beasts up it, on account of the difficulty of the ascent. Indeed, he himself was scarcely able, with a few of his followers, to get up this very steep path.

The prior and the workmen were wondering how on earth they would get the millstone down from the top of this precipitous peak, since it was clear that the yoked oxen, carrying such a burden, would be quite unable to negotiate the path. Some of the workmen, in despair, left the millstone and went down the mountain again, regarding their work in hacking it out as having been wasted. But the prior, after carefully thinking to himself, and after some further discussion with the men who stayed behind, said; 'Boys, the only way we can do this is for you to heave this millstone up smartly, and then to push it over the edge of the mountain, in the name and belief of our most revered St. Brigit; because we ourselves, whatever we try, are not going to be able to get this millstone down such a rocky slope—unless, that is, St. Brigit, to whom nothing is impossible (since all things are possible to

[1] An obvious case—Adomnán, *Vit. Col.* ii. 16 (milk, spilt from pail, is miraculously restored when C. blesses it; a careless youth thus saved from censure).

[2] *Vita Secunda*, cap. 8.

him who believes) can in some way get it for us to a place where we can bring the oxen to drag it away'.

So, firm in their faith, the men heaved the stone up, and over on to the slope. Gradually it started to roll down the side of the mountain, here by-passing boulders, there bounding right over them, and trundling across boggy patches on which neither men nor oxen would have been able to stand, until it was near the foot of the mountain. It rolled well in front of the awestruck onlookers, and it came to a halt, without being broken in any way, on the level ground where the team of oxen stood waiting. And from there, the oxen drew it all the way back to the mill, and it was carefully fitted to the nether millstone.

We might almost call this an early case of the luck of the Irish. I have no doubt at all that this is a true story, and I imagine it was very exciting to see the stone rolling down one of the Red Hills near Kildare (which are sandstone, with near-by limestones and grits, all suitable for milling). What this story gives us (and the actual miraculous element is negligible) is a factual account of the production of a millstone in the seventh century. Certain upland outcrops are known to be suitable quarries; I have myself seen such partially shaped, but undetached, medieval millstones on the high granite moors of west Cornwall; the not uncommon Scottish place-names such as *Cnoc nam bradhan* ('Hill of the querns')[1] point to other sites, and there are some examples from Argyll. In the admirable Mid-Argyll Survey,[2] a number of millstone and quern quarries are listed, and at two of these—one near Dun Cragach,[3] one near Ormsary[4]—millstones respectively 4 feet 9 inches and 4 feet 3 inches across have been marked out and for some reason not detached. It was a stone of this nature, not just a quern, that the Kildare workmen were after; another story in the same Life, which I omit here, shows that the mill was a full-sized water-powered mill, probably of the vertical spindle variety where the water is fed on to horizontal vanes below the stones.[5]

It would be repetitious to give further instances, and what has gone before will suffice to draw attention to the archaeological

---

[1] There are two hillocks so named on Iona alone.
[2] Campbell and Sandeman 1964. [3] Ibid. 102, no. 615.
[4] Ibid. 102, no. 616. [5] See Cruden 1947; Lucas 1953; Fahy 1956.

richness of this particular Life. Nor, of course, is this the only Life so distinguished; it merely happens to be one that comparatively few people have read.

Our tardiness in appreciating the value of insular hagiography as a source for the material culture of the period, both secular and ecclesiastical, follows from the sad fact that hardly any students of these Lives—I except, in his day, Bishop Reeves[1]—have been familiar with the archaeology of the same era, admittedly an increasingly complex archaeology; and hardly any archaeologists have bothered to examine, in the necessary detail, all the insular Lives of the pre-Norse age. A notable instance of what happens through this failure to collate the evidence is provided in the case of Iona. All editors of Adomnán's *Life of Columba*—Reeves, J. T. Fowler, the Andersons, and as a commentator W. F. Skene— tried to locate the 'monastery' (by which they seem to have meant different things, anyhow) some distance north of the present Abbey. There are some very explicit clues in the Life which at once suggest that this is improbable, and the most preliminary field-work confirms this. When I began to excavate there a decade ago, I deliberately chose the south end, close to the Abbey, because the experience gained in some years of field-work in far less promising ground enabled me (as it had enabled O. G. S. Crawford)[2] to locate almost the whole course of the *vallum*; because what is known of comparable sites elsewhere makes it clear that Columba's monastic complex could not conceivably have occupied the entire eleven acres within the *vallum* enclosure, and because earlier discoveries in and around the Abbey (then in ruins) indicated that the very position of the Abbey was dictated by the position of previous churches and their surrounding huts and communal buildings. Despite the discouraging havoc caused by centuries of medieval and modern activity, this hypothesis proved to be the case, and I was able to locate at least some of the monastic structures.

Again, the extent of Ciarán's great monastery at Clonmacnois

---

[1] Cf. Reeves 1857—described, rightly, by Bullough (1965, 115) as '. . . one of the outstanding achievements of nineteenth century Insular scholarship'.

[2] Crawford 1933, 455 (sketch map).

is often assumed to have been, more or less, the extent of the modern central walled area. This, in addition to acting as a cemetery, contains the 'cathedral', all the subsidiary churches, and the Round Tower.[1] The Life of Ciarán (who lived in the sixth century) is, as we have it, a much later redaction (perhaps as late as 800, or later), and contains a good deal of archaeological material.[2] It describes, by implication and occasionally explicitly, the arrangements of a monastic foundation which must closely have resembled that on Iona. I find it hard to credit that the modern enceinte, which contains less than three acres in extent, is of irregular shape, and is not bounded by any bank or ditch, could represent the sixth-century enclosure. The traces that I have shown earlier, in Fig. 7, represent what I believe to be stretches of the original *vallum*, pertaining of course to a much larger enclosed tract.

We have, so far, discussed mainly Irish matters. In the restricted context of the earliest Christian archaeology of North Britain, what are the sources we should examine? Without now venturing into such deep waters as the origin and development of the *Vita* as a literary genre,[3] I would class them in two distinct groups.

The first, and from the viewpoint of present-day interpretation certainly the easier for the student to handle, is that of the Northumbrian writings of the late seventh and early eighth centuries. The common link is that all these works were produced by clerics within the greater Northumbrian monasteries—Lindisfarne, Whitby, Monkwearmouth-Jarrow, and (probably) Ripon— and can be called 'Northumbrian', either by subject, or by authorship, or by both.

The works, which are listed in more detail as an appendix to this chapter (p. 225), are, with their approximate dates; *The Life of St. Cuthbert*, by a monk of Lindisfarne (698–705); *The Life of (Pope) St. Gregory the Great*, by a monk of Whitby (704–14); *The Life of Bishop Wilfrid*, by Eddius Stephanus (710–20); *The History of Abbots Ceolfrid and Cynefrid*, by a monk of Monkwearmouth-Jarrow (716–20?); *The Lives of the Holy Abbots of Wearmouth and*

[1] Macalister 1909, frontispiece (plan).   [2] Kenney 1929, 378–80.
[3] Bullough 1965, espec. 17–22 and nn.

Jarrow, by the Venerable Bede (716 or later); *The Prose Life of St. Cuthbert*, by the Venerable Bede (720?); and *The Ecclesiastical History of the English Nation*, by the Venerable Bede (completed in 731 or (?) 732). This is the hard core of any inquiry. We must face the fact that, both as repositories of reliable information and as literary productions, these Northumbrian writings stand well above any comparable group of Lives produced by the Irish church, and its subsidiary regions. The *Life of Wilfrid*, that moody and magnificent prelate, is (as J. F. Webb so rightly states)[1] our first, full-length, insular historical biography.

Closely allied to this school, and often containing archaeological information of no less worth, are those other Lives which describe the spread of the Faith in relatively factual terms, from Northumbria to other English provinces, and then on to the Germanic areas of the Continent. Instances are Felix's *Life of St. Guthlac*,[2] Willibald's *Life of St. Boniface*,[3] Alcuin's *Life of St. Willibrord*,[4] and (despite its earlier date and Irish connections) I would add here Jonas's *Life of St. Columbanus*.[5]

The second group is made up of the whole corpus of Atlantic British writings, and this must commence with some works which are really offshoots of the late Classical tradition; the *Confessio* and *Epistola* of Patrick in the fifth century,[6] the *De Excidio* of Gildas in the sixth,[7] and one might include, as a late exercise, the important *Miracula Nynie Episcopi* poem of the eighth.[8] Less directly than the Northumbrian Lives, these sources can, in the hands of skilled commentators, be made to yield information about the early insular church; they must be made to do so, because in the initial centuries they are almost all that we possess. The 'Atlantic' Vitae commence with Cogitosus' *Life of St. Brigit*, which we have already noticed; Adomnán's *Life of Columba*,

---

[1] Webb 1965, 29.   [2] Ed. Colgrave 1956—composed 730–40.

[3] Ed. (transl.); Talbot 1954, 25–62—composed 755–68.

[4] Ed. (transl.); Talbot 1954, 3–22—composed 782(?)–96(?).

[5] Composed *circa* 640; for MSS., edd., transl., etc., see Kenney 1929, 203–4; cf. also Walker 1957.

[6] Text and comm.; Bieler 1952. Transl. Bieler 1953.

[7] Cf. here Davies 1968, and refs. therein.

[8] Ed. and transl. MacQueen W. 1960.

written about 695;[1] and two very difficult works, Muir-chú's *Life of Patrick* and Tírechán's *Memoir of Patrick*, both composed prior to 700.[2] There must, naturally, have been many other Lives composed during the eighth century, and some others during the seventh, which we now have only in the form of much later recensions, often hardly detectable as unitary productions. From North Britain we could point to two such hypothetical works, the lost (Celtic) *Vita* of St. Ninian, the subject of prolonged study by Professor John MacQueen,[3] and a lost Life of St. Kentigern or Mungo (of Glasgow), the nature and very language of which are matters of some dispute.[4]

This western British material is much more difficult to grasp, and to use as evidence, either for the rise of Christianity or for details of the Christian archaeology of the region. Some items, like the Voyage of St. Brendan, which is primarily an essay in the secular idiom known as *imram*, the heroic magical sea-quest for an unknown land;[5] or the so-called Tripartite Life of St. Patrick,[6] which largely ignores the unities of time, space, and action; these are at the moment still, as literature, within the provinces of the philologist and the student of folklore. Again, neither the *De Excidio* of Gildas, nor the rather later History ascribed to Nennius, can be described as 'history' in quite the sense in which one would apply this term to Bede's work. Years of the most intensive study are, only now, beginning to explain what these exceptionally tortuous writings mean and (in the case of Nennius) what disparate earlier sources underlie them.

I referred earlier to something I called 'the period of incomprehension'. To explain this, one might begin by emphasizing that a great many lives of saints which are quoted in anthologies, or popularized in loose translations, stem, not from the early Christian era, but from the full Middle Ages. Those delightful tales of saints who play with birds and animals do occasionally

[1] On the wider setting of this Life, see Bullough 1965.
[2] See Kenney 1929, 329–35.
[3] MacQueen J. 1961; MacQueen J. 1962.
[4] MacQueen J. 1955; Jackson 1958.
[5] Most recent transl.; Webb 1965, 33–68 (refs., ibid. 29).
[6] Stokes 1887; cf. Kenney 1929, 342–4.

appear in the earlier Lives (of Cuthbert and Columba, for example), but the anecdotes normally employed to illustrate this *rapport* are drawn from medieval sources. There are four major compilations, three of Irish provenance and one of Welsh. The Irish collections are the *Codex Insulensis*, probably of the very early fourteenth century, largely edited by Charles Plummer;[1] the *Codex Salmanticensis*, edited recently by Professor Heist for the Bollandists;[2] and the *Codex Kilkenniensis*, not yet edited.[3] These are in Latin, and the editions are not translated; what is to some extent the counterpart in Irish of the *Codex Insulensis* group, almost all from a seventeenth-century corpus, has been edited by Charles Plummer,[4] in this case with English versions. The non-Irish collection is that known by various titles—'Lives of the Cambro-British Saints', or *Vitae Sanctorum Britanniae*—and is contained in British Museum MS. Cotton Vespasian A. xiv. The Lives are in Latin, and have been edited by A. W. Wade-Evans, with English translations.[5] There are other, later, collections—John of Tynemouth's, Colgan's, Lives in the Book of Lismore, Nicholas Roscarrock's, etc.—and indeed a continuous if thin tradition right up to the days of Sabine Baring-Gould. In addition, there are some individual works, including Jocelin's *Life of Kentigern*,[6] Ailred's *Life of Ninian*,[7] and many isolated later Lives of Irish and English (*sensu* late Anglo-Saxon) origin. As we are discussing North Britain, I have omitted any mention of a smaller sequence of Lives that more particularly concern south and west Wales, Cornwall, and Brittany. This begins with the very early *Life of St. Samson*, and continues, through such works as the three ninth-century Breton *Lives* of Winwaloe, Malo, and Paul, to a series of medieval Cornish and Breton productions—most of them edited, in part or in whole, and amply discussed, by the late Canon Doble and several Breton hagiologists.

By and large there is a gap between the early Lives and the late ones, a trough between two crests in the course of insular

---

[1] Plummer 1910; cf. Kenney 1929, 306–7.
[2] Heist 1965; cf. Kenney 1929, 304–5.　　　　[3] Kenney 1929, 305–6.
[4] Plummer 1922. See also Plummer 1910.
[5] Wade-Evans 1944.　　　[6] Forbes 1874, 27–120.　　　[7] Ibid. 1–26.

hagiographical output. Historically, this corresponds to the disruption of much of Church life in the ninth to eleventh centuries associated with the political and social troubles of various wars, invasions, and the long period of Norse settlement. The revival, under Norman-French stimulus, and in the milieu of the great monastic foundations, naturally took account of the pre-Norse patron saints, whose names and ascriptions had seldom been lost entirely, even if the shrines and relics had been despoiled in Viking raids. But whether in every case a relevant early Life still existed in any written form; and if so, whether it could still be read; and in that case, whether all the aspects of the earlier life and its surroundings could still be understood, are questions to which one would be reluctant in most cases to give a firm answer.

I have come to suspect that, between roughly the eighth and the twelfth centuries, the physical nature of the Church in the British Isles, and of most of its tangible and visible accessories, had changed radically; so radically that Lives like those in the *Codex Salmanticensis* (written in the fourteenth century from lives composed two centuries before) or those in Cotton Vespasian A. xiv, compiled somewhere on the Welsh border about 1200, cannot possibly be employed as quarries for archaeological evidence concerning the earliest stages of insular Christianity. This does not imply that they may not, with all due caution, be employed in the secondary capacity of supporting evidence, particularly if we can assume that given episodes (aspects of which we can perhaps reconstruct through our *ex post facto* knowledge) are derived from earlier, lost, Lives—Lives, that is, in which such episodes, doubtless phrased in a different way, would have possessed more direct relevance. It does mean that, over the centuries, knowledge of the exact nature and function of certain monuments, or sites, or objects, germane only to the earliest Christian world, had been lost, or preserved only in a very garbled tradition; when such things appear, fleetingly, in medieval sources, the writer can no longer fully comprehend that which he purports to describe, because a 'period of incomprehension' stands between him and the original.

We can find an instance in Jocelin's twelfth-century *Life of Kentigern*. In chapter 41 there is a mention[1] of a cemetery in the church of the Holy Trinity at Glasgow, a cemetery with a high stone cross, and a church in which Kentigern's episcopal chair was placed. Chapter 9 gives us[2] the earlier history of this cemetery. There was a holy old man called *Fregus* (probably for 'Fergus') who died at a place known as Kernach. There follows a purely folkloristic episode, in which the body of Fregus is placed on a wain drawn by two untamed bulls—this is a mode of locative divination—and the bulls mysteriously draw the wain to *Cathures*, which is later called *Glascu* (i.e. Glasgow). The wain came to a halt near a certain cemetery which had, long before this, been consecrated by St. Ninian. Kentigern now buried Fregus in this cemetery, in which, oddly, no other man had yet lain. This was the first burial in that place, where afterwards very many bodies were peacefully lain to rest; the tomb of the man of God, Fregus, is to the present time encircled by a delicious density of overhanging trees, etc., etc.

Jocelin, a monk of Furness, clearly could not resolve the paradox of a cemetery consecrated long before by Ninian, which, however, contained no burials and was thus not yet really a cemetery, with his need to depict Fregus's burial as the first grave within it, and his desire to record the divine choice of Cathures, or Glasgow, as the seat of Kentigern's bishopric—a choice manifested through the action of the dumb beasts which drew the cart with Fregus's body. We cannot entirely unravel this ourselves, but in the lost *Vita* from which this story almost certainly derives, I think the stress would have been on the supposed continuity; from the cemetery, founded and consecrated by Ninian in person (probably an enclosed cemetery of the sixth century, in fact), to the subsequent Holy Trinity Church founded as his seat by Kentigern. This, in the lost *Vita*, would give a perfectly recognizable picture of a developed cemetery enriched by its first stone church, to which it was desired to attach the prestige of an original, a Ninianic, consecration. The grave of Fregus, who may have been a local saint, is less likely to have been the first burial than to have

---

[1] Forbes 1874, 110.   [2] Ibid. 50–2.

been the first *special* burial—that is, with a leacht, or an enclosure, or some above-ground element. Jocelin's statement that Fregus's tomb is 'encircled by trees' (that is, in some fashion distinguished from the other graves) must reflect this. The lesson for us is that, by Jocelin's day, the distinction between a martyrial grave and any other grave, and the general concept of the primary enclosed cemetery and its subsequent development, were surely both meaningless ideas.

The Life of the Welsh saint, Cadoc, contained in Cotton Vespasian A. xiv,[1] itself embodies what seem to be the *acta* of some separate person who worked in the south of Scotland; the interpolated portions are not too difficult to sort out. On one occasion, this other saint (whom we must also call 'Cadoc'), founds a monastery somewhere in Strathclyde, and a *vallum* is dug around it. In this proceeding the saint unearths the collar-bone (*os collare*) of an ancient hero of incredible stature, a collar-bone so vast that a champion on horseback could ride through it. The next day, a phantasm in the shape of a giant appears, as it might be to claim his bone, and reveals himself as Caw of Prydyn, a bygone local tyrant.

Despite the late date and unidentified source, this tale may go back to a real happening, the recovery of the jawbones of a whale in alluvial gravels in the course of constructing a ditch. Those who know the 'Jawbone Arch' in the Meadows, in Edinburgh, will realize that the man-on-horseback statement is no exaggeration. Remains of whales, stranded in remote prehistory, are known from the upper reaches of the Forth,[2] and could presumably occur in the upper Clyde; the suggestion that the monastery in question was at Cambuslang thus gains force. But, in the same Life, another story[3] of a jeering rustic who insists on peering through a hole in in a wall (a hole through which kings have put their hands to swear oaths) at three of Cadoc's disciples, resting in marble sarcophagi in the porticus or side-aisle of a church, looks like a muddle; I imagine the original tale dealt with an unbeliever or pagan, who

---

[1] Wade-Evans 1944, 81–5 (*Vita Cadoci*, cap. 26).
[2] Clark 1952, 62–72, fig. 30 (map).
[3] Wade-Evans 1944, 101 (cap. 36).

impiously tried to look through a *confessio* in the side or end of a stone shrine, laughed at what he saw, and was blinded by divine anger as a result.

The difficulties inherent in any attempt to reconstruct details of early Christian practice, or monuments, from sources composed many centuries after the pre-Viking age are not of course insuperable, and the foregoing examples show how (with caution) one can make inspired guesses at what the lost original source may have contained. In discussing the nature, rather than the details, of the miracle stories about St. Ninian given in the eighth-century poem *Miracula Nynie Episcopi*, John MacQueen has compared some of them with the later versions contained in Ailred's twelfth-century Life of the saint.[1] His point, and it is a valuable one, is that the stories have features which seem to belong to the Celtic hagiographical tradition, rather than to a Northumbrian Anglian one, and that, after the eighth century, miracle stories of this or any type were not likely to be added to a Galloway tradition. I have tried to apply the same sort of approach to the poem from an archaeological angle, and have argued[2] that, despite the florid prose and the rhetorical form of the poem (which was written for Alcuin of York by one of his pupils), it does contain, at second-hand, traces of specific references to an early church at Whithorn, a stone shrine with Ninian's remains near the altar, the retreat at Physgyll cave, and a monastic establishment of seventh-, rather than fifth-century, character.

I want to conclude this chapter by drawing attention to a form of documentary evidence—the study of place-names—that we have already mentioned here and there in specific lines of inquiry. In the context of insular Christianity, this is a field of research which has hardly been explored. Yet some years of preliminary work, with which we associate the names of Dr. W. F. H. Nicolaisen and Professor Melville Richards, suggest that the whole question of Irish settlement in Britain—religious missions as well as secular colonization—might be greatly clarified, and can now only be further defined, through the construction of linguistic distribution-maps. The underlying assumption is that, in a

[1] MacQueen J. 1962, espec. 122.   [2] Thomas 1966a, 110–12.

linguistically mixed population—south-west Wales in the post-Roman period, for instance, with both native Welsh and a substantial Irish colony—many simple terms (like the names for basic features; 'road', 'hill', 'church') can be borrowed from one language into another, sometimes with a change of emphasis or slight variation of meaning. These loans can survive for a very long time, both as creative place-name elements and as individual nouns in common speech. A striking and obvious parallel can be drawn from South Africa, with its background of Dutch and English bilingualism; we think of words like *dorp* and *veld*. The latter, going back to the ordinary Dutch linguistic and semantic equivalent of our 'field', has now come to mean what we might call 'plain' or 'prairie'; and it does so both as a productive place-name factor and as a common South African noun used alike by speakers of English and Afrikaans.

In post-Roman Britain, we therefore think of Melville Richards's discussion of a Pembrokeshire dialect word *meid(i)r* or *moydir*, meaning 'lane', which would be the equivalent of the Irish *bóthar* 'road' (though not immediately derived from it).[1] I have now studied the history and detailed distribution of a Cornish word *bounder*, also meaning 'lane';[2] and I think that it represents an Old Cornish **bou-en*, a hypothetical collective or generic noun meaning something like 'store cattle, beef cattle', and a common suffix *tir*, 'land'. The Irish *bóthar*, O'Rahilly suggested, goes back to **bou-itro*, 'cow passage';[3] if the Welsh *meid(i)r*, *moydir*, is for an older **moudr*, **boudr*, a still earlier form involving **bou* (or **beu*) and *tir*, as in Cornwall, seems possible. The point is that in both south-west Wales and Cornwall (where *bounder* has a confined spread) a specific sort of lane[4] may have come into being in areas of Irish settlement (Fig. 99), because it represents a facet of field lay-out or farm-system which was

[1] Richards 1962, 128–34; cf. Richards 1960.
[2] Forthcoming, probably in *CA*.
[3] O'Rahilly, T. F., in *Celtica* i (1946), 160.
[4] The meanings include 'that part of a farm not enclosed into fields but used as access, (*a*) from the farm to a highway, (*b*) from one farm to another on a linked tenement, (*c*) from a farm's townplace to its open grazing, (*d*) from one area of grazing to another, and (*e*) from one lot of buildings to another'.

introduced or popularized by Irish settlers.[1] In both areas the word evolved for this lane or cow-passage was based on Irish usage.

A clearer example is the Scottish distribution (Fig. 100) of the word *Slew-*, as a place-name prefix. In Ireland, *sliabh* has the usual meaning 'high mountain', but in Scotland the use is far less emphatic, and can be determined, as Nicolaisen has shown,[2] more as

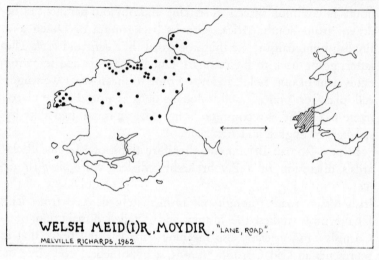

WELSH MEID(I)R, MOYDIR, "LANE, ROAD".
MELVILLE RICHARDS, 1962

FIG. 99.

'hill' or 'elevated moorland'. Scottish *Slew-* is rare, except for a dense grouping in the Rinns of Galloway, and, as Nicolaisen writes,[3] '. . . a very large part of the distribution pattern is . . . astonishingly identical with that of the early Dalriadic settlement of Gaelic speakers in Scotland from the middle of the fifth century onward'.

Now there is no doubt that this line of inquiry could be extended to wholly ecclesiastical terms. The first target should be the Old Irish *cell, cill,* in the sense of 'developed enclosed cemetery'. Where this occurs outside Ireland—for instance, in the Isle of Man, where it has also become a noun (keeill)—its pattern should be examined most closely in the light of the pre-800 spread of

[1] Cf. Crampton 1967.   [2] Nicolaisen 1965.   [3] Ibid. 102.

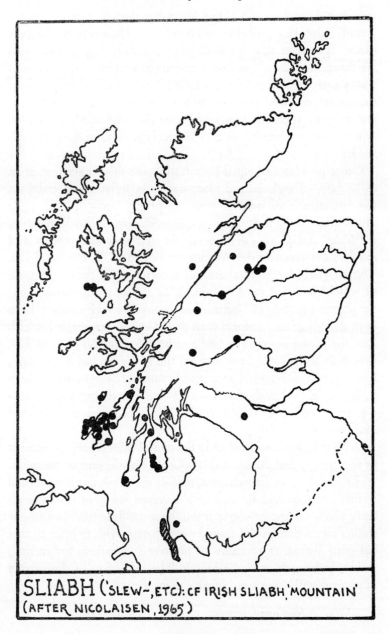

SLIABH ('SLEW-',ETC): CF IRISH SLIABH 'MOUNTAIN'
(AFTER NICOLAISEN, 1965)

FIG. 100.

Irish based monasticism. MacQueen has shown,[1] with great in-
genuity, that this probably holds true for Galloway in the pre-
Norse age. One day we shall have the full map of names in
*kil-*throughout Scotland, distinguishing those names which arose at
a very early stage from those which are post-800 and follow from
the spread of Gaelic into areas of former British, or mixed British
and English, speech. On a lesser scale this may apply to Wales,
where a limited number of ecclesiastical names with the prefix *cil-*
are known.

Other problems of equal importance are; the occurrence, at an
early date, of ecclesiastical place-names in Ireland, especially on
the eastern side of Ireland, with the prefix *Land-* or *Lann-*; the
distribution of the northern element *andóit, annait*; the distribution
in Wales and Cornwall respectively of the words *merthyr* and
merther; the recently defined question of the Old English **ecles,*
'church' (British **eglēs*), alone and in compounds, the distribution
of which[2] is not at once susceptible to any obvious explanation;
the precise meaning of Cornish *lan*, the use of which seems to have
been slightly more complex than that of the corresponding Welsh
llan; the possibility that an Old and Middle Cornish element *kil-,*
kyl-, is in some cases derived from the Irish *cill*; and the reasons,
if any, for the differential patterns of a number of 'cemetery' words
(*reilig, cladh*, etc.) in the far North. This is an exciting and promising field, and one which is ripe for prolonged and detailed
examination.

With this, we reach, not only the end of this cursory assessment
of the literary and documentary sources, but the end of the book.
As I stressed in the first chapter, neither the book nor the original
lecture-series should be seen as a received body of doctrine on
early Christian archaeology; it will be some little time before our
studies attain that level. I should nevertheless, wish to offer all that
has gone before as a variety of positive suggestions for further,
active, and much-needed research. The attraction of the subject
in general will, I am sure, speak for itself.

[1] MacQueen, J. 1956.   [2] Cameron 1968.

Appendix: The 'Northumbrian Lives'

THE PURPOSE OF THIS NOTE is to provide, for the student who wishes to examine these works as a source for the Christian archaeology of North Britain, details of the best editions and translations.

The Life of St. Cuthbert, by a monk of Lindisfarne:

Text and translation: Colgrave, B., *Two Lives of St. Cuthbert* (C.U.P., 1940), pp. 61–139.

The Life of Gregory the Great, by a monk of Whitby:

Text and translation: Colgrave, B., *The Earliest Life of Gregory the Great by an anonymous monk of Whitby* (Univ. of Kansas, Lawrence, 1968).

Other translations: Jones, C. W., *Saints' Lives and Chronicles in Early England* (N.Y., 1947), pp. 97–121.
Whitelock, D., in *English Historical Documents*, i (1955), pp. 687 ff. (parts only).

Commentaries: Colgrave, B., in Chadwick, N. K., ed., *Celt and Saxon* (C.U.P., 1963), chap. 3.

The Life of Bishop Wilfrid, by Eddius Stephanus:

Text and translation: Colgrave, B., *The Life of Bishop Wilfrid, by Eddius Stephanus* (C.U.P., 1927).

Another translation: Webb, J. F., in *Lives of the Saints* (Penguin Books, 1965), pp. 133–206.

The History of Abbots Ceolfrid and Cynefrid, by a monk of Monkwearmouth-Jarrow:

Text: Plummer, C., *Venerabilis Baedae Opera Historica*, 2 vols. (O.U.P., 1896), at i, pp. 388–404; notes at ii, pp. 371–7.

Translations: Boutflower, D. S. *The Life of Ceolfrid . . . by
                                 an unknown author of the eighth century*
                                 (Sunderland, 1912).
                                 Whitelock, D., in *English Historical Docu-
                                 ments*, i (1955), pp. 697–708.

The Lives of the Holy Abbots of Wearmouth and Jarrow, by the Venerable
    Bede:

Text: Plummer, C., *Venerabilis Baedae Opera
                                 Historica*, 2 vols. (O.U.P., 1896), at i, pp. 364–
                                 87; notes at ii, 355–70.
Translation: Stevens, J., *The Ecclesiastical History of the
                                 English Nation by the Venerable Bede* (Every-
                                 man Library, 1910 and reprints), pp. 349–65.

The Prose Life of St. Cuthbert, by the Venerable Bede:

Text and translation: Colgrave, B., *Two Lives of St. Cuthbert*
                                 (C.U.P., 1940), pp. 143–307.
Other translations: Stevens, J. (revised by Jane, L. C.), *The
                                 Ecclesiastical History of the English Nation by
                                 the Venerable Bede* (Everyman Library, 1910
                                 and reprints), pp. 286–348.
                                 Webb, J. F., *Lives of the Saints* (Penguin
                                 Books, 1965), pp. 71–129.

The Ecclesiastical History of the English Nation, by the Venerable Bede:

Bibliography: *English Historical Documents*, i (1955), pp. 581–
                                 8.
Text: Plummer, C., *Venerabilis Baedae Opera His-
                                 torica*, 2 vols. (O.U.P., 1896), i, text, ii, notes,
                                 with indices.
Text and translation: Colgrave, B., and Mynors, R. A. B., *Bede's
                                 Ecclesiastical History* (O.U.P., 1969).
Translations: Stevens, J. (revised by Jane, L. C.), *The
                                 Ecclesiastical History of the English Nation by
                                 the Venerable Bede* (Everyman Library, 1910
                                 and reprints).
                                 Sherley-Price, L., *Bede: A History of the
                                 English Church and People* (Penguin Books,
                                 1955, and reprints).

Abbreviations

PERIODICALS

AA², *AA⁴*	*Archaeologia Aeliana* (Society of Antiquaries of Newcastle upon Tyne), second and fourth series.
Ant. J.	*The Antiquaries Journal* (London).
Arch. Cambr.	*Archaeologia Cambrensis* (Cambrian Archaeological Association).
Arch. J.	*The Archaeological Journal* (London).
BBCS	*Bulletin of the Board of Celtic Studies* (Cardiff).
BROB	*Berichten van de Rijksdienst voor het Oudheidkundig Bodemonderzoek* (Amersfoort, Netherlands).
CA	*Cornish Archaeology* (Cornwall Archaeological Society).
EC	*Études Celtiques* (Paris).
JBAA	*Journal of the British Archaeological Association* (London).
JCHAS	*Journal of the Cork Historical and Archaeological Society* (Cork).
JRS	*Journal of Roman Studies* (London).
JRSAI	*Journal of the Royal Society of Antiquaries of Ireland* (Dublin).
Med. Arch.	*Medieval Archaeology* (Society for Medieval Archaeology, London).
OC	*Old Cornwall* (St. Ives and Marazion).
PRIA	*Proceedings of the Royal Irish Academy* (Dublin).
PSAS	*Proceedings of the Society of Antiquaries of Scotland* (Edinburgh).
RC	*Revue Celtique* (Paris).
SHR	*Scottish Historical Review.*
TDGNHAS	*Transactions of the Dumfriesshire and Galloway Natural History and Antiquarian Society* (Dumfries).
UJA	*Ulster Journal of Archaeology* (Belfast).
WAM	*Wiltshire Archaeological and Natural History Magazine* (Wiltshire A. and N. H. Society, Devizes).
WHR	*Welsh History Review.*

Bibliography

AITKEN, W. G. 1955. 'Excavation of a Chapel at St. Ninian's Point, Bute', *Trans. Buteshire Natur. Hist. Soc.* 14 (1955), 62–76.

ANDERSON, A. O. 1948. 'Ninian and the Southern Picts', *SHR* 27 (1948), 45.

—— and ANDERSON, M. O. *Adomnán's Life of Columba* (Edinburgh, 1961).

ANDERSON, J. 1876. 'Notes on the Survival of Pagan Customs in Christian Burial, etc.', *PSAS* 11 (1875–6), 363–406.

——1880. 'Notice of an Ancient Celtic Reliquary', *PSAS* 14 (1879–80), 431–5.

—— 1881. *Scotland in Early Christian Times*, 2 vols. (Edinburgh, 1881).

—— 1907. 'Notice of Bronze Brooches, etc., in Oronsay and . . . Colonsay', *PSAS* 41 (1906–7), 437–50.

ASHBEE, P. A. 1960. *The Bronze Age Round Barrow in Britain* (1960).

ASHLEY, A. 1958. *The Church in the Isle of Man* (St. Anthony's Hall Publn. no. 13, Borthwick Inst. Hist. Research, York, 1958).

BAILEY, R. 1963. 'The Clogher Crucifixion: a Northumbrian Parallel and its Implications', *JRSAI* 93 (1963), 187–8.

BARRUOL, G. 1964. 'L'autel et les cancels paléochrétiens de Limans, Basses-Alpes', *Cahiers Archéologiques* 14 (1964), 68.

BATTISCOMBE, C. F., ed. 1956. *The Relics of St. Cuthbert: Studies by various authors* (O.U.P., for Durham, 1956).

BECKERLEGGE, J. J. 1953. 'Ancient Memorial Inscription on a stone at Hayle', *OC* 5, pt. 4 (1953), 173–8.

BECKWITH, J. 1963. *Coptic Sculpture* (1963).

BERSU, G., and WILSON, D. M. 1966. *Three Viking Graves in the Isle of Man* (Society for Medieval Archaeology, Monograph no. 1, 1966).

BEVERIDGE, E. 1911. *North Uist: its Archaeology & Topography* (Edinburgh, 1911).

BIELER, L. 1952. *Libri Epistolarum Sancti Patricii Episcopi* (2 vols.: i, Intro. and Text, ii, Comm.); Dublin, Stationery Office (1952).

—— 1953. *The Works of St. Patrick* (Ancient Christian Writers, vol. 17) (Westminster, Md., and London, 1953).

—— 1963. *The Irish Penitentials* (*SLH*, vol. v) (Dublin: Dublin Institute for Advanced Studies, 1963).

—— 1966. *Ireland—Harbinger of the Middle Ages* (1966).

—— 1968. 'St. Patrick and the British Church', in *CIB* (1968), 123–30.

BINCHY, D. A. 1962. 'St. Patrick and his Biographers, Ancient and Modern', *Studia Hibernica* 2 (1962), 7–173.

BÖHNER, K. 1958. *Die Fränkischen Altertümer des Trierer Landes*, 2 vols. (Berlin, 1958).

BOWEN, E. G. 1954. *The Settlements of the Celtic Saints in Wales* (Cardiff, 1954).

BRUCE, J. C. 1889. 'A Roman Inscription from Portugal', *AA*² 13 (1889), 200.

BRUCE, J. R., and CUBBON, W. 1930. 'Cronk yn How, an Early Christian and Viking Site', *Arch. Cambr.* 85 (1930), 267–99.

BRYCE, T. H., and KNIGHT, G. A. F. 1930. 'Report on a Survey of the Antiquities on Eileach an Naoimh', *Trans. Glasgow Archaeol. Soc.*, N.S. 8, pt. 2 (1930), 62–102.

BULLEN, R. A. 1912. *Harlyn Bay and the Discovery of its Prehistoric Remains* (3rd rev. edn., Padstow 1912).

BULLOCH, J. 1963. *The Life of the Celtic Church* (Edinburgh, 1963).

BU'LOCK, J. D. 1965. 'Early Christian Memorial Formulae', *Arch. Cambr.* 105 (1956), 133–41.

BULLOUGH, D. A. 1965. 'Columba, Adomnán, and the Achievement of Iona', *SHR* 43 (1964), 111–30, contd. in *SHR* 44 (1965), 17–33.

BURN, A. R. 1969. 'Holy Men on Islands in pre-Christian Britain', *Glasgow Archaeol. Journ.* I (1969), 2–6.

CAMERON, K. 1968. '*Eccles* in English Place-Names', *CIB* (1968), 87–92.

CAMPBELL, Marian, of KILBERRY, and SANDEMAN, M. 1964. 'Mid-Argyll: An Archaeological Survey', *PSAS* 95 (1961–2), 1–125.

CHADWICK, N. K. 1955. *Poetry and Letters in Early Christian Gaul* (1955).

NB

CHADWICK, N. K. 1961. *The Age of the Saints in the Early Celtic Church* (O.U.P. 1961).

—— 1963. *Celtic Britain* (1963).

CHADWICK, O. 1968. *John Cassian* (2nd edn., Cambridge, 1968).

CHAMPNEYS, A. 1910. *Irish Ecclesiastical Architecture* (1910).

CHITTY, D. J. 1966. *The Desert A City: an Introduction to the Study of Egyptian and Palestinian Monasticism under the Christian Empire* (Oxford, 1966).

CLARK, J. G. D. 1952. *Prehistoric Europe—The Economic Basis* (1952).

COCKERTON, R. W. P. 1962. 'The Wirksworth Slab', *Derbyshire Archaeol. J.* 82 (1962), 1–20.

COFFEY, G. 1909. *R.I.A. Collection: Guide to the Celtic Antiquities of the Christian Period preserved in the National Museum, Dublin* (Dublin, 1909).

COLGRAVE, B. 1927. *The Life of Bishop Wilfrid by Eddius Stephanus* (Cambridge, 1927).

—— 1940. *Two Lives of St. Cuthbert* (Cambridge, 1940).

—— 1956. *Felix's Life of St. Guthlac* (Cambridge, 1956).

—— 1968. *The Earliest Life of Gregory the Great by a . . . monk of Whitby* (Lawrence, Kansas, 1968).

COLLINGWOOD, R. G., and RICHMOND, Sir IAN 1969. *The Archaeology of Roman Britain* (revised edn. 1969).

COLLINGWOOD, W. G. 1927. *Northumbrian Crosses of the Pre-Norman Age* (1927).

CRAINE, D. 1958. *Peel Castle, Isle of Man: Official Guide* (Douglas, 1958).

CRAMPTON, C. B. 1967. 'Ancient Settlement Patterns in Mid-Wales', *Arch. Cambr.* 116 (1967), 57–69.

CRAWFORD, O. G. S. 1933. 'Iona', *Antiquity* 7 (1933), 453–67.

—— 1934a. 'Coludes burh', *Antiquity* 8 (1934), 202–4.

—— 1934b. 'The Magic of St. Columba', *Antiquity* 8 (1934), 168–75.

CRIPPS, W. 1893. 'A Bronze Grave Chalice from Hexham Priory Church', *AA²* 15 (1890–93), 192.

CROLY, G. 1843. *Syria, Arabia, Egypt* (1843).

CRUDEN, S. E. 1947. 'The Horizontal Water-Mill at Dounby, Orkney', *PSAS* 81 (1946–7), 43–7.

CRUDEN, S. E. 1965. 'Excavations at Birsay, Orkney', in Small, A., ed. *The Fourth Viking Congress* (Edinburgh, 1965), 22–31.

CULICAN, W. 1965. 'The Ends of the Earth: Spain under the Visigoths', in Talbot Rice, D., ed. *The Dark Ages* (1965), 175–95.

CURZON, Hon. R. 1849. *Visits to Monasteries in the Levant* (1849, and many reprints).

DANIEL, G. E. 1950. *The Prehistoric Chamber Tombs of England and Wales* (Cambridge, 1950).

—— 1960. *The Prehistoric Chamber Tombs of France* (1960).

DANNHEIMER, H. 1967. 'Der Holzbau am Rande des Reihengräberfeldes von München-Aubing', *Germania* 44 (1967), 326–37.

DARLING, F. FRASER 1939. *A Naturalist on Rona* (Oxford, 1939).

DAVEY, N. 1964. 'A Pre-Conquest Church and Baptistery at Potterne', *WAM* 59 (1964), 116–23.

DAVIES, W. H. 1968. 'The Church in Wales', *CIB* (1968), 131–50.

DAWES, E. and BAYNES, N. H. 1948. *Three Byzantine Saints* (Oxford, 1948).

DE FLEURY, C. R. (ed. G.) 1883. *La Messe*; vol. i (Paris, 1883).

DELEHAYE, H. 1955. *Les Légendes hagiographiques* (Subsidia Hagiographica 18a) (4th edn., Soc. Bollandistes, Brussels, 1955).

DE PALOL, P. 1967. *Arqueología Cristiana de la España Romana* (España Cristiana, serie monografica, i), Madrid and Valladolid (1967).

DE PAOR, L. 1955. 'A Survey of Sceilg Mhichíl', *JRSAI* 85 (1955), 174–87.

DE PAOR, M. and L. 1958. *Early Christian Ireland* (1958).

DILLON, M. 1954. (ed.) *Early Irish Society* (Thomas Davis Lectures) (Dublin, 1954).

DOBLE, G. H. 1927. *St. Docco & St. Kew* (Cornish Saints, 12) (Truro, 1927).

DOWDEN, J. 1898. 'Observations and Conjectures on the Kirkmadrine Epigraphs', *PSAS* 32 (1897–8), 247–74.

DUKE, J. A. 1932. *The Columban Church* (Edinburgh, 1932).

DUNRAVEN, Earl of. 1875. (ed. Stokes, M.) *Notes on Irish Architecture*, 2 vols. (1875).

DURLIAT, M. 1957. 'Les autels de Septimania du Ve au VIIIe siècle', *Actes du V Congr. Internat. d'archéol. chrét.* 1954, Rome–Paris (1957), 539–50.

DYGGVE, E. 1951. *History of Salonitan Christianity* (Oslo: Instituttet for Sammenlignende Kulturforskning, ser. A. xxi, 1951).

ELIADE, M. 1954. *The Myth of the Eternal Return* (New York, 1954).

—— 1958. *Patterns in Comparative Religion* (1958).

—— 1961. *Images and Symbols: Studies in Religious Symbolism* (1961).

EVANS, E. E. 1957. *Irish Folk Ways* (1957).

FAHY, E. M. 1956. 'A Horizontal Mill at Mashanaglass, co. Cork', *JCAHS* 61 (1956), 13–57.

FEHRING, G. P. 1967. 'Frühmittelalterliche Kirchenbauten unter St. Dionysius zu Esslingen am Neckar', *Germania* 44 (1967), 354–74.

FERGUSON, Sir S. 1886. 'On Sepulchral Cellae', *Trans. Roy. Irish Acad.* 27 (1877–86), 57–66.

FORBES, A. B. 1874. *Lives of S. Ninian and S. Kentigern* (Historians of Scotland, v) (Edinburgh, 1874).

FOSTER, I. LL. 1965. 'The Emergence of Wales', in: Foster, I. LL. and Daniel, G. E., eds. *Prehistoric & Early Wales* (1965), 213–35.

FOX, Sir C. 1923. *The Archaeology of the Cambridge Region* (Cambridge, 1923).

FREND, W. H. C. 1955. 'Religion in Roman Britain in the Fourth Century', *JBAA* 18 (1955), 1–18.

GARDNER, K. S. 1960. 'Dark Age Remains on Lundy', *13th Report Lundy Field Society* (1959–60), 53–64.

—— 1962. 'Archaeological Investigations on Lundy 1962', *15th Report Lundy Field Society* (1962), 22–33.

GRABAR, A. 1946. *Martyrium* (2 vols.; Paris, 1943–6).

GREEN, C. J. S. 1967. 'Interim Report on Excavations at the Copse Site in the Roman Cemetery, Poundbury', *Proc. Dorset Natur. Hist. Archaeol. Soc.* 89 (1967), 133–5.

—— 1968. 'Interim Report on Excavations in the Roman Cemetery, Poundbury', *Proc. Dorset Natur. Hist. Archaeol. Soc.* 90 (1968), 171–3.

GRIEVE, S. 1923. *The Book of Colonsay and Oronsay* (2 vols.; Edinburgh, 1923).

GROOME, F. H. 1892. (ed.) *Ordnance Gazetteer of Scotland* (6 vols., n.d., ?1892).

GROSJEAN, P. 1945. 'Notes d'hagiographie celtique', *Analecta Bollandiana* 63 (1945), 65–130.

—— 1958. 'Les Pictes Apostats dans l'Épitre de S. Patrice', *Analecta Bollandiana* 76 (1958), 354–78.

HAARHOFF, T. J. 1958. *Schools of Gaul* (Witwatersrand Univ. Press, Johannesburg, 1958).

HALBERTSMA, H. 1961. 'Bonifatius' levenseinde in het licht der opgravingen', *BROB* 10–11 (1960–61), 395–444.

HALLIDAY, Sir W. R. 1925. *The Pagan Background of Early Christianity* (Liverpool, 1925).

HANSON, R. P. C. 1968a. *St. Patrick: His Origins and Career* (Oxford, 1968).

—— 1968b. 'Summary and Prospect', *CIB* (1968), 207–13.

HARRISON, R. M. 1963. 'Church and Chapels of Central Lycia', *Anatolian Studies* 13 (1963), 117–51.

HASELOFF, G. 1951. *Der Tassilokelch* (Munich, 1951).

HEIST, W. W. 1965. *Vitae Sanctorum Hiberniae ex codice olim Salmanticensi nunc Bruxellensi* (Subsidia Hagiographica 28) (Soc. Bollandistes, Brussels, 1965).

HENDERSON, C. 1928. 'Parochial History of Cornwall', in *The Cornish Church Guide* (Truro, 1928), 51–222.

HENDERSON, I. 1958. 'The Origin Centre of the Pictish Symbol Stones', *PSAS* 91 (1957–8), 44–60.

—— 1967. *The Picts* (1967).

HENRY, F. 1940. *Irish Art in the Early Christian Period* (1940).

—— 1947. 'The Antiquities of Caher Island (Co. Mayo)', *JRSAI* 77 (1947), 23–38.

—— 1957. 'Early Monasteries, Beehive Huts, and Dry-Stone Houses in the Neighbourhood of Caherciveen and Waterville (Kerry)', *PRIA* 57 C (1957), 45–166.

—— 1963. *L'Art Irlandais I* (Zodiaque, 1963).

—— 1964. *L'Art Irlandais II* (Zodiaque, 1964).

—— 1965. *Irish Art in the Early Christian Period (to A.D. 800)* (1965).

HENSHALL, A. S. 1958. 'The Long Cist Cemetery at Parkburn, Lasswade, Midlothian', *PSAS* 89 (1958), 252–83.

HEWISON, J. K. 1893. *The Island of Bute in the Olden Times* (2 vols.; Edinburgh, 1893).

HILLGARTH, J. 1961. 'The East, Visigothic Spain, and the Irish', *Studia Patristica* 4 (Berlin, 1961), 442.

—— 1962. 'Visigothic Spain and Early Christian Ireland', *PRIA* 62 C (1962), 167–94.

HOARE, F. R. 1954. *The Western Fathers* (1954).

HOULDER, C. 1968. 'The Henge Monuments at Llandegai', *Antiquity* 42 (1968), 216–21.

HUGHES, K. 1958. 'B.M. MS. Cotton Vespasian A. xiv (*Vitae Sanctorum Wallensium*); its purpose and provenance', in Chadwick, N. K., ed. *Studies in the Early British Church* (Cambridge, 1958), 183–200.

—— 1966. *The Church in Early Irish Society* (1966).

HULST, R. S. 1964. 'Een grafveld uit de voor-Romeinse IJzertijd te Nijnsel, gem. St.-Oedenrode, prov. Noord-Brabant', *BROB* 14 (1964), 74–83.

HUTCHISON, R. 1866. 'Notice of Stone Cists Discovered Near the "Catstane", Kirkliston', *PSAS* 6 (1864–6), 184–98.

HYSLOP, M. 1963. 'Two Anglo-Saxon Cemeteries at Chamberlains Barn, Leighton Buzzard, Bedfs.', *Arch. J.* 120 (1963), 161–200.

JACKSON, E. D. C. and FLETCHER, Sir E. 1968. 'Excavations at the Lydd Basilica, 1966', *JBAA* 31 (1968), 19–26.

JACKSON, K. H. 1948. 'On Some Romano-British Place-names', *JRS* 38 (1948), 54–8.

—— 1950. 'Notes on the Ogam Inscriptions of Southern Britain', in Fox, C. and Dickins, B., eds. *Early Cultures of North-West Europe* (Cambridge, 1950), 197–215.

—— 1958. 'The Sources for the Life of St. Kentigern', in Chadwick, N. K., ed. *Studies in the Early British Church* (Cambridge, 1958), 273–357.

—— 1969. *The Gododdin: The Oldest Scottish Poem* (Edinburgh, 1969).

JAMES, E. O. 1952. 'Archaeology, Folklore, and Sacred Tradition', *Advancement of Science* 34 (Sept. 1952).

JENKINS, F. 1965. 'St. Martin's Church at Canterbury: a survey of the earliest structural features', *Med. Arch.* 9 (1965), 11–15.

JESSUP, R. F. 1959. 'Barrows and Walled Cemeteries in Roman Britain', *JBAA* 22 (1959), 1–32.

JONES, A. H. M. 1964. *The Later Roman Empire* (3 vols.; Oxford, 1964).

KENDRICK, Sir T. D. 1939. 'Gallen Priory Excavations 1934–35', *JRSAI* 69 (1939), 1–20.

—— and SENIOR, E. 1937. 'St. Manchan's Shrine', *Archaeologia* 86 (1937), 105–18.

KENNEY, J. F. 1929. *The Sources for the Early History of Ireland: I, Ecclesiastical* (New York, 1929).

KERMODE, P. M. C. 1907. *Manx Crosses* (1907).

—— 1912. 'Cross-slabs Recently Discovered in the Isle of Man', *PSAS* 46 (1911–12), 53–76.

—— 1930. 'Note on Early Cross-Slabs from the Faeroe Islands', *PSAS* 65 (1930–1), 373–8.

—— and HERDMAN, W. A. 1914. *Manks Antiquities* (2nd edn. Liverpool, 1914).

KNIGHT, G. A. F. 1933. *Archaeological Light on the Early Christianizing of Scotland* (2 vols.; 1933).

KRAUTHEIMER, R. 1965. *Early Christian and Byzantine Architecture* (Pelican History of Art, 1965).

KURTH, Betty 1945. 'The Iconography of the Wirksworth Slab', *Burlington Magazine* 86 (May 1945), 114–21.

LAFONTAINE-DOSOGNE, J. 1967. *Recherches sur le monastère et sur l'iconographie de S. Syméon Stylite le Jeune* (Brussels, 1967).

LASSUS, J. 1947. *Sanctuaires chrétiens de Syrie* (Paris, 1947).

LAWLOR, H. C. 1925. *The Monastery of St. Mochaoi at Nendrum* (Belfast, 1925).

LAWLOR, H. J. 1897. *Chapters on the Book of Mulling* (Edinburgh, 1897).

LEASK, H. G. 1955. *Irish Churches and Monastic Buildings: I, The First Phases and the Romanesque* (Dundalk, 1955).

LEVISON, W. 1905. *Vita Bonifatii auctore Willibaldo; Vitae Sancti Bonifatii, recensit Wilhelm Levison* (Sciipt. Rer. Germ. in usum schol., Hanover, 1905).

LEWIS, M. J. T. 1966. *Temples in Roman Britain* (Cambridge, 1966).

LIONARD, P. 1961. 'Early Irish Grave-Slabs', *PRIA* 61 C (1961), 95–169.

Lucas, A. T. 1953. 'The Horizontal Mill in Ireland', *JRSAI* 83 (1953), 1–36.

MacAlister, R. A. S. 1896. 'The Antiquities of Ardoileán, co. Galway', *JRSAI* 26 (1896), 197–210.

—— 1909. *The Memorial Slabs of Clonmacnois, King's County* (Dublin, 1909).

—— 1916. 'The History and Antiquities of Inis Cealtra', *PRIA* 33 C (1916), 93–174.

—— 1946. *Monasterboice, Co. Louth* (Dundalk, 1946).

MacNeill, Eoin 1937. *Phases of Irish History* (Dublin, 1937).

—— 1964. *St. Patrick* (ed. John Ryan) (Dublin, 1964).

MacQueen, J. 1955. 'Yvain, Ewen, and Owein ap Urien', *TDGNHAS* 33 (1954–5), 107–31.

—— 1956. '*Kirk-* and *Kil-* in Galloway Place-Names', *Archivum Linguisticum* (Glasgow) 8 (1956), 135–49.

—— 1961. *St. Nynia: a Study of Literary and Linguistic Evidence* (Edinburgh, 1961).

—— 1962. 'History and Miracle Stories in the Biography of Nynia', *Innes Review* 13 (1962), 115–29.

MacQueen, W. 1960. 'Miracula Nynie Episcopi', *TDGNHAS* 38 (1959–60), 21–57.

McRoberts, Mgr. D. 1961. 'The Ecclesiastical Significance of the St. Ninian's Isle Treasure', *PSAS* 94 (1960–1), 301–14.

MacWhite, E. 1961. 'Contributions to a study of ogam memorial stones', *Zeitschrift fur Celtische Philologie* 28 (1960–1), 294–308.

Mason, T. H. 1936. *The Islands of Ireland; Their Scenery, People, Life, and Antiquities* (1936).

Maxwell, Sir H. E. 1885. 'St. Ninian's Cave, Glasserton', *Ayr. & Galloway Archaeol. Collections* 5 (1885) 1–10.

Meates, G. W. 1955. *Lullingstone Roman Villa* (1955).

Meehan, D. 1958. *Adomnán's De Locis Sanctis* (*SLH*, vol. iii) (Dublin Institute for Advanced Studies, Dublin, 1958).

Megaw, B. R. S. 1950. 'The Monastery of Kirk Maughold', *Proc. Isle Man Natur. Hist. Antiq. Soc.* 5 pt. 11 (1950).

—— 1958. 'The Calf of Man Crucifixion', *Journ. Manx Mus.* 6 (1958), 236–7.

MITCHELL, Sir A. 1880. *The Past in the Present: What is Civilization?* (Edinburgh, 1880).

—— 1884. 'On White Pebbles in Connection with Pagan and Christian Burials, etc.', *PSAS* 18 (1883–4), 286–91.

MOAR, P. 1944. 'Newly discovered Sculptured Stones from Papil, Shetland', *PSAS* 78 (1943–4), 91–9.

MODDERMAN, P. J. R., and ISINGS, C. 1961. 'Een grafveld uit de Romeinse tijd op de Gaalse Heide, gem. Schayk (N-Br.)', *BROB* 10–11 (1960–1), 318–46.

MOHRMANN, C. 1961. *The Latin of St. Patrick* (Dublin Institute for Advanced Studies, Dublin, 1961).

MOMIGLIANO, A. 1963. ed. *The Conflict between Paganism and Christianity in the Fourth Century* (Oxford 1963).

MORRIS, J. 1966a. 'Dark Age Dates' in; Jarrett M. G., and Dobson B., eds. *Britain and Rome* (Kendal, 1966), 145–85.

—— 1966b. 'The Dates of the Celtic Saints', *Journ. Theolog. Studies* 17 (1966), 342–91.

—— 1968a. 'The Date of St. Alban', *Hertfords. Archaeol.* 1 (1968), 1–8.

—— 1968b. 'The Literary Evidence', *CIB* (1968), 55–74.

MUNRO, R. W. 1961. ed. (*Dean*) *Monro's Western Isles of Scotland and Genealogies of the Clans* (Edinburgh, 1961).

NASH-WILLIAMS, V. E. 1950. *The Early Christian Monuments of Wales* (Cardiff, 1950).

NICOLAISEN, W. F. H. 1965. 'Scottish Place-Names; 24, *Slew-* and *sliabh*', *Scottish Studies* 9 (1965), 91–106.

NISBET, H. C., and GAILEY, R. A. 1962. 'A Survey of the Antiquities of North Rona', *Arch. J.* 117 (1962), 88–115.

NORMAN, E. R., and ST. JOSEPH, J. K. S. 1969. *The Early Development of Irish Society; the evidence of aerial photography* (Cambridge, 1969).

O'DELL, A. C. *et al.* 1959. 'The St. Ninian's Isle Silver Hoard', *Antiquity* 33 (1959), 241–68.

—— 1960. *St. Ninian's Isle Treasure* (Edinburgh, 1960).

OHLSON, G. 1968. 'A method of measurement and the use of terminology in a report on human skeleton posture', *Acta Archaeologica* 39 (Copenhagen 1968), 255–61.

O'KELLY, M. J. 1952. 'St. Gobnet's House, Ballyvourney, co. Cork', *JCHAS* 57 (1952), 18–40.

—— 1958. 'Church Island near Valencia, co. Kerry', *PRIA* 59 C (1958), 57–136.

—— 1967. 'Knockea, Co. Limerick', in Rynne, E., ed. *North Munster Studies* (Limerick, 1967), 72–101.

O'NEIL, H. E. 1964. 'Excavation of a Celtic Hermitage on St. Helen's, Isles of Scilly', *Arch. J.* 121 (1964), 40–69.

O'RAHILLY, C. 1924. *Ireland & Wales; their Historical and Literary Relations* (1924).

Ó RÍORDÁIN, S. P. 1947a. 'Roman Material in Ireland', *PRIA* 51 C (1947), 35–82.

—— 1947b. 'The Genesis of the Celtic Cross', in Pender, S., ed. *Féilscríbhinn Torna* (Cork, 1947), 108–14.

OSWALD, A. 1956. *The Church of St. Bertelin at Stafford and its Cross* (City of Birmingham Museum and Art Gallery, Birmingham, 1956).

PAINTER, K. S., and TAYLOR, C. C. 1967. 'The Roman Site at Hinton St. Mary, Dorset: ii, The Later History, etc.', *Brit. Mus. Quarterly* 32 (1967), 15–35.

PEACOCK, D. P. S., and THOMAS, C. 1967. 'Class "E" Imported Post-Roman Pottery; a Suggested Origin', *CA* 6 (1967), 35–46.

PEATE, I. C. 1940. *The Welsh House; a Study in Folk Culture* (1940).

PEERS, Sir C., and RADFORD, C. A. R. 1943. 'The Saxon Monastery of Whitby', *Archaeologia* 89 (1943), 27–88.

PETRIE, G. 1845. *The Ecclesiastical Architecture of Ireland* (2nd edn., Dublin, 1845).

PHILP, B. 1969. 'Keston', *Current Archaeology* 14 (May 1969), 73–5.

PIGGOTT, S. 1954. *The Neolithic Cultures of the British Isles* (Cambridge, 1954).

—— 1962. ed. *The Prehistoric Peoples of Scotland* (1962).

—— 1965. *Ancient Europe, from the Beginning of Agriculture to Classical Antiquity* (Edinburgh, 1965).

—— 1968. *The Druids* (1968).

PLUMMER, C. 1896. *Venerabilis Baedae Opera Historica* (2 vols.; Oxford, 1896).

—— 1910. *Vitae Sanctorum Hiberniae* (2 vols.; Oxford, 1910).

PLUMMER, C. 1922. *Bethada Náem nÉrenn; Lives of Irish Saints* (2 vols.; Oxford, 1922).

RADFORD, C. A. R. 1935a. 'Tintagel; the Castle and Celtic Monastery —Interim Report', *Ant. J.* 15 (1935), 401–19.

—— 1935b. *Tintagel Castle, Cornwall*: H.M.S.O. Guide (1935).

—— 1950. 'Excavations at Whithorn 1949', *TDGNHAS* 27 (1948–9), 85–126.

—— 1951a. 'St. Ninian's Cave', *TDGNHAS* 28 (1950–1), 96–8.

—— 1951b. 'Report on the Excavations at Castle Dore', *Journ. Roy. Inst. Cornwall*, N.S. I, pt. 1, Appendix (1951).

—— 1955a. 'An Early Cross at Staplegorton', *TDGNHAS* 32 (1954–5), 179–80.

—— 1955b. 'Two Scottish Shrines: Jedburgh and St. Andrews', *Arch. J.* 112 (1955), 43–60.

—— 1956. 'Imported Pottery found at Tintagel, Cornwall', in Harden, D. B., ed. *Dark-Age Britain* (1956), 59–70.

—— 1957a. 'Excavations at Glastonbury Abbey 1956', *Antiquity* 31 (1957), 171.

—— 1957b. 'Excavations at Whithorn (Final Report)', *TDGNHAS* 34 (1957), 131–94.

—— 1959. *The Early Christian and Norse Settlements, Birsay* (H.M.S.O. Guide, Edinburgh, 1959).

—— 1962. 'The Celtic Monastery in Britain', *Arch. Cambr.* 111 (1962), 1–24.

—— 1968. 'The Archaeological Background on the Continent', in *CIB* (1968), 19–36.

RAFTERY, B. 1969. 'A late Ogham Inscription from Co. Tipperary', *JRSAI* 99 (1969), 161–4.

RAFTERY, J. 1944. 'Air Photography and Archaeology', *JRSAI* 74 (1944), 119–23.

RAHTZ, P. A. 1968a. 'Sub-Roman Cemeteries in Somerset', in *CIB* (1968), 193–6.

—— 1968b. 'Glastonbury Tor', in Ashe, G., ed. *The Quest For Arthur's Britain* (1968), 139–54.

REEVES, W. 1847. *Ecclesiastical Antiquities of Down, Connor, and Dromore* (Dublin, 1847).

REEVES, W. 1857. *The Life of S. Columba . . . written by Adomnán* (Dublin, 1857).

—— 1860. 'Saint Maelrubha; His History and Churches', *PSAS* 3 (1857–60), 258–96.

RENAUD, J. G. N. 1959. 'Nogmaals de kerk van Zelhem', *BROB* 9 (1959), 189–98.

RICHARDS, M. 1960. 'The Irish Settlements in South-West Wales: a Topographical Approach', *JRSAI* 90 (1960), 133–52.

—— 1962. 'Welsh *Meid(i)r*, *Moydir*, Irish *Bóthar*, "Lane, Road" ', *Lochlann* 2 (1962), 128–34.

RICHARDSON, J. T., and RICHARDSON, J. S. 1902. 'Prehistoric Remains near Gullane', *PSAS* 36 (1901–2), 654–8.

RICHMOND, Sir I. A. 1932. 'The Irish Analogies for the Romano-British Barn Dwelling', *JRS* 22 (1932), 96–106.

RITCHIE, J. 1920. *The Influence of Man on Animal Life in Scotland* (Cambridge, 1920).

ROE, H. 1960. 'A Stone Cross at Clogher, co. Tyrone', *JRSAI* 90 (1960), 191–206.

ROSEHILL, Lord. 1871. 'Note of the Opening of a Group of Cists Near Lauder', *PSAS* 9 (1870–1), 223–7.

RUSSELL, V., and POOL, P. A. S. 1964. 'Excavation of a Menhir at Try, Gulval', *CA* 3 (1964), 15–26.

SALIN, E. 1955–9. *La Civilisation Mérovingienne* (4 vols.; Paris, 1950–9).

SALWAY, P. 1965. *The Frontier People of Roman Britain* (Cambridge, 1965).

SAVORY, H. N. 1960. 'Excavations at Dinas Emrys, Beddgelert, Caerns., 1954–56', *Arch. Cambr.* 109 (1960), 13–77.

SAWYER, E. H. 1930. 'The First Monasteries', *Antiquity* 4 (1930), 316–26.

SCHAFFRAN, E. 1941. *Die Kunst der Langobarden in Italien* (1941).

SCHERER, C. 1905. *Die Codices Bonifatiani in der Landesbibliothek zu Fulda* (Festgabe zum Bonifatiusjubileum, Fulda, 1905).

SCHOVE, D. J. 1950. 'Visions in North-West Europe (A.D. 400–600) and Dated Auroral Displays', *JBAA* 13 (1950), 34–49.

SIMPSON, D. D. A., and SCOTT-ELLIOT, J. 1964. 'Excavations at Camp Hill, Trohoughton, Dumfries', *TDGNHAS* 41 (1964), 125–34.

SIMPSON, W. D. 1954. *Dundarg Castle* (Edinburgh, 1954).

SIMPSON, W. D. 1958. 'Eileach an Naoimh Reconsidered', *Scottish Gaelic Studies* 8, pt. 2 (1958), 117–29.

—— 1960. 'Dundarg Castle Reconsidered', *Transactions of the Buchan Club* 17, pt. 4 (1960), 9–25.

SMITH, I. F., and SIMPSON, D. D. A. 1964. 'Excavation of Three Roman Tombs and a Prehistoric Pit on Overton Down', *WAM* 59 (1964), 68–85.

STEAD, I. M. 1961. 'A Distinctive Form of La Tène Barrow in Eastern Yorkshire and on the Continent', *Ant. J.* 41 (1961), 44–62.

STEER, K. A. 1958. 'Arthur's O'on; a lost shrine of Roman Britain', *Arch. J.* 115 (1958), 99–110.

STOJKOVIC, I. N. 1957. 'Rapport préliminaire sur la recherche des monuments chrétiens a Doclea', *Actes du V Cong. Internat. d'archéol. chrét.* 1954, Rome-Paris (1957), 567–72.

STOKES, W. 1862. *Three Irish Glossaries* (1862).

—— 1887. *The Tripartite Life of St. Patrick, etc.* (Rolls Series, 2 vols., 1887).

—— 1905. *Félire Óengusso Céli Dé: The Martyrology of Oengus the Culdee* (Henry Bradshaw Society, vol. 29, 1905).

STUART, J. 1866. 'Account of Graves recently discovered at Hartlaw, etc.', *PSAS* 6 (1864–6), 55–61.

SWARZENSKI, G. 1954. 'An Early Anglo-Irish Portable Shrine', *Bulletin of the Museum of Fine Arts, Boston*, 52 (1954), 50–62.

TALBOT, C. H. 1954. *The Anglo-Saxon Missionaries in Germany* (1954).

TAYLOR, H. M., and TAYLOR, J. 1963. 'Pre-Norman Churches of the Border', in Chadwick, N. K., ed. *Celt and Saxon: Studies in the Early British Border* (Cambridge, 1963), 210–57.

—— 1965. *Anglo-Saxon Architecture* (2 vols.; Cambridge, 1965).

THOM, A. 1967. *Megalithic Sites in Britain* (Oxford, 1967).

THOMAS, C. 1953. 'The Carnsew Inscription', *OC* 5, pt. 3 (1953), 125–30.

—— 1957. 'Some Imported Post-Roman Sherds from Cornwall and their origin', *Proc. West Cornwall Field Club*, ii, pt. 1 (1957), 15–19.

—— 1959. 'Imported Pottery in Dark-Age Western Britain', *Med. Arch.* 3 (1959), 89–111.

—— 1961. 'A New Pre-Conquest Crucifixion Stone from west Cornwall', *Ant. J.* 41 (1961), 89–92.

THOMAS, C. 1962. *Phillack Church: an Illustrated History, etc.* (Gloucester, 1962).

—— 1964. 'The Interpretation of the Pictish Symbols', *Arch. J.* 120 (1964), 31–97.

—— 1966a. 'Ardwall Isle: The Excavation of an Early Christian Site of Irish Type, 1964–5', *TDGNHAS* 43 (1966), 84–116.

—— 1966b. 'A Cross-Incised Slab from Ludgvan Churchyard', *CA* 5 (1966), 86–7.

—— 1967a. *Christian Antiquities of Camborne* (St. Austell, 1967).

—— 1967b. 'An Early Christian Cemetery and Chapel on Ardwall Isle, Kirkcudbright', *Med. Arch.* 11 (1967), 127–88.

—— 1968a. 'The Evidence from North Britain', *CIB* (1968), 93–122.

—— 1968b. *Christian Sites in West Penwith* (Guide, for Society for Medieval Archaeology, 1968 Conference: Cornwall Archaeological Society, Penzance, 1968).

—— 1969a. 'Are These the Walls of Camelot?' *Antiquity* 43 (1969), 27–30.

—— 1969b. 'Lundy, 1969', *Current Archaeology* no. 16 (Sept. 1969), 138–42.

THOMPSON, A. H. ed. 1935. *Bede—His Life, Times and Writings* (Oxford 1935, re-issued 1969).

THOMPSON, E. A. 1958. 'The Origin of Christianity in Scotland', *SHR* 37 (1958), 17–22.

TOYNBEE, J. M C. 1953. 'Christianity in Roman Britain', *JBAA* 16 (1953), 1–24.

—— 1964. 'The Christian Roman Mosaic at Hinton St. Mary, Dorset', *Proc. Dorset Natur. Hist. Archaeol. Soc.* 85 (1964), 1–10.

TROLLOPE, E. 1860. 'Roman Remains in the Vicinity of Padstow, Cornwall', *Arch. J.* 17 (1860), 311–14.

VAN DER MEER, F., and MOHRMANN, C. 1958. *Atlas of the Early Christian World* (1958).

VENDRYES, J. 1920. 'Les vins de Gaule en Irlande et l'expression *fín aicneta*', *RC* 38 (1920), 19–24.

—— 1956. 'Sur un emploi du mot *AINM* "nom" en irlandais', *EC* 7 (1955–6), 139–46.

VOLBACH, W. F. 1961. *Early Christian Art* (1961).

WADE-EVANS, A. W. 1944. *Vitae Sanctorum Britanniae et Genealogiae* (Cardiff, 1944).

WAINWRIGHT, F. T. 1955. (ed.) *The Problem of the Picts* (Edinburgh, 1955).

WAKEMAN, W. F. 1893. *A Survey of the Antiquarian Remains on the Island of Inismurray (Inis Muireadhaigh)* (Dublin, 1893).

WALKER, G. S. M. 1957. *Sancti Columbani Opera* (*SLH*, vol. ii) (Dublin Institute for Advanced Studies, Dublin, 1957).

WALL, J. 1966. 'Christian Evidences in the Roman Period: The Northern Counties', *AA*[4] 43 (1965), 201–25, and *AA*[4] 44 (1966), 147–64.

WARD-PERKINS, J. B. 1938. 'The Sculpture of Visigothic France', *Archaeologia* 87 (1938), 79–128.

WATERMAN, D. M. 1967. 'The Early Christian Churches and Cemetery at Derry, co. Down', *UJA* 30 (1967), 53–75.

WATSON, G. R. 1968. 'Christianity in the Roman Army', *CIB* (1968), 51–4.

WATSON, W. J. 1926. *The History of the Celtic Place-Names of Scotland* (Edinburgh, 1926).

WEBB, J. F. 1965. (ed. and transl.) *Lives of the Saints* (Penguin Books, 1965).

WERCKMEISTER, O. K. 1963. 'Three Problems of Tradition in pre-Carolingian Figure Style; From Visigothic to Insular Illumination', *PRIA* 63 C (1963), 167–89.

WESSEL, K. 1965. *Coptic Art* (1965).

WESTLAKE, H. F. 1921. 'An Early Pewter Coffin-Chalice and Paten found in Westminster Abbey', *Ant. J.* i (1921), 56.

WILLIAMS, H. 1912. *Christianity in Early Britain* (Oxford, 1912).

WILLIAMS, Sir I. 1968. (ed. and transl. J. E. Caerwyn Williams) *The Poems of Taliesin, annotated by Sir Ifor Williams* (Dublin Institute for Advanced Studies, Dublin, 1968).

WILSON, D. M., and BLUNT, C. E. 1961. 'The Trewhiddle Hoard', *Archaeologia* 98 (1961), 75–122.

WILSON, D. R. 1968. 'An Early Christian Cemetery at Ancaster', *CIB* (1968), 197–9.

WILSON, P. A. 1964. 'St. Ninian and Candida Casa: Literary Evidence from Ireland', *TDGNHAS* 41 (1964), 156–85.

WILSON, P. A. 1966. 'Romano-British and Welsh Christianity: Continuity or Discontinuity?', *WHR* 3, pt. 1 (1966), 5–21, and *WHR* 3, pt. 2 (1966), 103–20.

—— 1968. 'The Cult of St. Martin in the British Isles', *Innes Review* 19 (1968), 129–43.

ZIMMER, H. 1910. 'Über direckte Handelsverbindungen Westgalliens mit Irland in Altertum und frühen Mittelalter' (in five parts), *Sitz. d. kon. preuss. Akad. d. Wissenschaft* (Berlin), 1909, 363–400, 430–76, 543–613; 1910, 1031–1119.

ZSCHOKKE, F. 1963. 'Surgical Instruments in the Service of Art', *Roche Image: Medical Photo Reports* (Roche Products Ltd., London), 3 (1963), 29–32.

Indexes

I. Technical Terms

LATIN

Agnus Dei, 119–20
altare, 167
antae, 75
antependium, 183
antitas, 89
ara, 167, 181
brandea, 136–7, 191, 194
cancella, -us, 160–1
cella memoriae, 58, 67, 88, 140–4, 168
cemiterium, 85
cippus, 183
clymiterium, 85
commutatio, 138
confessio, 143, 178, 220
diaconus, 102
episcopus, 102
fenestella, 143
frontale, 183
lectus, 144, 171
martyrium, 89, 105
memoria, 103–5
mensa, 178–9, 181
nomina (nomena), 105–6
paruchia, 19–20, 43, 90, 137
plebs, 19–20
porticus, 14
praepositus, 44, 210
presbyter, 102
reliquiae, 66–7, 88, 105–6
sacerdos, 14, 102
sarcophagus, 49, 147, 219
sepes, 33
sigillae, 198
stipes, 178
theca, 154
transenna, 160–1
translatio, 138, 141
vallum (monasterii), 29–31, 33, 35–7, 43, 83–4, 212, 219
virtus, see 'Virtue'
Vitae, see 'Lives of Saints'

BRITISH

*egles, 224
*lano-, 85, 88

IRISH

(OLD, MIDDLE, AND MODERN)

AILITHIR (ogam), 106
altoir, 169–70
andóit, 89, 137, 224
ANM (ogam), 106
aregal (airecal), 40
caincell, 161
cell, cill, 68, 87–9, 143, 168–75, 222
cellurach, 50
cillin, 50
cos, 177
dairthech, 69
disert, 33
dún, 29
fert(a), 40, 66–7, 88
land-, lann-, 68, 87–8
leacht, 58, 67, 144
lecht, 171
lis, 29, 40
martir, 89, 105
martra(e), 89
nemed, 89
ráith, ráth, 29, 40
relic(c), 66–7, 88–9, 105
rúam, 89
tech (mór), 40, 208
tuath, 20

SCOTTISH GAELIC

annait, 89, 224
cladh, 67, 224
reilig, 88, 224

MANX

keeill, 222
rhullick, 88

WELSH

llan, 87, 224
merthyr, 68, 89, 224

CORNISH

kil-, kyl-, 224
lan, 87, 224
merther, 89, 137, 224

GERMAN

Blockaltar, 175–6, 181
Kastenaltar, 175–6, 178
Sarcophagaltar, 175–6
Tischaltar, 175
Totenmemoria, 147–8

ENGLISH

Altars, defined, 167–8
— cavity-, 176–81
— portable, 190–8
Altar-frontals, *see* 'Frontals'
Altar-graves, 58, 168–9
Altar-linen, 183
Burial chalices, 197
Burial portable altars, 196–7
Burials, contracted, 48
— extended, 48
Cemeteries, developed, 51, 81–5, 218
— enclosed, 50, 218
— undeveloped, 51
— walled, 49–50
Chalices, 198–200
Chancel-screens, 160–3
Chi-rho, 11, 100–1, 107–9, 112–16
Church, diocesan, 13, 16–17
— orientation of, 69–71
— timber, 207–9
Circular shrines, 66
Cist (-graves), long, 49, 54
— short, 48, 53
Communal hermitage, 44
Crosses, 'arm-pits' of, 122
— consecration (altars), 182
— 'face-', 128–31
— freestanding, 39, 121–3, 126
— hexafoil, 120–1
— initial, 107–12
— primary, 112–18, 124, 155, 181
— wooden, 118, 122–3, 133
Cross-slabs, primary, *see* 'Crosses, primary'
— recumbent, 126–8
Croziers, 40, 119–20, 165
Cruck construction, 75–6
Diocesan church, 13, 16–17
Double shrines, 152–4
Eremitic monastery, 44–6, 81
Finials, gable, 76–8
Frontals, 183–90.
Graves, cist-, 48–54
— dug, 49–50

— lintel, 49–56
— special or specially marked, 58–64, 219
Grave-goods, 48
Grave-markers, primary, 113–14
Grave-surrounds, circular, 59–63, 171
— rectangular, 63–4, 171
Hermitages, 85
— communal, 44
'Incomprehension, period of', 215–20
Inhumation, 48
Lintel graves, 49–56
Lives of Saints, defined, 203–6
Martyrial tombs or graves, 138–41, 144
Memorial (tomb)stones, inscribed, 11, 94, 98
— ogam, 94–7
— pictorial, 97–8
Monastery, defined, 21
— erematic, 44–6, 81
Monastic cells, 25–6, 82–5
Monastic enclosure, *see* '*vallum*'
Name-stones, 121
Oratories, Gallerus type, 75–6
— timber, 68–75, 81
Orientation, of churches, 69–71
— of graves, 49
Pillow-stones, 121
Relics, cult of, defined, 135
— corporeal, 135, 165
— incorporeal (representative), 135, 163
Relic-cavity, altar, 178–81, 198
Reliquary-coffins, 81, 141, 150, 159
Reliquaries, portable, *see* 'Shrines, house-shaped (portable)'
Shrines, circular, 66
— corner-post, 73, 150–60
— double (corner-post), 152–4
— grooved, 149
— house-shaped (portable), 163–6
— house-shaped (stone), 149–50
— self-shaped, 165–6
— slab, 73, 141–4
— solid, 150
Special graves, 58–64, 219
Staff rood, 122
Timber churches and oratories, 68–75, 207–9
Tombs, martyrial, 138–41, 144
Tombstones, *see* 'Memorial (tomb)-stones'
'Virtue' (*virtus*), 134–5, 147, 170

II. Names of Places

III. GENERAL

PRINTED IN GREAT BRITAIN
AT THE UNIVERSITY PRESS, OXFORD
BY VIVIAN RIDLER
PRINTER TO THE UNIVERSITY